The Joy of Kierkegaard

BibleWorld
Series Editors: Philip R. Davies and James G. Crossley, University of Sheffield
BibleWorld shares the fruits of modern (and postmodern) biblical scholarship not only among practitioners and students, but also with anyone interested in what academic study of the Bible means in the twenty-first century. It explores our ever-increasing knowledge and understanding of the social world that produced the biblical texts, but also analyses aspects of the Bible's role in the history of our civilization and the many perspectives—not just religious and theological, but also cultural, political and aesthetic—which drive modern biblical scholarship.

Recently Published

Linguistic Dating of Biblical Texts: An Introduction to Approaches and Problems
Ian Young and Robert Rezetko

Sex Working and the Bible
Avaren Ipsen

Jesus in an Age of Terror: Scholarly Projects for a New American Century
James G. Crossley

On the Origins of Judaism
Philip R. Davies

The Bible Says So!: From Simple Answers to Insightful Understanding
Edwin D. Freed and Jane F. Roberts

From Babylon to Eternity: The Exile Remembered and Constructed in Text and Tradition
Bob Becking, Alex Cannegieter, Wilfred van der Poll and Anne-Mareike Wetter

Judaism, Jewish Identities and the Gospel Tradition: Essays in Honour of Maurice Casey
Edited by James G. Crossley

A Compendium of Musical Instruments and Instrumental Terminology in the Bible
Yelena Kolyada

Secularism and Biblical Studies
Edited by Roland Boer

Jesus beyond Nationalism: Constructing the Historical Jesus in a Period of Cultural Complexity
Edited by Halvor Moxnes, Ward Blanton and James G. Crossley

The Production of Prophecy: Constructing Prophecy and Prophets in Yehud
Edited by Diana V. Edelman and Ehud Ben Zvi

The Social History of Achaemenid Phoenicia: Being a Phoenician, Negotiating Empires
Vadim S. Jigoulov

Biblical Resistance Hermeneutics within a Caribbean Context
Oral A. W. Thomas

Three Versions of Judas
Richard G. Walsh

The Archaeology of Myth: Papers on Old Testament Tradition
N. Wyatt

Power and Responsibility in Biblical Interpretation: Reading the Book of Job with Edward Said
Alissa Jones Nelson

Bible and Justice: Ancient Texts, Modern Challenges
Edited by Matthew J.M. Coomber

Simulating Jesus: Reality Effects in the Gospels
George Aichele

An Introduction to the Bible (Third Edition)
J.W. Rogerson

The Joy of Kierkegaard

Essays on Kierkegaard as a Biblical Reader

Hugh Pyper

SHEFFIELD OAKVILLE

Published by Equinox Publishing Ltd.
UK: Unit S3, Kelham House, 3, Lancaster Street, Sheffield S3 8AF
USA: DBBC, 28 Main Street, Oakville, CT 06779

www.equinoxpub.com

First published 2011

British Library Cataloguing-in-Publication Data

A catalogue record for this book is available from the British Library.

ISBN-13   978-1-84553-271-0 (hardback)
          978-1-84553-272-7 (paperback)

Library of Congress Cataloging-in-Publication Data

Pyper, Hugh S.
  The joy of Kierkegaard: essays on Kierkegaard as a biblical reader/Hugh Pyper.
    p. cm.—(Bibleworld)
  Includes bibliographical references and index.
    ISBN 978-1-84553-271-0 (hb)—ISBN 978-1-84553-272-7 (pb) 1. Kierkegaard, Søren,
1813-1855. I. Title. II. Series.
  BX4827.K5P97 2011
  230'.044092—dc22
                                    2010038331

Typeset by S.J.I. Services, New Delhi
Printed and bound in the UK by the MPG Books Group

CONTENTS

Preface   vii

Acknowledgments   xi

Abbreviations   xiii

1. The Joy of Kierkegaard   1

2. Kierkegaard's Canon: The Constitution of the Bible and
    of the Authorship in *Concluding Unscientific Postscript*   14

3. The Apostle, the Genius and the Monkey: Reflections on
    Kierkegaard's 'The Mirror of the Word'   32

4. Your Wish Is My Command: The Peril and Promise of the
    Bible as 'Letter from the Beloved'   43

5. The Lesson of Eternity: The Figure of the Teacher in
    Kierkegaard's *Philosophical Fragments*   52

6. Cities of the Dead: The Relation of Person and *Polis* in
    Kierkegaard's *Works of Love*   67

7. Adam's *Angest*: The Language of Myth and the Myth of
    Language   81

8. Beyond a Joke: Kierkegaard's *Concluding Unscientific
    Postscript* as a Comic Book   99

9. 'Sarah Is the Hero': Kierkegaard's Reading of Tobit in
    Fear and Trembling   115

10. How Edifying Is Upbuilding? Paul and Kierkegaard in
    Dialogue   130

11. Forgiving the Unforgivable: Kierkegaard, Derrida and the
    Scandal of Forgiveness   145

    Bibliography   161

    Index of Biblical References   165

    Index of Authors   167

PREFACE

This collection of essays represents nearly twenty years of writing on the work of Kierkegaard, although my reading of him goes back forty years at least. They share the aim of showing that the Bible is a key to understanding Kierkegaard and that what passionately concerned him was the task of showing how the most troubling, puzzling and offensive passages of the Bible bring a message of good news and of joy.

When, for example, Kierkegaard in the guise of Johannes Climacus explores the story of Abraham and Isaac in *Fear and Trembling*, we would be quite wrong to suppose that, through philosophical reflection, he came up with the notion of the teleological suspension of the ethical and then cast around for a biblical story to illustrate his point. Quite the contrary: it is as he reads the story of Abraham's preparedness to sacrifice his son Isaac, which is not only an Old Testament passage, but is held up by Paul in the New Testament as a paradigm example of true faithfulness, that the need for philosophical reflection becomes apparent. How can this appalling tale, which has shocked the ethical sensibilities of many philosophers, be taken as an example for Christian conduct? The answer must either be that Paul is quite mistaken and morally suspect for suggesting this, or that something other than Kantian morality is at stake here, something that opens up seemingly impossible possibilities for us.

This is just one example among many of the way in which difficult biblical texts engender Kierkegaard's most creative thought. Contrary to some superficial assessments of his work, however, this does not stem from some perverse fascination on his part with the cruelty, suffering and meaninglessness at the heart of human existence. These things cannot be glossed over, but what Kierkegaard is about is disrupting his readers' superficial accommodation with the despair that this awareness can engender. This accommodation can be made either through sheer spiritlessness, which is lumpishly unaware of its own inadequacy, or a deliberate refusal to acknowledge the danger. Such a refusal may be wilful blindness, or a defiant embrace of despair, or else depend on an elaborate system of distraction. Such distractions can be aesthetic, but the ethical can also be used to distract. The idea that works alone can answer the problem boils down to masking the void through busyness.

What Kierkegaard constantly promotes for his readers is the message that only by admitting our despair can we hope to be caught up in a joy that is grounded in the eternal and changeless love of God. One of the main instruments by which this can be effected is through the encounter with the scandal of the good news of the gospel as it is transmitted in the Bible. Whether or not his faith is well founded, or convincingly and consistently expressed, is a legitimate question, but in these essays I hope to show that reading him in this light is fruitful and potentially enlightening and life-enhancing.

Since some of these essays were written, there has been a welcome increase in the recognition of the importance of the Bible in Kierkegaard's work. The interestingly different contributions of L. Joseph Rosas III, Timothy Polk and Jolita Pons have moved the debate on in significant ways.[1] The recent publication of two collections under the editorship of Lee Barrett and Jon Stewart dedicated to the Old and New Testaments in the magisterial series of *Kierkegaard Research: Sources, Reception and Resources* is a very welcome and thorough contribution to this endeavour and will be indispensable for future researchers in these topics.[2] The fact that the Bible is the topic of the first volume of this series which covers an astonishing range of sources for understanding Kierkegaard in philosophy, theology and aesthetics is testimony in itself to a renewed sense of the fundamental importance of Scripture to his authorship.

In presenting these essays, however, I have not undertaken a wholesale revision in the light of these later contributions. The aim is to make my own work over this period, warts and all, available in a more convenient form for those who might be interested. The essays have only been lightly revised from their original forms but at certain points I have taken leave to insert a new footnote to acknowledge this work and to point the reader to points of convergence and difference with subsequent work. On re-reading these essays myself, however, I have to say that, overall, I stand by what I have written. Although much more could be said on all these topics and although I hope I continue to learn as I re-read Kierkegaard and the work of those who study him, there is little here that I would repudiate.

This long engagement with Kierkegaard has been enriched and made all the more enjoyable by conversations in person, by letter and in print, with a wide range of scholars, students and friends. It would be impossible to name them all. I hope they recognize themselves in these pages. There are some, however, that I will take the risk of singling out. Dr Hugh Saxton, my father's cousin, has something to answer for the inspired but somewhat unusual gift of an introduction to Kierkegaard as a gift for a twelve-year-old boy.

Throughout my engagement with Kierkegaard, George Pattison has been a constant and supportive presence. I owe him and other friends in the Søren Kierkegaard Society of the United Kingdom a great debt from many hours of conversation and discussion. If I single out Steven Shakespeare, John Lippitt and Simon Podmore in this group, it is in recognition of longstanding intellectual and personal friendships.

Friends and colleagues at the Søren Kierkegaard Research Centre in Copenhagen have also been conversation partners over many years. Again, if I make particular mention of Niels Jørgen Cappelørn, Jon Stewart, Pia Soltøft and Joakim Garff, they stand proxy for others who have been unfailingly welcoming and interested in Copenhagen.

Robert Perkins, the editor of the International Kierkegaard Commentary series has been a source of encouragement and a fine model of scholarly integrity along with his wife, Sylvia Walsh. Some of the following pieces are all the better in their final form from the editorial insights of Robert and his team.

I, along with many others, have benefited from the hospitality, wisdom and friendship to be found at the Howard and Edna Hong Library at St Olaf College, Northfield, Minnesota. The support and companionship of friends such as Leo Stan, Søren Landkildehus and Jamie Turnbull has been an enrichment to my life and I know they would join me in appreciation for the unstinting generosity—material, intellectual and spiritual—of Gordon Marino and Cynthia Lund. While acknowledging gratefully my indebtedness I owe to these friends and to many other scholars, it behoves me to point out that in all that follows I bear the responsibility for any errors.

Along with all the English-speaking students of Kierkegaard of my generation, I owe a particular debt to Howard and Edna Hong. Howard's recent death for once fully justifies the clichéd verdict that it marks the end of an era. Their extraordinary partnership gave us the gift of access to Kierkegaard's world through their life's work in editing and translating his *Journals and Papers* and collected works. This was not just a herculean feat but also a labour of love: their love of Kierkegaard, of the most exacting but imaginative scholarship, and above all of each other. The library that bears their name is a unique and precious legacy, both as an unrivalled collection of resources for scholars and as a space for thinking, for conversation and for friendship. I treasure the time that I spent as a guest in the basement of their house. Howard, I know, was characteristically amused when I introduced myself to others in his hearing as a 'sub-Hong'; I think he knew it was a badge of pride for me. I would like to dedicate this volume to their memory.

Notes

1. L. Joseph Rosas III, *Scripture in the Thought of Søren Kierkegaard* (Nashville: Broadman and Holdman, 1994); Timothy Houston Polk, *The Biblical Kierkegaard: Reading by the Rule of Faith* (Macon: Mercer University Press, 1997); Jolita Pons, *Stealing a Gift: Kierkegaard's Pseudonyms and the Bible* (New York: Fordham University Press, 2004).
2. Lee C. Barrett and Jon Stewart, *Kierkegaard Research: Sources, Reception and Resources. I. Kierkegaard and the Bible.* Tome 1. *The Old Testament* (Farnham: Ashgate, 2010); Lee C. Barrett and Jon Stewart, *Kierkegaard Research: Sources, Reception and Resources. I. Kierkegaard and the Bible.* Tome 2. *The New Testament* (Farnham: Ashgate, 2010).

ACKNOWLEDGMENTS

The provenance of the essays in this book is given below. All but two are previously published and acknowledgment is hereby given for the permission to republish these articles.

'The Joy of Kierkegaard.' *Søren Kierkegaard Newsletter* 47 (2004), pp. 10–16.

'Cities of the Dead: The Relation of Person and *Polis* in Kierkegaard's *Works of Love.'* In *Kierkegaard: The Self in Society.* Edited by G. Pattison and S. Shakespeare; London: Macmillan, 1998, pp. 125–38.

'"Sarah is the Hero": Kierkegaard's Reading of Tobit in *Fear and Trembling.'* In *Studies in the Book of Tobit: A Multidisciplinary Approach.* Edited by M. Bredin; The Library of Second Temple Studies; London: T & T Clark, 2006, pp. 59–71.

'Kierkegaard's Canon: The Constitution of the Bible and the Authorship in *Concluding Unscientific Postscript.'* In *Kierkegaard Studies Yearbook 2005; Concluding Unscientific Postscript.* Edited by N.J. Cappelørn, H. Deuser and J. Stewart; Berlin: Walter de Gruyter, 2005, pp. 53–70.

'Forgiving the Unforgivable: Kierkegaard, Derrida and the Scandal of Forgiveness.' *Kierkegaardiana* 22 (2002), pp. 7–24.

'Beyond a Joke: Kierkegaard's *Concluding Unscientific Postscript* as a Comic Book.' In *Concluding Unscientific Postscript to 'Philosophical Fragments'.* Edited by R. L. Perkins; International Kierkegaard Commentary, 12; Macon, GA: Mercer University Press, 1997, pp. 149–68.

'Adam's *Angest*: The Myth of Language and the Language of Mythology.' In *Kierkegaard Studies Yearbook* 2001. Edited by N.J. Cappelørn, H. Deuser and J. Stewart; Berlin: Walter de Gruyter, 2001, pp. 78–95.
'The Apostle, the Genius and the Monkey: Reflections on the Mirror of the Word.' In *Kierkegaard on Art and Communication*. Edited by G. Pattison; Basingstoke: Macmillan Press, 1992, pp. 125–36.

The two previously unpublished papers are adaptations of addresses delivered on the following occasions.

'How Edifying is Upbuilding? Paul and Kierkegaard in Dialogue.' Keynote paper for conference on Kierkegaard's *Eighteen Upbuilding Discourses*, Christ Church, Oxford, 16th–18th April, 2010.

'"Your Wish is My Command": The Peril and Promise of the Bible as "Letter from the Beloved."' Paper for the Kierkegaard, Religion and Culture Group of the AAR, AAR/SBL Annual Meeting, Atlanta, GA, 22nd–25th November, 2003.

Abbreviations

References to Kierkegaard's works are standardly given as page numbers in the following editions of his works with the following abbreviations. References to entries in the *Journals and Papers* are to the entry numbers in the Hong and Hong edition.

BA   *The Book on Adler.* Translated by Howard V. Hong and Edna H. Hong; Princeton: Princeton University Press, 1995.

C   *The Crisis and a Crisis in the Life of an Actress.* In *Christian Discourses* and *The Crisis and a Crisis in the Life of an Actress.* Translated by Howard V. Hong and Edna H. Hong; Princeton, NJ: Princeton University Press, 1997.

CA   *The Concept of Anxiety.* Translated by Reidar Thomte in collaboration with Albert B. Anderson; Princeton: Princeton University Press, 1980.

CD   *Christian Discourses.* In *Christian Discourses* and *The Crisis and a Crisis in the Life of an Actress.* Translated by Howard V. Hong and Edna H. Hong; Princeton, NJ: Princeton University Press, 1997.

CI   *The Concept of Irony* together with 'Notes on Schelling's Berlin NSBL Lectures.' Translated by Howard V. Hong and Edna H. Hong; Princeton: Princeton University Press, 1989.

COR   *The Corsair Affair.* Translated by Howard V. Hong and Edna H. Hong; Princeton: Princeton University Press, 1982.

CUP1   *Concluding Unscientific Postscript to 'Philosophical Fragments'.* 2 vols.;

CUP2   Translated by Howard V. Hong and Edna H. Hong; Princeton: Princeton University Press, 1992.

EO1   *Either/Or.* 2 vols.; Translated by Howard V. Hong and Edna H. Hong;

EO2   Princeton: PrincetonUniversity Press, 1987.

EPW   *Early Polemical Writings.* Translated by Julia Watkin; Princeton: Princeton University Press, 1990.

EUD   *Eighteen Upbuilding Discourses.* Translated by Howard H. Hong and Edna H. Hong; Princeton: Princeton University Press, 1990.

FSE   *For Self-Examination.* In *For Self-Examination* and *Judge for Yourself!* Translated by Howard V. Hong and Edna H. Hong; Princeton: Princeton University Press, 1990.

FT   *Fear and Trembling.* In *Fear and Trembling* and *Repetition.* Translated by Howard V. Hong and Edna H. Hong; Princeton: Princeton University Press, 1983.

JC   'Johannes Climacus.' In *Philosophical Fragments* and 'Johannes Climacus.' Translated by Howard V. Hong and Edna H. Hong; Princeton: Princeton University Press, 1985.

JFY   *Judge for Yourself!* In *For Self-Examination* and *Judge for Yourself!* Translated by Howard V. Hong and Edna H. Hong; Princeton: Princeton University Press, 1990.

JP   *Søren Kierkegaard's Journals and Papers.* Edited and translated by Howard V. Hong and Edna H. Hong, assisted by Gregor Malantschuk; Bloomington and London: Indiana University Press. Volume 1, 1967; 2, 1970; 3 and 4, 1975; 5–7, 1978.

LD   *Letters and Documents.* Translated by Hendrik Rosenmeier; Princeton: Princeton University Press, 1978.

P   *Prefaces.* In *Prefaces* and 'Writing Sampler.' Translated by Todd W. Nichol; Princeton: Princeton University Press, 1998.

PC   *Practice in Christianity.* Translated by Howard V. Hong and Edna H. Hong; Princeton: Princeton University Press, 1991.

PF   *Philosophical Fragments.* In *Philosophical Fragments* and 'Johannes Climacus.' Translated by Howard V. Hong and Edna H. Hong; Princeton: Princeton University Press, 1985.

PV   *The Point of View for My Work as an Author.* Translated by Howard V. Hong and Edna H. Hong; Princeton: Princeton University Press, 1998.

R   *Repetition.* In *Fear and Trembling* and *Repetition.* Translated by Howard V. Hong and Edna H. Hong; Princeton: Princeton University Press, 1983.

SLW   *Stages on Life's Way.* Translated by Howard V. Hong and Edna H. Hong; Princeton: Princeton University Press, 1988.

SUD   *The Sickness unto Death.* Translated by Howard V. Hong and Edna Hong; Princeton: Princeton University Press, 1980.

TA   *Two Ages: The Age of Revolution and the Present Age. A Literary Review.* Translated by Howard V. Hong and Edna H. Hong; Princeton: Princeton University Press, 1978.

TD   *Three Discourses on Imagined Occasions.* Translated by Howard V. Hong and Edna H. Hong; Princeton: Princeton University Press, 1993.

MLW   *'The Moment' and Late Writings.* Translated by Howard V. Hong and Edna H. Hong; Princeton: Princeton University Press, 1998.

UD   *Upbuilding Discourses in Various Spirits.* Translated by Howard V. Hong and Edna H. Hong; Princeton: Princeton University Press, 1993.

WA   *Without Authority.* Translated by Howard V. Hong and Edna H. Hong; Princeton: Princeton University Press, 1997.

WL   *Works of Love.* Translated by Howard V. Hong and Edna H. Hong; Princeton: Princeton University Press, 1995.

WS   'Writing Sampler.' See *Prefaces.*

Other Abbreviations

KR: SRR   *Kierkegaard Research: Sources, Reception and Resources.* Ed. Jon Stewart; Farnham: Ashgate.

The Joy of Kierkegaard

The title of this chapter and this book, 'The Joy of Kierkegaard', is the same as that of a module that I once taught at a leading British university. As part of the process of getting the module accepted, I had to present the paper work for the proposed module to the relevant Faculty committee. The philosophers present fell off their chairs laughing. 'That'll be the shortest module ever taught', they chortled. 'Well', I replied, 'if that's what you think, that's all the more reason why I should teach it. Why don't you all enrol and you might learn something?' Needless to say, they did not take me up on this, but the module went ahead and was much appreciated by the students.

At one level, of course, their reaction was quite understandable. The melancholy Dane, the father of existentialism, inventor of angst, favourite philosopher of anguished teenagers, the writer of *The Concept of Dread*, *Sickness unto Death* and *The Gospel of Suffering*—these stereotypes hardly convey a bundle of fun. To be fair, a casual, or even a more than casual, reading of the journals with their constant allusions to suffering and misunderstanding and isolation tends to bear this out.

Yet my strong conviction is that joy is at the heart of what Kierkegaard was about. When I am asked what description bests sums up Kierkegaard—philosopher, theologian, religious thinker, a kind of poet, novelist, preacher—these days I have an answer: he is an evangelist, in its root meeting as a bearer of good news. What he burns to communicate is good news, while knowing that the majority of his hearers cannot tell good news from bad and have a tendency to mistake the disease for the cure and the cure for the disease.

The joy of Kierkegaard can itself mean different things. There is the sheer joy of reading Kierkegaard's writings, an experience that is well summed up in a paragraph introducing another book and another writer not always thought of as a bundle of laughs, Dostoyevsky's *The Brothers Karamazov*:

The Brothers Karamazov is a joyful book. Readers who know what it is 'about' may find this an intolerably whimsical statement. It does have its moments of joy, but they are only moments. The rest is greed, squalor, lust, unredeemed suffering, and a sometimes terrifying darkness. But the book is joyful in another sense, in its energy and curiosity, in its formal inventiveness, in the mastery of its writing. And therefore, finally, in its vision.[1]

There is in even the darkest passage of Kierkegaard the sheer joy of the writing, the dazzling verbal display, but also so often the teasing tone that leads you up the garden path only to pull the rug out from under you, to mix a jolly metaphor. Kierkegaard is a great comic writer, in the sense that Dostoevsky, Proust and Joyce are great comic writers. They give us the joy of recognition, putting in front of us figures and arguments and voices caught with the deftest of sketch-lines, but irresistibly alive and recognizable.

At times, he sets out to make us laugh. One passage where this always works with me is the remarkable disquisition on boredom in the section of *Either/Or* entitled 'Rotation of Crops':

> The gods were bored; therefore they created human beings. Adam was bored because he was alone; therefore Eve was created. Since that moment, boredom entered the world and grew in quantity in exact proportion to the growth of population. Adam was bored alone; then Adam and Eve were bored together; then Adam and Eve and Cain and Abel were bored *en famille*. After that the population of the world increased and the nations were bored *en masse*. To amuse themselves, they hit upon the notion of building a tower so high that it would reach the sky. This notion is just as boring as the tower was high and is a terrible demonstration of how boredom had gained the upper hand. (EO1, 286)

We smile at the sly *aperçus*, and then are brought up with a shock, which has its own pleasure, rather like a cold wave breaking over us, of recognizing ourselves. I might interject here my own experience of Kierkegaard as providing this variation on the old practice of finding your fortune in a random verse of the Bible or Virgil in the *sortes virgiliensis*. It was on my fortieth birthday that I was thumbing through *Concluding Unscientific Postscript* and came across this remarkable passage:

> Often enough one encounters men who are full grown, confirmed, and men of heart who in spite of being older in years do everything or leave undone like a child and who even in their fortieth year would undeniably be regarded as promising children if it were the custom for every man to become two hundred and fifty years. (CUP, 490)

Yet this passage can also serve as a warning. There is rather a gulf between being amused by Kierkegaard and getting to grips with the joy of Kierkegaard, and we need to watch ourselves around here. After all, it is boredom, *Either/Or* reminds us, that underlies the search for amusement and in the name of that search all sorts of ridiculous, immoral and thoughtless things are done which in the end turn out to make life more boring than ever.

Recognizing the joy of Kierkegaard is not simply a matter of appreciating the humour of Kierkegaard and the key place of humour in his thought, though this too is a vital counter to the lazy characterization of him as melancholic.[2] Humour marks the necessary transition from the ethical to the religious, for Kierkegaard, although I am not a great believer in too formulaic an application of the notion of stages in his work. This means is more important in his thought than humour, except the religious. This is well explained in a passage from his *Concluding Unscientific Postscript*:

> On the whole the comic is present everywhere, and every existence can at once be defined and assigned to its particular sphere by knowing how it relates to the comic. The religious person is one who has discovered the comic on the greatest scale and yet he does not consider the comic as the highest, because the religious is the purest pathos. But if he looks upon the comic as the highest, then his comic is *eo ipso* lower, because the comic is always based on a contradiction, and if the comic itself is the highest, it lacks that contradiction in which the comic exists and in which it makes a showing. That is why it holds true without exception that the more competently a person exists, the more he will discover the comic. (CUP, 462)

Discovering the comic is something that comes with a deepening awareness of the contradictions of the world and its incongruities, but to rest in the comic, to see it as the highest, argues that we have some way of rising above the world and fails to acknowledge the pathos of our own comic contradiction in being aware of the comedy of our own existence. Humour, the comic and joy are not unrelated, but they are not by any means identical for Kierkegaard.

What I want to suggest about joy in Kierkegaard comes in a different category. I think that W.H. Auden captures this particularly well in one of his poems. Auden was profoundly influenced by Kierkegaard. He himself describes his first encounter with his writings as bowling him over in the same way as his first encounter with Simone Weil, Pascal or Nietzsche. Although Auden later came to see Kierkegaard as a partial thinker, one who heretically homed in on the crucifixion, failing to balance it with the incarnation and the resurrection (an opinion we might wish to question later), he never lost his admiration for him. This stanza from his poem 'In Sickness and in Health' is I think as fine a summary of how I would understand Kierkegaard's thought on joy as I have found.

> Beloved, we are always in the wrong,
> Handling so clumsily our stupid lives,
> Suffering too little or too long,
> Too careful even in our selfless loves:
> The decorative manias we obey
> Die in grimaces round us every day,
> Yet through their tohu-bohu comes a voice
> Which utters an absurd command—Rejoice.[3]

This stanza would bear a lot of reading. Note how it starts with the word 'beloved', even although what it goes on to chronicle are the imperfections and stupidity and clumsiness of those addressed who fall among the collective 'we' of the title. Despite all our faults, or perhaps because of all our faults, we are, the poet proclaims, beloved. The poem then develops into a thought which directly echoes one of Kierkegaard's most characteristic aphorisms: 'The joy of it: that before God we are always in the wrong.'[4] How can that be a cause of joy? The answer is that this realization saves us from the error of focussing on our errors, and reminds us that it is not our prerogative to choose how we are judged.

In *The Gospel of Sufferings*, all but one of the seven chapter headings contains the word 'joy', as do the series of aphorisms and paradoxes which form the headings of the second part of *Christian Discourses*, 'States of Mind in the Strife of Suffering':

> The joy of it, that one suffers only once but is victorious eternally;
> The joy of it, that hardship does not take away but procures hope;
> The joy of it, that the po0rer you become the richer you are able to make others;
> The joy of it, that the weaker you become, the stronger God becomes in you;
> The joy of it, that what you lose temporally you gain eternally;
> The joy of it that when I 'gain everything' I lose nothing at all;
> The joy of it, that adversity is prosperity. (CD, vi)

That suffering itself is not the problem is clear from these paradoxes. A similar structure of paradox is to be found too in *The Sickness unto Death*. There it is our inability, or unwillingness to embrace suffering, and ultimately to undergo death that is the cause of our true suffering and despair. The sickness unto death itself is the inability to die, precisely, suffering too long, refusing to end our despair because we fear what will actually cure us, the death to self. What Auden seems to imply, in line with Kierkegaard, is that the problem has more to do with how we approach the suffering and that, in particular, appropriate timing is called for. Auden reproaches us with suffering both too little and too long, thereby depriving ourselves of the good news of suffering. But what do these categories imply and can Kierkegaard, and Auden, really have it both ways?

The paradigmatic New Testament example of the one who suffers too long is the sick man at the pool of Bethsaida in John 5 who has lain there for thirty-eight years, never making it to the pool at the healing moment when the water is troubled. Jesus asks him a key question, 'Do you want to be made well?' The man's reply is not a 'yes' or a 'no' but a recital of his grievances. I was very struck teaching this story many years ago to a rather motley class of children in a very rough inner London comprehensive. One forthright young lady said, 'What an idiot that sick man was!' When I asked her why, and whether she had any sympathy for his plight, she said, and I apologise for the language, 'Well, even if he could only shuffle on his bum an inch a day, in thirty-eight years he could have got to the edge of the pool, and then when the water bubbled up, he could just have rolled himself over and got in first. But he didn't have the bottle!'

That is a good account of what might be meant by 'suffering too long'. When suffering becomes an excuse for inaction or when it is allowed to become the defining aspect of a human life, the sufferer is in the wrong. This notion is also a corrective to another potential misrelationship to suffering. If suffering is the necessary pathway to joy, and the inevitable experience of the Christian in the world, should we not embrace suffering itself as a good? This, however, is something that Kierkegaard warns against, and which his journal entries strongly deny. It is a kind of frivolity to entertain that thought, he says, one that could only occur to someone who has not truly experienced suffering. Paul was not enjoined to see the suffering of his thorn in the flesh as in itself a good, and certainly not expected to seek out thorns to impale himself upon. Suffering in itself is not a good, anymore than despair is. It is given to us to be striven against, not embraced. The fact that it can be turned to good, or that the struggle against it can be life-changing, does not make it a good in itself.

In this poem, Auden goes on to chide us for our carefulness even in our selfless loves. How reminiscent of the Kierkegaard who in *Works of Love* tells us that love can never be deceived, and that we should carry on loving even the one who attempts to deceive us. He may deceive us, but not love, because love remains undeceived by his attempts to evade it. It is a bold kind of selfless lover who can open himself to such deceit. Auden also takes on the aesthetic and its self-deception as our 'decorative manias' die around us. Yet the final line is the one that arrests me in this context. Auden sees this confusion, this *tohu-bohu*, overcome by an absurd command: 'Rejoice!'

Joy, then, is both absurd in itself and something which is commanded, although the idea of commanding someone to rejoice is strange in its own right. Surely nothing is less convincing than a display of joy to order, which cannot help recalling the well drilled spontaneous enthusiasm fostered by some former communist regimes. In this line I do think that Auden catches the essence of what Kierkegaard has to say about joy.

Let us look at this in two stages. Firstly, I want to understand the absurdity of joy, and secondly, I want to look more closely at the absurdity of a command to rejoice, or what we might call a duty of joy.

Firstly, the absurdity of joy. The absurd, the paradox, is of course something that is entirely characteristic of Kierkegaard's thought, and I would argue, of biblical thought. I teach the Hebrew Bible, when I am permitted to, and have to do an outline course in 20 lectures. I always begin by explaining to the students that this is a mugs' game and that, given my head, I have been known to spend four weeks lecturing on the first verse of Ecclesiastes. Having got that off my chest, I then go on to make them a promise that, when it comes down to it, I will perform the even more impossible feat of summing up the Hebrew Bible in one word. They have to sit through eleven weeks of lectures to hear it, but I will let you into the secret with rather less suspense, though I might give you a minute to think of it: the one word that sums up the entire Hebrew Bible. The word is: nevertheless.

I suspect my fondness for this word may be due to my Edinburgh heritage, either through nurture or nature, I am not sure which. Certainly the word is incisively explored by my fellow Edinburgh native, the inimitable Muriel Spark. She writes,

> It would need a scientific study to ascertain whether the word was truly employed more frequently in Edinburgh than anywhere else. It is my own instinct to associate the word, as the core of a thought-pattern, with Edinburgh particularly. I see the lip of tough elderly

women in musquash coats taking tea at MacVittie's, enunciating this word of final justification, I can see the exact gesture of head and chin and gleam of the eye that accompanied it. The sound was roughly 'niverthelace' and the emphasis was a heartfelt one. I believe myself to be fairly indoctrinated by the habit of thought which calls for this word. In fact I approve of the ceremonious accumulation of weather forecasts and barometer reading that pronounce for a fine day, before letting rip on the statement: 'Nevertheless, it's raining'. I find that much of my literary composition is based on the nevertheless idea. I act upon it. It was on the nevertheless principle that I turned Catholic.[5]

The biblical roots of this attitude are epitomized by the prophet Habakkuk:

Though the fig tree does not blossom
And though no fruit is on the vines
Through the produce of the olive fails
And the fields yield no food;
Though the flock is cut off from the fold
And there is no herd in the stalls,
Yet I will rejoice in the Lord;
I will exult in the God of my salvation. (Hab 3:17-19)

Yet I will rejoice: Habakkuk's nevertheless to God, and one that is bound to rejoicing. It is not because of what he sees or experiences that Habakkuk rejoices, but in spite of it. Time and again in the psalms, and in the stories of Israel, it is the 'nevertheless' that breaks through after the depths of lamentation have been plumbed. Yet there is another side to this, God's recurrent 'nevertheless' to the people of Israel, whose disobedience by rights should have led to their casting off and utter destruction. In the interplay of these neverthelesses we find the possibility of forgiveness and of love.

It is not a matter of 'because'. Indeed, in such a worldview joy itself can be the most acute source of suffering. When Johannes Climacus in *Fear and Trembling* confesses his admiration yet incomprehension when he contemplates Abraham, he sets out four exordia. These quasi-midrashic retellings of the sacrifice of Isaac offer four Abrahams who are easier to understand than the one depicted in Genesis. The second of these four is the Abraham who loses his joy. Describing the aftermath of the aborted sacrifice, Climacus writes, 'From that day henceforth, Abraham was old; he could not forget that God had ordered him to do this. Isaac flourished as before, but Abraham's eyes were darkened, and he saw joy no more' (FT, 12). It is one thing to be required to undergo suffering; it is another to be expected to rejoice while we undergo it.

This is Climacus' way of pointing out the incomprehensibility that the biblical Abraham not only performed his appalling duty but also retained his joy. The Abraham who obeys in despair we can understand more easily. Indeed, despair is something that we can empathize with more readily than joy. That is not surprising as, according to *The Sickness unto Death*, despair is a universal condition and Kierkegaard brilliantly dissects and displays the varieties of despair that we fall into. But we misread that book entirely if we just see it as an anatomy of our condition, a description of the human heart offering us the consolation of a bleak solidarity of despair, which is how it has been taken up in some quarters. Kierkegaard, or rather Anti-Climacus, explicitly warns against this in the preface: 'Just one more comment, no doubt unnecessary, but nevertheless I will make it: once and for all may I point out that in the whole book, as the title indeed declares, despair is interpreted as a sickness not as a cure' (SUD, 6). Kierkegaard's tongue is in his cheek here; he knows full well that this 'unnecessary' warning is all too necessary. Climacus does go on to say that, strange as it may seem, despair is good news.

> Is despair an excellence or a defect? Purely dialectically, it is both. If only the abstract idea of despair is considered, without any thought of someone in despair, it must be regarded as a surpassing excellence. The possibility of this sickness is man's superiority over the animal, and this superiority distinguishes him in quite another way than does his erect walk, for it indicates infinite erectness or sublimity, that he is spirit. The possibility of this sickness is man's superiority over the animal, to be aware of this sickness is the Christian's superiority over the natural man; to be cured of this sickness is the Christian's blessedness. (SUD, 14–15)

The possibility of blessedness is only available to us because we are constituted to despair. That may seem a strange sort of good news, but it falls in the same explicitly medical category as receiving the diagnosis that one has a life-threatening but curable disease, even though one feels healthy enough except for some indefinable pang, but that the cure itself may be slow and painful. To be told one has the disease is a terrible shock that may lead some patients to spin off into denial and others to despair. Yet there can be a sense of relief at having at least a diagnosis, which may lead to the confidence that this enemy, though formidable, is not above defeat. What is named and described is already more controllable than the anonymous fear or the unknown threat.

Kierkegaard often uses this forensic sort of metaphor, and much of his work could be understood as the attempt to persuade his hearers that they are sick so that they will seek a cure for the disease that is killing them spiritually unawares. It is only in the encounter with the offer of a cure that we realize how ill we have been and the true nature of sin can be realized. In Kierkegaard's thought, it is in the encounter with Christ that we become aware of both the disease and the possibility of cure.

Yet human perversity is such that the identification of the cure and the disease can be reversed. The one who points out the falseness of our sense of security can be quickly recast as the champion, if not indeed the cause, of the sickness. After all, we felt perfectly healthy until he intervened. The escape into denial or defiance, which itself constitutes despair, can then be seen as the cure. Here is the offence of which Kierkegaard so often speaks. It can be healing, but can result in the healer, the God-man, or his apostle, falling victim to the fear that he engenders. The anger that should be vented on the disease is vented on the physician. Yet for those who come to accept that they are in need of a cure, the discovery that the bearer of the bad news is also the bearer of the good news of healing paradoxically makes the bad news into joyful tidings.

Indeed, it leads to the further absurd but joyful discovery that joy is commanded. Kierkegaard sets this out in *Stages on Life's Way*:

> It is now obvious what must be understood religiously by self-torment. It is a matter of discovering *by oneself* the full possibility of danger, and *by oneself* at every moment its actuality (this the esthete would call self-torment and the esthetic lecture would prevent one from it by imitation religious gilding), but it is simultaneously a matter of being joyous. Where then, is the self-torment? It is at the halfway point. It is not at the beginning, for then I am speaking esthetically, but it is due to one's being *unable to work one's way through to joy*. And this, declares the religious person, is not comic; neither does it lend itself to evoking esthetic tears, for that is reprehensible and one *shall* work one's way through. (SLW, 470–71; emphasis in original)

One *shall* work one's way through. This is where the notion of joy as duty and commandment comes into its own. It is a task and a duty and something that takes courage. As Kierkegaard puts it in a journal entry, 'It takes moral courage to grieve; it takes religious courage to rejoice' (JP, 2179).

Joy is not an optional extra, or a subjective sense of satisfaction, but an orientation, and a command, as Auden intimates. It is as absurd and as important as that other problematic order, the command to love. The idea that one can love on command has been challenged as meaningless and offensive by philosophers. No less absurd is a command to be joyful,

surely. Kierkegaard's defence of this seeming absurdity is expounded at
length in *Works of Love*, where, rather than being an impossible burden,
the command to love is demonstrated to be a source of power and
freedom for the human subject. 'You shall love. There is nothing difficult
in one sense in the syntax of this sentence, but nevertheless it is a source
of offence. It seems to rob love of its spontaneity, its romance and its
arbitrariness. All this Kierkegaard acknowledges, but then we read, in
emphatic script in the original, '"You shall love." *Only when it is a duty
to love, only then is love eternally secured against every change, eternally
made free in blessed independence, eternally and happily secured against
despair*' (WL, 29).

It is the very obligation that frees us, as Kierkegaard explains: 'Alas,
we very often think that freedom exists and that it is law that binds
freedom. Yet it is just the opposite; without law, freedom does not exist
at all, and it is law that gives freedom' (WL, 38). The imperative to love is
also the counter to despair: '...there is only one security against despair:
to undergo the change of eternity through duty's *shall*' (WL, 39). In
Works of Love, Kierkegaard explains despair as a misrelation to eternity.
Only eternity can be the object of our infinite passion, and so when that
passion is directed anywhere else, despair results. Joy, I would contend,
is the manifestation of this passionate relation to eternity, and while the
misrelation persists, there can be no joy. The command brings joy, as it
brings love. A journal entry reads, 'If this is properly interpreted, every
man who truly wants to relate himself to God and be intimate with him
really only has one task—to rejoice always' (JP, 2187). Rejoicing brings
the relation, the relation causes joy, all through the task.

Another take on this, one which gives quite another colour to the
same ideas, is to be found in *Judge for Yourself!*, in the story of little
Ludwig. It is part of a discussion of Kierkegaard's beloved lily and the
bird, one where, in contrast to the rather forbidding prose of *Sickness
unto Death*, he offers a delightfully lyrical hymn to the joy of those who
trust absolutely in God. Little Ludwig makes his appearance precisely to
deal with the paradox that joy is our task, and yet we can only undertake
the task because of the relationship with God that underpins it.

> Every day little Ludvig is taken for a ride in his stroller, a delight that
> usually lasts an hour, and little Ludvig understands very well that it is a
> delight. Yet the mother has hit upon something new that will definitely
> delight little Ludvig even more; would he like to try to push the stroller
> himself? And he can! What! He can? Yes, look, Auntie, little Ludvig can
> push the stroller himself! Now, let us be down to earth but not upset

> the child, since we know very well that little Ludvig cannot do it, that
> it is really his mother who is actually pushing the stroller, and that it is
> really only to delight him that she plays the game that little Ludvig can
> do it himself. And he, he huffs and puffs. And he is sweating, isn't he?
> On my word, he is! The sweat stands on his brow, in the sweat of his
> brow he is pushing the stroller—but his face is shining with happiness;
> on could say he is drunk with happiness, and, if possible, he becomes
> even more so every time Auntie says: Just look at that! Little Ludvig can
> do it himself. (JFY, 185)

This is a remarkable bit of writing as Kierkegaard teeters on the brink of
sentimentality to make the point that the joy of the task and the fact that
God accomplishes it are not incompatible. Characteristically, however,
just as we are beginning to think that Kierkegaard is turning into Patience
Strong or another such sentimental versifier, over the page we find little
Ludvig again—only, now he is grown up. He now knows that his mother
was pushing the stroller, but, instead of disillusioning him, this gives
him a new joy, a joy of the recollection of her love which could think of
providing such joy to her child, along with a mature awareness of the
fact that the task, and the joy, are not his, but God's. Joy, then, is both
duty and gift, both task and reward.

What we have been saying here is echoed in some remarkable words
often attributed to Nelson Mandela in his 1994 inaugural speech, but are
in fact by Marianne Williamson:

> Our deepest fear is not that we are inadequate. Our deepest fear is
> that we are powerful beyond measure. It is our light, not our darkness,
> that most frightens us. We as ourselves, 'Who am I to be brilliant,
> gorgeous, talented, fabulous?' Actually, who are you not to be? You
> are a child of God. Your playing small doesn't serve the world. There's
> nothing enlightened about shrinking so that other people won't feel
> insecure around you. We are all meant to shine, as children do. We
> were born to make manifest the glory of God that is within us. It's not
> just in some of us, it's in everyone. And as we let our own light shine,
> we unconsciously give other people permission to do the same.[6]

The pity is that we think of joy in terms of a philosophy of scarcity. It is
a precious thing, and if we have it, we conclude, we need to keep hold of
it. More selflessly, we become self-conscious about our joy. What right
have we to rejoice when other people are in pain and suffering and in
poverty? The mistake is that we think that joy is *our* joy. If we have joy,
we seem to think, other people are deprived of it and we are deprived by
their joy, as if there were not enough to go around. If joy is commanded,
such calculation becomes irrelevant. The knowledge that joy is not a

matter of our subjective state, but part of our duty before God, takes our focus away from our selves. Joy is a gift, not our gift to others, or a gift to us, but a gift such as is spoken of in that verse of James which Kierkegaard so often refers to and called his favourite: 'every good gift and every perfect gift is form above, and cometh down from the Father of Lights, which who is no variableness, neither shadow of turning' (Jas 1:17). If joy is God's joy, then it is not limited except by our failure to make it manifest, to live up to that duty.

If this is so, one final question occurs: did Kierkegaard himself live up to this vision? Is there really a 'joy of Kierkegaard'? That is probably an impertinent question, and one that strays into a realm of spiritual judgment that is not ours to make. There are passages in the journal which do speak of an unutterable joy, like the following:

> Therefore my voice will shout for joy at the top of my lungs, louder than the voice of a woman who has given birth, louder than the angels' glad shout over a sinner who is converted, more joyful than the morning song of the birds, for what I have sought I have found, and if men robbed me of everything, if they cast me out of their society, I would still retain this joy. If everything were taken from me, I would still continue to have the best—the blessed wonder over God's infinite love, over the wisdom of his decisions. (JP, 2184)

Yet, as we have seen, Kierkegaard's reputation in some quarters has been as a pedlar of gloom, and angst, and as we read through some of his journals and the account of the attack on Christendom we can understand those who feel a sense of sympathetic disappointment that this brilliant and difficult man in the end of a tortured life succumbed to bitterness and loneliness. Nevertheless, and I use that word quite consciously, as so often, we have choices to make about how we weigh the evidence.

I read of Kierkegaard's last days with more than the usual sense of unwarranted intrusion that such accounts may induce. There in cold print we can now all read the doctor's notes and can only imagine the chagrin with which an intensely private and physically reserved man would feel to know that this is so, as the body with which he had so uncomfortable a relationship asserted its feeble but ungainsayable demands.

Nevertheless, among these pages is the remarkable account by Kierkegaard's nephew, Troels Frederik Troels-Lund, of his last parting from his uncle, an account where Troels is at pains to underscore his own awareness that what he says could be taken as the romanticism of an impressionable young man, but which he stands by:

When I extended my hand to him, the others had already turned toward the door, so it was as though we were alone. He took my hand in both of his own—how small, thin and transparently white they were—and said only "Thank you for coming to see me, Troels! And now, live well!' But these ordinary words were accompanied by a look of which I have never since seen the equal. It radiated with an elevated, transfigured, blessed brilliance, so that it seemed to me to illuminate the entire room. Everything was concentrated in the flood of light from these eyes: profound love, beatifically dissolved sadness, an all-penetrating clarity, and a playful smile. For me it was like a heavenly revelation, an emanation from one soul to another, a blessing, which infused me with new courage, strength and responsibility.[7]

Joy as gift and duty seems to me epitomized in this encounter. That his nephew would write this, whatever the cold eye of the camera would have made of that moment, is to me earnest enough that Kierkegaard, in whatever measure, was what I think he would agree that we are all called to be, a prophet of joy. This joy is not Kierkegaard's possession, but a gift that he passes on to his readers so that we too could be prophets of the joy that Kierkegaard knew: the joy of Kierkegaard.

Notes

1. Richard Pevear, 'Introduction,' in Fyodor Dostoevsky, *The Brothers Karamazov* (London: Vintage, 1990), xi–xviii (xi).
2. The fact that an anthology by Thomas C. Oden entitled *The Humor of Kierkegaard* (Princeton: Princeton University Press, 2004) is currently available is testimony to this. Not many other philosophers have been accorded that kind of recognition and not many could sustain it.
3. W.H. Auden, *Collected Poems* (ed. Edward Mendelson; London: Faber & Faber, 1994), pp. 317–20 (319).
4. This point is also made by John Fuller in his *W.H. Auden: A Commentary* (London: Faber & Faber, 1998), p. 392, where he mentions that this very phrase from Kierkegaard is quoted in a letter from Auden to Stephen Spender of the same year.
5. Muriel Spark, 'What Images Return,' in Douglas Dunn (ed.), *Scotland: An Anthology* (London: Fontana, 1992), pp. 117–120 (119). Originally published as 'Edinburgh-born,' *New Statesman*, 10 August 1962, 180.
6. Marianne Williamson, *A Return to Love: Reflections on the Principles of* A Course in Miracles (New York: HarperCollins, 1992), pp. 190–191.
7. Bruce Kirmmse, *Encounters with Kierkegaard: A Life as Seen by His Contemporaries* (Princeton: Princeton University Press, 1996), p. 190. The source for Kirmmse's translation is Troels Frederik Troels-Lund's memoir, *Et Liv: Barndom og Ungdom* (Copenhagen: H. Hagerups Forlag, 1924), pp. 235–41.

KIERKEGAARD'S CANON: THE CONSTITUTION OF THE
BIBLE AND OF THE AUTHORSHIP
IN *CONCLUDING UNSCIENTIFIC POSTSCRIPT*

Questions of canonicity form an *inclusio* for *Concluding Unscientific Postscript*. The book begins with Climacus' discussion of the irrelevance of historical and theological debates about the canon of the Scriptures to Christian faith and ends with the 'First and Last Explanation', signed by Kierkegaard himself, which discusses the canon of his own authorship. This circling back to the initial question is fitting in view of the fact that these questions themselves lead to a series of circularities in our reading of *Postscript*. Furthermore, in the body of *Postscript* there is another more elaborate discussion of the constitution of the canon of the authorship in 'A Glance at a Contemporary Effort in Danish Literature', where Climacus comments on the interrelationships between not one but three 'canons': the set of pseudonymous works, behind which Climacus implies there is a single author; Magister Kierkegaard's *Upbuilding Discourses*; and Climacus' own *Philosophical Fragments*, with the present text *Postscript* assigned its canonical role as a sequel. These discussions have their own problems of canonical status: what is the significance of the fact that 'A Glance...' is described as an appendix, and that the 'Explanation' is on unnumbered pages, following on Climacus' revocation of *Postscript*? Are these texts part of *Postscript* or not?

The question of what constitutes a canon and how awareness of a text's place in a canon shapes our reading of it can be applied to our reading of *Postscript* itself. How does Kierkegaard's understanding of the canon of his own writings in the 'Explanation' relate to Climacus' version in 'A Glance...', and how does the internal variety of voices in *Postscript* relate to voices outside the text, in particular the *Point of View of my Work as an Author* where another account of the Kierkegaardian canon and the role of *Postscript* within it is given? If we need to invoke other of Kierkegaard's writings to elucidate *Postscript*, which can we legitimately choose, and why?

These are wide-ranging issues and this essay cannot hope to do more than point out that this aspect of *Postscript* suggests there could be creative analogies and tensions between Kierkegaard's understanding of the biblical canon and his conception of his own production as an authorship. In this connection, consider the following statement by the biblical theologian Paul Noble:

> The formal model...I am proposing is that the biblical canon be construed as analogous to the 'collected works' of a single author. This (divine) author wrote them (over a considerable period of time) by assuming a variety of authorial *personae*, each with its own distinctive character, historical situation, etc. As one moves, therefore, from one book to another one encounters a diversity of 'implied authors', each of whom must be understood on their own terms; yet behind them all is a single, controlling intelligence, working to an overall plan. Because of this, these diverse works therefore can—and for a full understanding, must—be read together as a unified canon.[1]

Noble stresses that this is a formal proposal which does not purport to account for the Bible and its origins historically but gives a methodological framework for interpretation. However, everything he says here of the biblical canon could be a description of Kierkegaard's authorship. Indeed, this may lead us to wonder whether the model of the biblical canon lies somewhere behind the construction of the authorship. Looked at in this light, Matthew, Mark, Luke and John could be construed as pseudonyms of the divine author, not entirely dissimilar to Kierkegaard's pseudonyms.

This is not an unprecedented thought. Luther hints at this when he says that it is a mistake to speak of four Gospels; there is one gospel, but it is communicated in different texts. Kierkegaard himself writes as follows in the *Upbuilding Discourses in Various Spirits*: 'Whether you consult the Scriptures of the Old Covenant or the New, there is only one view on this. There are many replies, but they all say the same thing. The reply is always the same; only the voice is different, so that the reply, by means of this difference, might win different people' (UD, 92). The communicative function of the concept of canon is thus a live issue in both biblical studies and in Kierkegaard's authorship.

What leads Climacus, however, to open his *Postscript* with this question of the canon? The answer is to be found in a paradox that besets the Christian tradition and Lutheranism in particular. To cut a long story short, in the very act of making the Bible the central authority for the Christian, Luther disturbs a consensus over the biblical canon which it had taken the Western church several centuries to achieve through its acceptance of Jerome's Vulgate translation and the pragmatic solution it enshrined. In what follows, the focus is on the development of the canon of the New Testament, although there are important concerns over the canonical shape of the Old Testament and its relation to the New to be borne in mind as well. Kierkegaard himself remarks, 'It is not easy to have both the Old and the New Testament, for the O.T. contains altogether different categories' (JP, 206).[2]

Bruce Metzger provides an authoritative overview of the historical development of the New Testament canon which acknowledges that this is not a simple or universally agreed story.[3] While there seems to have been a general acceptance by the end of the second century of the core of the New Testament as we now understand it—the four Gospels, the Acts of the Apostles and the Pauline epistles—there was less agreement over the other epistles and Revelation. In addition, books such as the Epistles of Clement and Barnabas and the Shepherd of Hermas were quoted by several Church fathers as Scripture.

In the first quarter of the fourth century, Eusebius of Caesarea tried to clarify the situation by listing apostolic or pretended apostolic writings in three groups:

1. Books which all the churches and authorities he had consulted agreed should be included, which he called the *homolegumena*. These were the four Gospels, Acts, the Pauline epistles, including Hebrews (though Eusebius notes that this had been disputed), 1 Peter and 1 John. He also mentions the Apocalypse of John in this category, but notes that this judgment is very controversial.

2. Books which were disputed, yet well known and widely accepted, which he calls the *antilegomena*. These were the Epistles of James, Jude, 2 Peter and 2 and 3 John.

3. Spurious books: these include the acts of Paul and the Shepherd, but Eusebius also includes the Apocalypse of John here, and mentions Hebrews again.

In what seems to have been an attempt to clear up confusion, Eusebius simply bears witness to the confused state of the question. In Metzger's view, Eusebius himself is torn between his responsibility as a historian to record which books have been accepted or not and his theological instincts. His confused categories reflect the fact that he regrets that certain generally accepted books, particularly the Apocalypse, have been misused, as he sees it, by heretical groups such as the Montanists. Whatever the truth of this, the canonical status of seven of the books in the present New Testament is shown to be disputed even in Eusebius' day.

The first statement that the canon of the New Testament comprises the twenty-seven books recognized today is to be found in Athanasius' Thirty-Ninth Festal Epistle, but although Athanasius is characteristically definitive on this matter, his opinions, particularly his inclusion of John's Apocalypse, were not universally accepted at the time. In any case, the need for a sharp delineation of the canon was more strongly felt in the Latin Church than the Greek, so Metzger contends. This went along with a starker view in the Latin Church that the books to be rejected were devoid of spiritual worth; the Greek Church was more ready to live with a collection of texts which it acknowledged had degrees of value.

In practical terms, the contents of the canon were settled in the West with Jerome's new Vulgate translation. Whatever the theoretical arguments and ambiguities, a translator ends up having to make clear *de facto* decisions as to what texts are to be translated. So, for instance, Jerome decided to include both Hebrews and Revelation in his New Testament, even though he was not following the accepted practice of the day in this. Jerome acknowledged that the churches of the West in his day did not receive Hebrews and those of the East did not receive Revelation, but the ancient writers quoted both as Scripture and so he includes both.

Although by use and custom Jerome's canon prevailed, it was not until the Council of Florence, held from 1439–43, that Rome finally pronounced definitely on which books were to be received in the canon of the New Testament. This was in the context of a rapprochement with the Eastern Church. It also coincided with the rise of humanist scholarship which began to reopen critical questions about the authorship of New Testament books. Erasmus, for instance, queried several of the disputed books, although he later expressed the desire not to contradict Church teaching. Luther's one-time colleague Andreas Bodenstein, commonly known as Karlstadt, was not so constrained when in 1520 he consigned seven disputed books (corresponding to Eusebius' *antilegomena*) to a clear third rank in the canon on the grounds of doubt about their authorship.

When we come to Luther himself, we find that he divides the New Testament books into three categories. First are those books which teach all that is necessary to know: John's Gospel and first epistle, Paul's letters to the Romans, Galatians and Ephesians and 1 Peter.[4] In the second rank are the synoptic Gospels, the other Pauline epistles, Acts, 2 Peter and 2 and 3 John.

The third group contains Hebrews, Jude, James and John. In his New Testament of 1522, Luther places these last four at the end of the text and on the title page lists them in a separate block, without numbers, at the end of the numbered list of the other books. He gives his reasons for doubting their apostolicity: Hebrews teaches that there can be no repentance after baptism, James teaches justification by works, Jude repeats 2 Peter and quotes from apocryphal texts and the visions of Revelation are not the concern of an apostolic author. Although Luther makes some general appeal to the ancient doubts about these books, this is not the primary ground for his arguments. His particular list of questionable books and his re-ordering of the New Testament are unprecedented.[5]

What becomes clear is that, for Luther, what matters in a text is apostolicity, which is a quality of a text, not an author: 'Whatever does not teach Christ is not [yet][6] apostolic, even though St Peter or St Paul does the teaching. Again whatever preaches Christ would be apostolic, even if Judas, Annas, Pilate and Herod were doing it.'[7] Luther's stated criteria for canonicity are thus theological. As Jaroslav Pelikan observes, however, whatever Luther the theologian thinks, Luther the translator, just like Jerome, is faced once more with the practical question of which books are to be included. In the event, he does not seek to suppress even those books he regards as doubtful or of limited use, contenting himself with his reordering.

Luther's order was followed by such translations as Tyndale's in England and the Gustavus Adolphus Bible in Sweden (1618), which goes so far as to label the four disputed books as 'Apocryphal', and indeed by Danish translations until the early nineteenth century.[8] This is evidence that the issue of the New Testament canon was a constant point of discussion for Lutheran theologians. They had to reconcile the central place given to the Bible by the doctrine of *sola scriptura* with Luther's own reopening of the question of what constituted that Scripture.

That debate lies behind Climacus' concerns at the beginning of *Postscript*, but there is a more immediate manifestation of this continuing argument within the Danish Church. It had come to a head in the notorious events surrounding N.F.C. Grundtvig's publication of his pamphlet *Kirkens Gienmæle* [*The Church's Rejoinder*] in 1825. This seminal work in Grundtvig's public career was a polemical retort to H.N. Clausen's book *Catholicismens og Protestantismens Kierkeforfatning, Lære og Ritus*

[*Catholicism and Protestantism: Their Church Constitutions, Doctrines and Rites*].[9] Grundtvig's reading of Clausen was partial at best and in the course of the pamphlet he attacked Clausen with such vehemence that the latter successfully sued him for libel.

Although moving beyond it, the argument between them has its roots in the Lutheran problem of the canon. Both Grundtvig and Clausen were seeking to counter the difficulties critical scholarship was posing for the classical Reformation stance of reliance on Scripture alone. It is in this rejoinder that Grundtvig announced his 'matchless discovery' [*mageløse opdagelse*], a turn of phrase which Climacus seizes upon satirically in *Postscript*. What Grundtvig asserted was the determinative place in Christian faith of the Church as a community of believers bound together by the oral traditions of the prayers and creeds which predate and validate the Bible. The ground of certainty is thus this church tradition, as opposed to Clausen's advocacy of the role of the scientific researches of professional theologians and biblical scholars.

Clausen, whose importance for Kierkegaard is, I believe, still underestimated, was an admirable scholar who was well acquainted with the most current biblical research and showed a masterly fluency in synthesizing and communicating it. He was much influenced by Friedrich Schleiermacher who, in his own discussion of the formation of the canon, uses the metaphor of an individual refining and ordering his own thoughts to express the Spirit's role in the Church's process of selection and agreement of what constitutes Scripture.[10] This process is gradual and Schleiermacher states explicitly that 'the Church is only approximating ever more closely to a complete expulsion of the apocryphal and the pure preservation of the canonical'.[11] Schleiermacher interestingly does not privilege the opinion of the earliest witnesses, as many other theologians have done. He regards the sense for the truly apostolic as something that increases in the Church over time, so that earlier generations are more liable to make misjudgments than the later. Canonicity, for Schleiermacher, does not depend on the authorship of a book. Pseudonymous works could well be admitted to the canon, because what matters is that the Church has been led to accept them. Importantly, the contents of the canon are always open to renewed critical investigation by the Church. 'Doubt of the genuine can only issue in greater certainty', he writes.[12] Such investigation is the business of professionally trained scholars, not a matter of appeal to tradition or authority.

Clausen follows Schleiermacher in much of this. He argues that Scripture is in a sense raw material for the Church, and the job of the professional theologian and biblicist is to clarify and elaborate through a constant process of critical engagement the teaching that had been given *in nuce* in the Bible. However, Clausen was never simplistic enough to think that scholars could answer everything and, along with this argument, acknowledged the authority of the spiritual heritage of the Church. There is a difference between the kind of answers which are sought by church historians to questions over the formation of the canon and the answers appropriate to the questions of the faithful believer. Yet a revelation which cannot be rationally comprehended and which does not yield fruits from rational investigation is no revelation for Clausen. The process of research is never-ending, but also endlessly enriching.[13]

Climacus seizes on Schleiermacher's term 'approximation' to undercut the whole argument. It is important to acknowledge that fundamentally he agrees with Clausen's analysis and pours scorn on what he sees as Grundtvig's naïve reliance in his counter-argument on an idealized concept of the Church that cannot hold up in reality and certainly cannot provide the historical grounding for Christianity that Grundtvig seems to imagine it will.

The problem is that approximation knowledge will not do in the life of faith, however. The reason for this is made clear by Jaroslav Pelikan when he points out that Kierkegaard came from an intellectual background which demanded intellectual assurance as the guarantee of the certainty of salvation. Given that background, Pelikan writes, 'All the more terrifying was it, therefore, to discover that in dealing with the Holy there was no guarantee of such certainty, indeed that such certainty was impossible and even hostile to the true knowledge of God.'[14]

As so often in Kierkegaard's writing, however, what might seem to be the point of despair becomes the reason for hope. The rhetoric of the discussion of the historical truth of Scripture in *Postscript* is designed precisely to instil and heighten the terror of uncertainty and to show the hollowness of the attempts to assuage this by clutching at some other promise of certainty. Climacus' line is that the question of faith is one of infinite interest. The question of the canon can only ever lead to an approximate knowledge. Therefore, this question is only relevant to faith insofar as it demonstrates that the Bible in itself can give no ground of certainty. This works both ways. Even supposing the impossible result that scholarship has definitively settled any question regarding the Scripture, that fact would still not advance the individual's faith one jot. Conversely, the disproof of the authenticity of Scripture would do no harm to the believer's faith. This leads Climacus to the following declaration:

> ...because these books are not by these authors, are not authentic, are not *integri*, are not inspired (this cannot be disproved, because it is a matter of faith), it does not follow that these authors have not existed and, above all, that Christ has not existed. To that extent, the believer is still equally free to accept it, equally free, please note, because if he accepted it by virtue of a demonstration, he would be on the verge of abandoning the faith. (CUP1, 30)

This declaration, however, leads to a problem which I can perhaps elucidate by asking the following slightly outré question: on these grounds, would Climacus have accepted the Book of Mormon as canonical Scripture?[15] He has made it clear that no argument from historical evidence and accusations of forgery could be used to disprove its status. On a theological level, the introduction to the book of Mormon holds out the following promise:

> We invite all men everywhere to read the Book of Mormon, to ponder in their hearts the message it contains, and then to ask God, the Eternal Father, in the name of Christ if the book is true. Those who pursue this course and ask in faith will gain a testimony of its truth and divinity by the power of the Holy Ghost. (see Moroni 10:3-5)

Compare this to the following passage from the Journals:

> Suppose that doubt hit upon and came up with a kind of probability that Paul's letters were not by Paul and that Paul never lived at all— what then? Well, scholarly orthodoxy might give up hope. The believer might quite simply turn to God in prayer, saying: How can all this hang together? I cannot cope with all this scholarship, but I stick to Paul's teaching, and you, my God, will not allow me to live in error, whatever the critics prove about Paul's existence [*Tilværelse*]. I take what I read here in Paul and this I refer to you, O God, and then you will keep me from being led into error though my reading. (JP, 212)

What is the formal difference here? The proof of the pudding could only be in the eating and Climacus seems to have undercut any arguments he could offer against someone whose faith was based on Mormon texts. Would he then have accepted them? If not, what is his basis for accepting the biblical canon as uniquely authoritative?

I suspect the principle answer to this would be the pragmatic but possibly entirely adequate one that he is addressing an audience of Danish Christians. Kierkegaard throughout his works seems simply to assume the standard canon, raising few questions about its provenance. He is not concerned to persuade non-Christians of the value of the Bible, or to educate them on its contents, but rather to get Christians to read and act upon it. His plea in the journals that the New Testament should be taken away so that people would appreciate it reflects this presupposition that the Bible is a given, but as such also merely part of the familiar scenery to most Danes. The idea of adding to the Bible does not enter into the discussion. No doubt he might have said that there was time enough to worry about additions to the Bible once one had actually taken the Bible in one's hands seriously.[16]

Given that pragmatic attitude which accepts the canon of Scripture as a given, Kierkegaard is able to chide Luther for his unbalanced use of the canon. 'He one-sidedly draws Paul forward and uses the gospels less', he writes (JP, 2507), and in the same journal entry we find specific criticism of Luther's disregard for James because of a dogmatic presupposition. Kierkegaard concedes out that Luther never denied James his place in the canon, but that his denigration of the book shows that he has a point of departure superior to the Bible, thus disproving his own position on the sufficiency of the Bible. Kierkegaard's point is Luther's inconsistency, and he carefully does not say that his own position assumes the sufficiency of the Bible.

Indeed, in *For Self-Examination* Kierkegaard cunningly enlists Luther as an ally in his recovery of James as not just a part of the canon, but as a central text, arguing that Luther would be the first person to insist that faith must issue in works when confronted by the spiritless complacency of contemporary Christians.[17] The danger he confronted of people strenuously trying to earn righteousness through fearsome disciplines of penitence hardly applies to contemporary Copenhagen, Kierkegaard argues. Indeed, as I have suggested elsewhere, in the *Concept of Dread* there is at least a hint that Kierkegaard is seeking to replace the Pauline reading of Genesis 3 and its particular understanding of original sin with a new understanding gained by reading Genesis through the lens of James.[18] Reactively, Kierkegaard, in common with every other Christian writer, does manifest a personal canon within the canon, one made up of those biblical writings that emphasize his particular concerns.

Ultimately, however, Kierkegaard is, as ever, not seeking a logical, consistent and satisfying solution to the problem of canonicity. What Kierkegaard wants to do at every turn is to recover the sense of the Bible as scandal. The very fact that its contents are disputed and disrupted is to him paradoxically part of its power. In a journal entry entitled 'A New

Proof for the Divinity of the Bible' Kierkegaard argues that, as God knows what faith requires, the New Testament is *not* harmonious: 'Precisely because God wants Holy Scripture to be the object of faith and an offense to any other point of view, for this reason there are carefully contrived discrepancies (which, after all, in eternity will readily be dissolved into harmonies); therefore it is written in bad Greek, etc.' (JP, 2877)

An important footnote in *Postscript* reinforces this insistence on the scandal of the Bible, and gets us closer to understanding the role of the problem of the canon in this regard:

> On the whole, the infinite reflection in which the subjective individual is first able to become concerned about his eternal happiness is immediately recognizable by one thing, that it is everywhere accompanied by the dialectical. Whether it is a word, a sentence, a book, a man, a society, whatever it is, as soon as it is supposed to be a boundary, so that the boundary itself is not dialectical, it is superstition and narrow-mindedness. In a human being there is always a desire, at once comfortable and concerned, to have something really firm and fixed that can exclude the dialectical, but this is cowardliness and fraudulence toward the divine. Even the most certain of all, a revelation, *eo ipso*, becomes dialectical when I am to appropriate it; even the most fixed of all, an infinite negative resolution, which is the individuality's infinite form of God's being within him, promptly becomes dialectical. As soon as I take away the dialectical, I am superstitious and defraud God of the moment's strenuous acquisition of what was once acquired. It is however, far more comfortable to be objective and superstitious, boasting about it and proclaiming thoughtlessness. (CUP1, 34–35 fn.)

The key word in this passage is 'boundary'. The desire to establish the canon beyond doubt is exactly such a desire to fix a boundary that is not dialectical. Living with the uncertainty of the boundary is faith. There is no uncertainty, however, if there is no sense that there should be a boundary or if any text could be regarded as scriptural. This is a point that the biblical critic Timothy Beal reinforces when he discussed the way in which the notion of intertextuality underlies but destabilizes the notion of canon.[19] Texts within a canon have resonances with texts outside it, and the boundary of the canon is fluid. This boundary is comparable to the boundary between the public and the private, or the boundary between the conscious and the unconscious, between something constructed by decision and exclusion and something constructed through organic growth and happenstance. All interpretation is a matter of decision, Beal reminds us, of cutting off the infinite possible ramifications as a result of conscious and unconscious choice. And it is in making, or evading, such choices, Kierkegaard insists time and again, that we as readers open ourselves to judgment.

Note too that in this passage the failure to embrace the dialectical leads to a fissure and a position which seems to embrace two contradictory postures which are shown to be to sides of the same coin: objectivity and superstition. It is not faith that leads to superstition but the lack of faith that superstitiously clings to an impossible objectivity. This is an important insight. Far from seeking objectively defensible criteria for the inclusion and exclusion of texts from the canon, Kierkegaard heightens the arbitrariness of the canon. Climacus' refusal to account for his acceptance of the canon is the point, just because it is arbitrary and offensive to reason and tradition alike; in short, it is scandalous.

Let us turn then to ask how this relates to Kierkegaard's understanding of the canonical shape of his own authorship. From the two accounts of this in *Postscript* we can gain a sense of this. In 'A Glance..', the fact that Climacus considers three distinct bodies of work and reads them in tension with each other reinforces the importance of the sense of diversity *almost* corralled into conversation that the canon can attain. Kierkegaard's plea for the integrity of the pseudonyms in the 'Explanation' is another example of this. Both, however, may seem to underplay the unity of the authorship and the 'Explanation' seems to consider the unity of authorship is of little interest to the reader.

This is rather belied by the way in which Kierkegaard argues in *Point of View*. He is prepared to come up with a declaration that unifies the whole authorship when he states that 'my entire work as an author revolves around: becoming a Christian in Christendom' (PV, 90). The structure of the authorship as a whole is shown there to be carefully planned and, if not exactly premeditated, the outcome of process of which he is merely the servant under the direction of divine governance.

That the canonical shape of the authorship is a matter of deep concern to Kierkegaard is evidenced in the prolonged and agonized discussion in the Journals over the publication of *The Crisis and a Crisis in the Life of an Actress*, where Kierkegaard debates with himself whether the publication of the aesthetic piece will disturb the careful construction of the authorship, but where he finally decides to publish it on what could be called canonical grounds.[20] His conclusion is as follows:

> Yes it was a good thing to publish that little article. I began with *Either/Or* and two upbuilding discourses; now it ends, after the whole upbuilding series—with a little esthetic essay. It expresses: that it was the upbuilding the religious, which should advance, and that now the

esthetic has been traversed; they are inversely related, or it is something of an inverse confrontation, to show that the writer was not an esthetic author who in the course of time grew old and for that reason became religious. (JP, 6238)

Indeed, Kierkegaard goes beyond that: 'Strange, strange about that little article—that I was so close to being carried away and forgetting myself. When one is overstrained as I was, it is easy to forget momentarily the dialectical outline of a colossal structure such as my authorship' (JP, 6242).

Yet, in quoting these journal entries, we reopen the criticisms that can be levelled at any canonical approach. What constitutes the Kierkegaardian canon, and who determines its bounds? In a canonical context, the Hong Edition displays the problem. The wonderful resource provided in their apparatus to each volume of the intertextual allusions between the Journals and the work in question both illuminates the text, but raises a question. How far are the Journals part of the canon? Are they to be read as equal partners with the published works? Beyond that general question, there is the more specific issue of passages in the apparatus that represent rejected material or discarded drafts form the published work. These are illuminating for scholarly readers, but precisely not part of the accepted canon. How should they inform our reading?

In any case, is it quite clear which works should be included in the canon? Is *The Concept of Irony* canonical? Kierkegaard nowhere includes it in any list he gives of the authorship; indeed, the journal entry quoted above says he 'began' with *Either/Or*. What of *The Book on Adler* and the *Point of View*, which are posthumously assembled and published? Are these, in their different ways, best regarded as Kierkegaardian apocrypha?

Neither is the canonical function of individual works fixed during his production. In the quotation above, quite naturally Kierkegaard regards *Crisis and the Crisis* as the end of the authorship, but that is only a temporary phase as other works follow it. On the other hand, he claims *Postscript* was to mark the end of the authorship when it was first produced. How far should or can we read the book with that in mind? In what ways does its meaning alter when it is no longer the final work of the canon, but a work of transition to a new phase?

At several junctures in the *Point of View*[21] Kierkegaard refers to *Postscript* as the 'turning point' of the authorship, sitting as it does between the aesthetic and religious works. It indicates how the issue of becoming a Christian is the driving force of the entire authorship, but does not explicitly state that this is the object of the pseudonymous works, because it is itself pseudonymous. Is this, however, what Kierkegaard envisaged as he wrote the text, or is it a function conferred on it in retrospect as the corpus of the authorship developed beyond it? Even if the second is true, however, is it not still a valid account of the meaning of the text as it develops?

If we want to understand further this matter of the changing functions of a work within the canon, a striking analogy might be found in the book of Malachi in the Old Testament. Malachi, which is often taken as the proper name of its author, simply means 'my messenger'. One commonly accepted critical hypothesis regards the very existence of a book of Malachi, and the further deduction of an authorial figure named Malachi, as an effect of canonization. This arises from the fact that the strange collection of diverse works which the Christian tradition knows as 'the minor prophets' is counted as a single book in Jewish tradition and carries the title 'The Book of the Twelve'. The hypothesis is that Malachi consists of the original final chapters of the book of Zechariah which comes immediately before it. These were separated off and given their own title in order to bring the number of books in the collection up to the biblically significant twelve. 'Malachi' is thus what we might call a canonical pseudonym, generated by the exigencies of the collection, and has no bearing on the authorship of these chapters.

In the Christian Old Testament, moreover, this odd fragment of a book comes to have a particular prominence as the final book of the canon. This is in contrast to the Hebrew Bible, where 2 Chronicles is the final book, which means that the Bible ends with an exhortation to go up to the temple in Jerusalem (2 Chron 36:10). The change in the Christian ordering may be due to the allusion in the final verses of Malachi (Mal 4:5-6) to the return of Elijah. This takes on a new meaning when the book is placed immediately before the New Testament with its early allusions to John the Baptist as the returned Elijah. From being a detached appendix to Zechariah, Malachi becomes a transitional work between the two Testaments, looking forward and back. The parallels to the detached 'Postscript' which becomes the pivotal work in Kierkegaard's authorship are intriguing.

What this reminds us is that the constitution of a canon is not simply a mechanical process of collection and ordering, but can itself be creative and recreative. Does *Postscript* itself become a different work when read in the context of the books which follow it and in the light of the *Point of View* and the *Journals and Papers*? If so, which is the 'real' meaning of the book?

This brings us full circle to the debates on canonical criticism in biblical studies that we cited at the beginning, debates which are far from settled. What Climacus says of the biblical canon applies also to the Kierkegaardian one. The canon is always only an approximation and needs to be dealt with as such. Biblical scholarship has no definitive solution to offer as to how this awareness should inform our reading and indeed Kierkegaard gives cogent reasons as to why such 'solutions' to the problems of canonicity cannot be adequate and are themselves a distraction. What the biblical experience may serve to clarify is that the way we deal with the questions of canonicity in any particular situation depends on what we are reading *for*. If we are reading as textual critics and editors of the Kierkegaardian corpus, we may answer such questions differently from those who are seeking 'Kierkegaard's' answer to philosophical or theological questions.

This debate may remind us that to read Kierkegaard is a complex process, which involves faithfulness to the particularity of texts but also an awareness of an unstable canonical context with all the questions that such a statement entails. If nothing else, I hope that this present essay makes clear that these questions of canon are vital for Kierkegaard himself, both in regard to the biblical text and his own productions. Both the conscious and unconscious consequences of his construction of his output as an authorship are illuminated by raising the question of canon and by the debates generated by this in biblical studies.

Notes

1. P.R. Noble, *The Canonical Approach: A Critical Reconstruction of the Hermeneutics of Brevard S. Childs* (Leiden: E.J.Brill, 1995), p. 341. As the subtitle indicates, Noble's work is a response to Brevard S. Childs, whose series of works on what he calls canonical criticism have been the spur to a revived interest in the topic among biblical scholars.

2. In terms of the limits of the canon, the fact that the Greek Septuagint contains a number of books not found in the Hebrew text of the Old Testament poses an obvious problem which Luther, following the lead of Jerome, solves by relegating the disputed books to a separate category of Apocrypha.

   Kierkegaard does make a number of references to the Apocryphal books, but these are mostly to single verses in passing. The *Cumulative Index* to the Hong edition states that Judith is cited four times, II Maccabees once, Sirach fourteen times, Susanna three times, Tobit five times and Wisdom of Solomon four times in the whole of the published works. Of these citations, only the treatment of the story of Sarah and Tobias in *Fear and Trembling* is more than a verse citation. In a number of cases, Kierkegaard does explicitly cite verses from the apocrypha as 'Scripture'. A particular case in point is his citation of Sirach 2:1 in part 5 of the *Gospel of Sufferings*, the discourse entitled 'The Joy of It That It Is Not the Road That Is Hard but That Hardship Is the Road'. The explicit point he is making in that discourse is that both the Old and New Testaments are at one in asserting that the road of perfection is in hardship, which he claims is a theme which outstrips all others in the number of passages which assert it. It is striking, then, that the three passages he selects to confirm this are Acts 14:22, 1 Thessalonians 3:3-4, and Sirach (see UD, 292). Sirach and Judith are certainly referred to as Scripture in Kierkegaard's works.

In *Fear and Trembling*, the plight of Sarah is dealt with very differently from the way in which the story of Abraham is used in the same work. Johannes de Silentio pores over the details of the canonical text from Genesis, but in the end the only options he allows his reader in reaction to the text are scandal or acceptance. Explaining Abraham away will not do. The apocryphal story of Sarah, however, is set alongside and treated on a par with the legend of Agnes and the merman, Shakespeare's Gloucester and Faust. De Silentio seems to regard Tobit as literature on the same level as these, which is a high compliment to the work, but not the same as treating it as part of Scripture. The case of Sarah is discussed in more detail in the chapter entitled '"Sarah is the Hero": Kierkegaard's Reading of Tobit in *Fear and Trembling*'. The difference in treatment does seem to be a consequence of the different canonical status of the books, but Kierkegaard's attitude to the apocrypha would bear further investigation in the light of accepted practice in the Danish Church of the time. W. Glenn Kirkconnell's 'Kierkegaard's Use of the Apocrypha: Is it "Scripture" or "Good for Reading"?', *KR:SRR* 1.1, pp. 253–64, is a thoughtful discussion.

3. Bruce Metzger, *The Canon of the New Testament: Its Origin, Development and Significance* (Oxford: Clarendon Press, 1987).

4. See the discussion in the section of Luther's *Preface* to the New Testament headed 'Which Are the Truest Noblest Books of the New Testament?' in 'Preface to the Epistles of St James and St Jude' (1546 [1522]) in *Luther's Works*. XXXV. *Word and Sacrament I* (ed. by T. Bachmann; Philadelphia: Muhlenberg Press 1960), pp. 361–62.

5. Some later Lutheran dogmaticians, e.g. Oecolampadius, did expand Luther's list to include further members of the seven 'antilegomena' on the grounds of their disputed status in the early church.

6. The softening addition of 'noch' before 'nicht' is not found in editions before 1530.

7. In *Luther's Works*, XXXV, p. 396.

8. Calvin and the Reformed tradition, although aware of the problems of authorship and historical disputes, never adopted this Lutheran practice. On the Catholic side, the decree *De Canonicis Scripturis* of the Council of Trent issued in 1546 added for the first time an anathema to the list of books of both Old and New Testaments as found in the Vulgate, making the acceptance of the canonical list an article of faith.

9. For further discussion in English of this dispute, see A.M. Allchin, *N.F.S. Grundtvig: An Introduction to his Life and Work* (London: Darton, Longman

and Todd, 1997), pp. 105–114 and B.H. Kirmmse, *Kierkegaard in Golden Age Denmark* (Bloomington: Indiana University Press, 1990), pp. 210–214. The two accounts are interestingly different in their degree of sympathy for Grundtvig's stance.

10. F.E.D. Schleiermacher, *The Christian Faith* (trans. H.R. Mackintosh and J.S. Stewart; Edinburgh: T & T Clark, 1976 [1928]), p. 603.
11. Schleiermacher, *Christian Faith*, p. 603.
12. Schleiermacher, *Christian Faith*, p. 603.
13. Clausen's view (and Climacus') is endorsed, if there were any doubt, by one of the leading contemporary scholars working on the New Testament canon. The final conclusion of Harry Y. Gamble's survey article, 'The New Testament Canon: Recent Research and the Status Quaestionis,' in *The Canon Debate* (ed. by L.M. McDonald and J.A. Sanders; Peabody, MA: Hendrickson Publishers, 2002), p. 294, is as follows:

> The history of the New Testament canon will not be adequately grasped until all of its dimensions have been comprehended. I have sought to suggest that these dimensions are far more numerous than is customarily thought. They include the social history of the early church, the history of theology and doctrine, the liturgical life of early Christian communities, the history of interpretation, the bibliographical practices of the church and the textual history of particular documents and collections of documents. It is a daunting task.

14. 'Kierkegaard: The Holy and the True,' in *Fools for Christ: Essays on the True, the Good and the Beautiful* (Eugene: Wipf and Stock, 1955), p. 25.
15. The first Mormon missionaries arrived in Jylland in 1850, much to the alarm of the local and national clergy. One of the State Church's most active workers in counteracting their influence was, interestingly enough, Kierkegaard's brother, Peter. The only specific reference to Mormons that I have come across in Kierkegaard's writings is a mention in a journal entry (JP, 1443) of a report by Jacobi that the Mormons believe that God is not omnipresent but moves with great rapidity from star to star. Kierkegaard is rather amused by what he sees as an uncharacteristic retrograde step in theology from the spiritual to the concrete, and surmises that the invention of the railway train and the telegraph may have had some influence here. He then goes on to speculate on the possibility that technological progress will fuel similar retrogressive analogies: a matter on which he may have had some prophetic insight.

   The introduction to the Book of Mormon claims that it 'contains, as does the Bible, the fullness of the everlasting gospel.' It not only contains parallels to the biblical histories which trace the migrations of various Jewish groups to the New World, but also contains what purport to be eye-witness accounts of Jesus' appearance in the New World and of his preaching. A large proportion of the book of 3 Nephi, for instance, closely matches Gospel texts. Chapters 12–14 are almost identical to Matthew 5–7. It does therefore literally contain New Testament material.

   Without wishing to offend any Latter-day Saints, the consensus of non-Mormon scholarship is that the Book of Mormon is a patchwork of biblical quotations and pseudo-biblical history, much of it with parallels in earlier literature such as Ethan Smith's *A View of the Hebrews* of 1823. It was put together by the Prophet Joseph Smith, possibly with some assistance from his companions at the time. Any claim to inspiration, and certainly to its being included as 'Another Testament of Jesus Christ' (its official subtitle), is summarily dismissed by most non-Mormons. There is no generally accepted evidence that any of the historical incidents it alludes to have occurred, or that the people mentioned in it ever existed.

In this context, however, consider this defence:

> So I assume ... that the enemies have succeeded in demonstrating what they desire regarding the [Book of Mormon], with a certainty surpassing the most vehement desire of the most spiteful enemy—what then? Has the enemy thereby abolished the [Church of Jesus Christ of Latter-day Saints or] Christianity? Not at all. Has he harmed the believer? Not at all, not in the least. Has he won the right to exempt himself from the responsibility for not being a believer? Not at all. That is, because these books are not by these authors, are not authentic, are not *integri*, are not inspired (this cannot be proved, since it is an object of faith), it does not follow that these authors have not existed, and above all, that Christ has not existed. To that extent, the believer is still equally free to accept it, equally free, please note, because if he accepted it by virtue of a demonstration, he would be on the verge of abandoning the faith. (CUP, 30)

Thus modified, Johannes Climacus seems to offer a spirited defence for the Book of Mormon against its sceptics. No historical or rational argument can disprove the believer's faith in the text's inspiration. If it leads its readers to a confrontation with the paradox of the God-Man, that is all that matters.

16. I suspect also that Kierkegaard would have pounced on the signed declarations of witnesses to the authenticity of the golden plates of Moroni to be found at the beginning of the Book of Mormon as a demonstration that Smith betrayed his claim to apostolicity by seeking quasi-legal confirmation. He would also have found the central Mormon teaching articulated by the fifth President of the Church, Lorenzo Snow, in the aphorism 'As man now is, God once was; as God now is, man may be', a fatal dilution of the paradox of the God-man.

17. See FSE, pp. 16–17.

18. See 'The Apostle, the Genius and the Monkey' in this volume.

19. See his article on 'Intertextuality' in *Handbook of Postmodern Biblical Interpretation* (ed. by A. K. M. Adam; St Louis: Chalice Press, 2000), pp. 128–130. There is a genealogy worth tracing here, in that the contemporary literary critical interest in intertextuality stems from the use of the term in the works of Julia Kristeva, who in turn was influenced by Mikhail Bakhtin's work on the interpenetration of languages and voices in texts. What is not much remarked upon is that the young Bakhtin is reported to have been sufficiently taken with Kierkegaard's work that he attempted to learn Danish to read it, although he had in the end to resort to German translations (see for this claim K. Clark and M. Holquist, *Mikhail Bakhtin*

[Cambridge: Belknap/Harvard, 1984], p. 24). My suspicion is that Bakhtin's insights into unity and diversity in the interplay of multiple voices within and between texts are more influenced than is recognized by what he learned from Kierkegaard. Kierkegaard, in turn, both illuminates and is educated by the Bible as a unity of diverse voices, genres and situations of communication.

20. I explore the significance of this incident for an understanding of the authorship as a whole in much greater depth in an article entitled 'The Stage and Stages in a Christian Authorship,' in R.L. Perkins (ed.), *International Kierkegaard Commentary. XVII. 'Christian Discourses'* and *'The Crisis and a Crisis in the Life of an Actress'* (Macon, GA: Mercer University Press, 2007), pp. 299–320.

21. See, for example, PV, p. 31.

The Apostle, the Genius and the Monkey: Reflections on Kierkegaard's 'The Mirror of the Word'

In Ezek 33:30-2 the prophet is given this rather disheartening warning (NEB):

> Man, your fellow countrymen gather in groups and talk of you under walls and in doorways and say to one another, 'Let us go and see what message there is from the Lord.' So my people will come crowding in, as people do, and sit down in front of you. They will hear what you have to say but they will not do it. 'Fine words!' they will say, but their hearts are set on selfish gain. You are no more to them than a singer of fine songs with a lovely voice, or a clever harpist; they will listen to what you say but will certainly not do it.

There in a nutshell is the problem of the religious author, the problem that Kierkegaard constantly confronts in his own work. The more skill such an author uses to catch people's attention and the more graphically he or she describes for them the awesome possibilities of the religious transformation, the more scope there is for the audience's attention to be devoted to the aesthetic titillation to be gained from contemplation of these possibilities as fantasies. In Kierkegaard's analysis, it is this flight from the realization of possibility which is at the heart of the aesthetic attitude. The aesthete attempts to cover up his or her despair at the necessity that he or she sees as ruling their life by escaping into a fantastic world of unrealizable possibilities. The task of the religious author is to persuade their audience that there are possibilities that can be made actual in their own lives, that change can occur. How this task, which Kierkegaard sees as his own, is to be achieved is the question I wish to address.

Kierkegaard explores one example of such a call to change in his version of the story of Nathan's parable found in 2 Samuel 12. This appears in his discourse 'What is Requited in Order to Look at Oneself with True Blessing in the Mirror of the Word?' (hereafter referred to as 'The Mirror of the Word'), the first part of *For Self-examination*. The biblical context of this parable is the sordid tale of King David's relations with Bathsheba. Lounging round his palace in Jerusalem when the rest of Israel are off at the battlefront, David catches a glimpse of Bathsheba bathing on the rooftop of her house. He summons her, has his way with her and sends her back home, only to learn that she has become pregnant by him. He hastily recalls Bathsheba's husband Uriah from the front and tries to entice him to sleep with Bathsheba in order to cover up the consequences of this adulterous liaison.

When Uriah will not comply, David sends him back to the scene of battle, carrying the orders for his own destruction. On the receipt of the news of Uriah's death, David promptly marries Bathsheba, who bears him a son. Everything seems hunky-dory. Until, that is, God sends the prophet Nathan to have a word with the king. Nathan tells the king a story about a rich man who stole the only lamb of his poor neighbour because he was too mean to slaughter one of his own flock to feed an unexpected guest.

In 'The Mirror of the Word', Kierkegaard presents the meeting between David and Nathan as a literary *conversazione*. The well-known belletrist Nathan has composed a short story which he brings for the renowned psalmist to criticize. Kierkegaard writes,

> I imagine that David listened to this attentively and thereupon declared his judgment, did not, of course, intrude his personality (subjectivity) but impersonally (objectively) evaluated this charming little work. Perhaps there had been a detail he thought could be different: he perhaps suggested a more felicitously chosen phrase, perhaps also pointed out a little fault in the structure, praised the prophet's masterly presentation of the story, his voice, gestures—in short, expressed his opinion the way we cultured people today tend to judge a sermon for the cultured—that is, a sermon that is itself also objective. Then the prophet says to him, 'Thou art the man.' Behold, the tale which the prophet told was a story, but this 'Thou art the man'—this was another story—it was the transition to the subjective. (FSE, 38; translation adapted)

This clearly sets David's inappropriate objective aesthetic attitude in opposition to the subjective religious appropriation of the text. The interesting thing is that this version of David's response is quite different from what is actually recorded in the biblical text. In 2 Samuel 12, Nathan arrives at God's behest and, without any preliminaries, presents the story baldly to the king. David's response is a blaze of anger. He blurts out, 'As the Lord lives, the man who did this deserves to die! He shall pay for

the lamb four times over, because he has done this and shown no pity'
(2 Sam 12:5-6, NEB).

This is a far cry from the urbane reaction of Kierkegaard's David. In
the biblical account, David leaps into the unresolved gap between the
rich man and the poor man in the story, appointing himself to the role
of the just judge who will redress this imbalance, only to be told that the
role he really plays is that of the unscrupulous oppressor. In Kierkegaard's
retelling, on the other hand, David stands back from the story as an
aesthetic critic without realizing that he is being given a description of
his own lived experience, something from which he cannot properly
distance himself.

Kierkegaard prefaces his recast version with the admission that he is
'modernizing' it to 'make it more vivid to us'. What his version does, in
fact, is to align David's perception of the story much more closely with
that of the modern biblical reader. As readers of the biblical text, we
are warned at the end of chapter 11 of 2 Samuel that Nathan has been
sent by God because 'what David had done was wrong in the eyes of the
Lord'. We are thus privileged spectators who can appreciate the irony of
David's ignorant self-judgment. We can experience the aesthetic thrill
of the ironic reversal. Kierkegaard's David is not the naive, impulsive
and inadvertent author of his own judgment represented in Samuel,
but a detached critic who mimics the modem Bible-reader in his or her
expectation of deriving just this aesthetic pleasure from the text, perhaps
with an indulgent smile at its primitive awkwardness of expression.

In a striking passage in his *Purity of Heart is to Will One Thing*,
Kierkegaard addresses this issue of the reader as critic:

> Alas, in regard to things spiritual, the foolishness of many is this, that
> they in the secular sense look upon the speaker as an actor and the
> listeners as theatregoers who are to pass judgment on the artist. But
> the speaker is not the actor—not in the remotest sense. No, the speaker
> is the prompter...
>
> In the most earnest sense, God is the critical theatregoer, who
> looks on to see how the lines are spoken and how they are listened to:
> hence here the customary audience is wanting. The speaker is then the
> prompter, and the listener stands openly before God. The listener, if I
> may say so, is the actor, who in all truth acts before God. (PH, 180–81)

In the biblical account, David takes on the role of the judge and thus
opens himself to judgment in his leap on the stage. Someone called onto
the stage to enact the role appointed for him is, however, just as much
under judgment if all he does is stand in the wings and pass remarks

on the performances of his fellow actors. The latter is precisely David's situation in Kierkegaard's version of the scenario. David sees Nathan's story as a performance on which he is called to give a critical judgment, whereas in fact Nathan is setting the stage and providing the script, in which David opts to act out the role of the insufferably complacent critic under the properly critical gaze of God. With his 'You are the man', Nathan, as it were, causes David to turn round and see the hidden audience which has already watched and judged what he thought was a cleverly concealed private transaction. As the phrase which ends 2 Samuel 11 has it, 'what David had done was wrong in the eyes of the Lord'. In the biblical version, David's ethical judgment of the actions of the characters within the story reveals his own ethical blindness. In Kierkegaard's alternative, it is David's stance as a reader which is laid open to judgment.

This discussion of Nathan's parable in the form of a critique of the aesthetic approach to the text comes in the middle of 'The Mirror of the Word', the discourse where Kierkegaard offers his most sustained discussion of the correct approach to the reading of the Bible. He does this in the form of an extended commentary on James 1:22-25 (cited here from the Revised Standard Version):

> But be doers of the word, and not hearers only, deceiving yourselves. For if any one is a hearer of the word and not a doer, he is like a man who observes his natural face in a mirror; for he observes himself and goes away and at once forgets what he looks like. But he who looks into the perfect law, the law of liberty, and perseveres, being no hearer that forgets but a doer that acts, he shall be blessed in his doing.

This passage has obvious resonances with the passage from Ezekiel with which this article begins. It also directly addresses the differentiation between the aesthetic and religious stances which is Kierkegaard's particular concern. The problem for Kierkegaard in his desire to make use of it is that it comes from James's epistle, never top of the Lutheran pops. Luther himself notoriously called it a 'right strawy epistle' in the general introduction to his German New Testament of 1522. In the preface to the epistles of James and Jude from the same work he says categorically that he does not consider the Epistle of James to be the work of an apostle. The reasons he gives are that it does not preach Christ crucified and preaches up the significance of works. In the much less formal context of the *Table Talk* Luther is far more dismissive, regarding the epistle as the work of a rather bumbling Jewish opponent to the Christian emphasis on faith. Given this history, how can Kierkegaard reinstate James as an authoritative supporter of his case?

In 'The Mirror of the Word', Kierkegaard craftily enlists Luther himself as his best witness for the reinstatement of James. Times have changed, and the last thing contemporary Danish Christians are tempted by is the idea of mortifying themselves by works to earn grace. Luther himself, writes Kierkegaard, said that 'Faith is a perturbing thing'. It stands to reason that the faithful life must issue in visible changes as a result of this perturbing force.

Yet, just as Luther is much more scathing about the epistle in private, Kierkegaard's *Journals* reveal a more direct condemnation of Luther. Luther rejects the author's apostolicity on the basis of the content of the letter. To Kierkegaard, this kind of argument was impermissible. He says of Luther, 'He himself best disproves his conception of the Bible, he who throws out the epistle of James. Why? Because it does not belong to the canon? No, this he does not deny. But on dogmatic grounds. Therefore he himself has a point of departure superior to the Bible' (JP, 2507). Kierkegaard offers an alternative to Luther's approach in another journal entry: 'How am I going to find out whether something is God's word or doctrine? Luther answers: By testing the doctrine—then all is lost and Christianity is a human invention. It happens the other way around, that I submit to a person's authority; but consequently the person is higher than the doctrine' (JP, 2512).

The same criticism lies behind Kierkegaard's long engagement with Pastor Adler, who claimed to have produced his rather long and incoherent books under direct revelation. In his *On Authority and Revelation*, Kierkegaard argues that, by subsequently trying to prove on doctrinal and aesthetic grounds that his works were genuinely revealed, Adler betrays a fundamental confusion over the category of revelation. In Kierkegaard's view, any appeal to the aesthetic or ethical merits of a work to prove its revealed status only shows that those who are defending the work do not accept its inspiration themselves. He uses the image of a royal pronouncement which is to be heard and obeyed, not subjected to literary criticism. He applies the same standards to biblical writing: 'If Paul is to be regarded as a genius, it looks very bad for him... As a genius Paul can sustain no comparison with Plato or Shakespeare, as an author of beautiful similes he ranks rather low' (OAR, 104–105).

Paul is not a genius but an apostle, and there is an absolute difference between the two. This distinction is not to be exposed by scrutinizing his works. Here surely Kierkegaard is in danger of going too far in denigrating the apostle. The whole point about Paul is not that such an ordinary man *could* become an apostle, but that such an extraordinary man *would*. It is a question not of Paul's skill, but of his obedience. Kierkegaard is entitled to argue that his extraordinariness has no bearing on his apostolicity, but in that case, there is no need to downgrade Paul as a writer in comparison to Shakespeare. The comparison has no validity. The author of 1 Corinthians 13 is a great writer, but that is neither here nor there for his apostolicity. As Kierkegaard himself explains

> It is not by appraising aesthetically or philosophically the doctrine that I must and can reach the conclusion that *ergo* he who has taught this doctrine was called by a revelation, *ergo* he is an apostle. The order of sequence is exactly the reverse: the man called by a revelation, to whom was entrusted a doctrine, argues from the fact that this was a revelation, that he has an authority. (OAR, 107)

For Kierkegaard, the apostle's authority is to be accepted without any recourse to argument. Unlike an earthly potentate, God cannot even supply credentials to his apostles. There are no objective markers open to aesthetic inquiry. All the apostle can do is to hold to the absurdity that he, a man like any other, not set apart by special gifts and skills like the genius, is the bearer of an authoritative message from the Lord. The religious reader accepts this authority unquestioningly, seeking only to know what benefit or transformation can be gained from truly listening to the words of the apostle. James comes under this category, so Luther's criticism of his epistle is irrelevant. Just as David, in Kierkegaard's version, mistook his role as a reader, so too has Luther.

In this regard, Nathan is an interesting figure. In the Old Testament, his first encounter with David, in 1 Samuel 7, shows the ambiguity of the prophet's or apostle's authority. When David comes up with the idea of building a temple to God, Nathan's initial reaction is to encourage him. That night, however, the word of God comes to Nathan and he returns to the king the next morning to tell him that it is not for him to build a house for God. So not all that Nathan says can be taken as authoritative just because he says it. In the Bathsheba episode, Nathan is the bearer of the authoritative word of God. We are not told that God supplies him with any form of words, however. There is nothing to indicate that, having received the divine revelation, he did not go off and himself compose an elegant short story as the best means of carrying out his commission. The mere fact that he may have employed such literary genius as he had no more detracts from the authority of his message to David than it enhances it. But Nathan's literary skill is not the point. In itself it does not give him the authority to confront the king. Even if the parable is his own production, it is a production 'under guidance'. It is Nathan's obedience to his divine commission, something that could well end up in his rejection by David with the possibility of very unpleasant consequences to his person, which is the source of his authority.

But how is that authority to be recognized? As Kierkegaard represents it, David's reading of the parable enacts the transition from the aesthetic to the religious. David first regards Nathan as a 'genius' offering a product of his literary skill for aesthetic appraisal. It is only when he accepts Nathan's application of the story to his own conduct that he makes the transition to the subjective. He ceases to criticize the story and submits to the judgment it reveals. There is no inevitability to this change of attitude, however. Many a prophet in the Bible finds himself and his divine message rejected. It is quite open to David to say to Nathan, 'What do you mean, I am the man?' It would also be mistaken to see this retort of Nathan's as a direct statement in contrast to the indirectness of the parable. The device only works because David was initially led to distance himself from the man in the story by the skilful indirection of Nathan's reference. It is only because David was convinced that he was *not* the man that his faculty of judgment could be exercised.

The crux of the matter is that David's repentance and his recognition that Nathan is the authoritative bearer of God's word of judgment are the same event. Repentance *involves* the recognition and acceptance that God has the authority to appoint whom he likes to bring one to judgment. The recognition of the authority of the bearer of God's word and the submission to God's judgment are the same process. David's shock of recognition is what allows him to confer on Nathan the right to speak such words of judgment to his king. If David had retorted, 'Who do you think you are?', there would *ipso facto* have been no movement of repentance in his heart. After the event, it is clear to David that Nathan has from the beginning had authority as a man entrusted with God's word and that therefore David should have submitted to him. As David experiences the encounter, however, authority and applicability have nothing to do with the case until he is confronted with the occasion of repentance.

Kierkegaard's defence of James's epistle is thus not as arbitrary as it looks. It is not a case of a kind of canonical fundamentalism that argues that the book must be accepted solely because it forms part of the canon, a precarious argument in the case of James anyway. That would be setting the Church's traditional assessment of James against

Luther's when the problem for Kierkegaard is the inappropriateness of any process of assessment. The truth of the matter for Kierkegaard is this: James is addressing exactly that process of the transition to the subjective which is repentance. Kierkegaard writes as one who has been brought to repentance by James, just as David was by Nathan, and who therefore has been brought to acknowledge James's apostolic authority in a way that rules out the kind of critical judgment that Luther wants to apply.

Once James is reinstated, his metaphor of the mirror of the word is taken up as an expression of the proper approach to the biblical text. Kierkegaard puts the point in an aphorism: 'The first requirement is that you must not look at the mirror, observe the mirror, but must see yourself in the mirror' (FSE, 25). But is this not the problem with mirrors? All we can see in them is ourselves. Kierkegaard himself prefaces his *Stages on Life's Way* with a quotation from Lichtenberg: 'Such works are mirrors: when an ape looks in, no apostle can look out' (SLW, 81). In his *Sudelbücher*, Lichtenberg expands this aphorism: 'A book is a mirror—if a monkey looks into it, certainly no apostle can look out. We have no words to speak of wisdom to the foolish. He who understands the wise is himself wise.'[1]

In using this metaphor, then, is Kierkegaard not obliged to acknowledge the truth of the Socratic contention which he so passionately opposes in the *Philosophical Fragments*, the contention that knowledge is essentially a matter of recollection? This is quite explicitly the implication of Lichtenberg's expanded version. If the text can do nothing but reflect back our own faces, are we not caught forever in the limitations of our own knowledge? How can we learn something radically new? Does it follow from the fact that we can grasp a new idea that we must in some sense have understood it already?

To adopt the terms of Lichtenberg's aphorism, this problem becomes acute when we encounter the monkeys who think they are apostles—or the cultural Christians of Kierkegaard's day who think they really are Christians. If we tell such monkeys that, believe it or not, there are actually monkeys masquerading as apostles, their response will be an outburst of righteous indignation. 'Who do these monkeys think they are? We apostles will soon make them change their tune!' How are they to be convinced of their error?

The biblical version of Nathan's parable works by holding up a mirror to the monkey, getting him to admit that there is a monkey in it, and then letting him see that it is his own reflection. David's wrath at the rich man means that he cannot but admit his own wrongdoing if he accepts Nathan's identification. The only recourse left to the monkey is to blame the mirror, which falsely reflects apostles as monkeys. In Kierkegaard's retelling, David is so busy criticizing what he takes to be the picture of a monkey which Nathan holds up to him that he fails to realize that the picture is a mirror.

Both responses are not unknown among readers of the biblical text. Either its authority is denied or it is treated as an aesthetic object with no consequences for the reader's life. For Kierkegaard this aesthetic denunciation of the mirror, or of the apostolicity of the writer of the text, because the reader dislikes what she sees in it, serves to reveal the aesthete's state of sinfulness. The root of sin is the denial of the authority of the rightful judge. Kierkegaard's use of the image of reflection is a radical critique of the subjectivism which it represents in Lichtenberg's aphorism. The importance of a mirror is this: it shows us not just what we want to see, but as much of what we are as we are willing to see. The trouble with the stubborn kind of monkey is that it lacks the capacity to see the mismatch between its reality and its illusion or that the two must be brought into line.

Kierkegaard's own account of his authorship represents it as a tactical approach to this problem. In addressing a readership which is locked into the aesthetic mode, even though it imagines itself to be religious, it is necessary to begin from within the aesthetic in order to establish communication. He says, 'It means that one doesn't begin *directly* with the matter one wants to communicate, but begins by accepting the other man's illusion as good money' (PV, 40). That this involves deception, Kierkegaard is quite happy to admit. He defends this strategy by pointing out, 'One must not let oneself be deceived by the word "deception". One can deceive a person for truth's sake, and (to recall old Socrates) one can deceive a person into the truth. Indeed it is only by this means, i.e. by deceiving him, that it is possible to bring into the truth one who is in an illusion' (PV, 40). The mode of communication of truth is dependent on the state of the addressee. The greatest of all indirect communicators is God. How else could communication bridge the infinite qualitative difference between God and humanity? In the *Concluding Unscientific Postscript* we read,

> no anonymous author can more cunningly conceal himself, no practitioner of the maieutic art can more carefully withdraw himself from the direct relationship, than God. He is present in the creation and present everywhere in it, but directly he is not there; and only when

the individual turns to his inner self, and hence only in the inwardness
of self-activity, does he have his attention aroused, and is enabled to
see God. *(CUP1, 218)*

What Kierkegaard sometimes obscures by his apparently sequential
system of life stages is actually the fundamental insight that justifies
his authorship: the affirmation that the religious does not abolish the
aesthetic but undermines its affectation of objectivity. In other words, the
religious does not deny the artist's role in presenting alternative possible
worlds to us, which involves the deception of acting as if they exist. It
does insist that we take these possibilities seriously and acknowledge our
responsibility to choose that form of life which engages most earnestly
and faithfully with the responsibility of choice. Where we make such a
choice we acknowledge in that act the authority of the one who provides
the occasion of our choosing. Genius or no, he is revealed as an apostle.
We can disregard an unflattering picture of ourselves as distorted, but
what we see in a mirror can stir us to realize the need for change, the
need for repentance.

Let me finish with a story which encapsulates many of the themes
we have been exploring. It is one of the *Para Handy* tales of the Scottish
author Neil Munro, a series of short stories recounting the adventures
of the captain and crew of a Clyde puffer, a small steam cargo boat
of a kind that plied the west coast of Scotland in the early twentieth
century. In the story entitled 'The Malingerer', the Captain and Dougie,
the mate, are confronted with the problem of what to do when the Tar,
the junior member of the crew, announces that he is ill and takes to
his bed, obviously hoping to avoid his share of the week's work. They
adopt the ingenious strategy of coddling the invalid, tiptoeing round
the ship, plying him with gruel and inviting the local joiner in to cast a
professional eye over his measurements, having solemnly averred that
the hunger pains he is suffering from are the infallible symptoms of the
'galloping convolvulus'. To cap the ploy, they paste a picture of a monkey
cut from a soap advertisement onto a mirror, and take it down below:

> The fo'c's'le was in darkness, and the Tar felt as if he was already dead
> and buried. 'Am I looking very bad?' he ventured to ask Dougie.

'Bad's no the the name for it,' said Dougie. 'Chust look at yourself in the
enchineer's looking-glass.' He produced from under his arm the engineer's
little mirror, on the face of which he had gummed the portrait of the
monkey cut out from the soap advertisement, which fitted neatly into the

frame. The Captain struck a match, and in its brief and insufficient light the Tar looked at himself, as he thought reflected in the glass.

'Man, I'm no' that awful changed either; if I had a shave and my face washed. I don't believe its convulvulus at all,' said he, quite hopefully, and jumped from his bunk. For the rest of the week, he put in the work of two men.[2]

Notes

1. Georg Christoph Lichtenberg, *Aphorismen, Schriften, Briefe* (Munich: Carl Hauser, 1974), p. 95.
2. Hugh Foulis (Neil Munro), *Para Handy and Other Tales* (Edinburgh: William Blackwood and Sons, 1948), p. 19.

Your Wish Is My Command: The Peril and Promise of the Bible as 'Letter from the Beloved'

Reading Kierkegaard frightens me. No doubt he would regard that as a compliment. After all, no one urges more strongly the importance of the category of offence in any communication of the divine. Yet at times his insistence on scandal seems to be a hostage to seriously disquieting and destructive appropriation of his writing. Take, for instance, the implication of Kierkegaard's metaphor of the Bible as 'Letter from the Beloved' in *For Self-Examination*. The metaphor is used to chide those who distract themselves from obeying the message of the Bible by appealing to critical scholarship, making the specious plea 'I certainly intend to comply—as soon as the discrepancies are ironed out and the interpreters agree fairly well' (FSE, 32). This is a conveniently endless undertaking in Kierkegaard's view. So far so good. However, Kierkegaard (of course) takes things further:

> Let us not discard the metaphor too soon. Let us assume that this letter from the beloved contained not only an expression of affection, as such letters ordinarily do, but that it contained a wish, something the beloved wished her lover to do. It was, let us assume, much that was required of him, very much; any third party would consider that there was good reason to think better of it, but the lover, he is off at once to fulfil his beloved's wish. (FSE, 26–27)

Again, so far so good. Yet Kierkegaard again presses the point:

> Let us assume that after some time the lovers met and the beloved said, 'But, my dear, that was not at all what I asked you to do; you must have misunderstood the word or translated it incorrectly.' Do you think that the lover would now regret rushing off straightway that very second to obey the wish instead of first entertaining some doubts, and then perhaps getting the help of a few additional dictionaries, and then having some more misgivings and then perhaps getting the word translated correctly and consequently being exempt—do you believe that he regrets the mistake, do you believe that he pleases his beloved less? (FSE, 28)

I have to answer, 'Yes, I *do* believe both of these things.' Imagine if the lover had misread the letter to say, 'Next time you see me, ignore me', or, 'See if you can't seduce my best friend', or, 'Offer our children through the fire to Molech', or even 'Break off our engagement.' Would the beloved really praise his zeal and would he really have no ground for regret in such cases? Remember, whether the beloved could have actually intended any such thing or whether any sober judge would consider such acts advisable or even allowable are not admissible considerations.[1]

These are trivial if troubling examples in comparison to the destruction of human lives and spirits that is daily wrought by those who claim, perhaps in all conscience, that they are following an instruction taken from a 'letter from the beloved' or, in other words, from a scriptural text. What of those who assert textual justification for terrorist acts, for instance? In this paragraph, Kierkegaard seems to offer such people the argument that their zealousness will render whatever they do acceptable in divine judgment even if it is exegetically unsound and, more worryingly, counter to God's wishes.[2]

Now, it would be rather stretching a point to argue that those who carry out violent acts of terrorism in God's name take encouragement from their assiduous study of Kierkegaard. However, in *Fear and Trembling* Johannes de Silentio does explicitly deal with the question of how to respond to a biblical reader who is sincerely tempted to emulate Abraham and kill his own son.[3] He does not have much sympathy for the preacher who berates the man for his presumption, nor for an approach that would seek to play down the fact that Abraham's intended act is murder. Johannes writes:

> But if there was one who, having heard the greatness as well as the dreadfulness in Abraham's deed, ventured to proceed along that path, I would saddle my horse and ride along with him. At every station before coming to Mount Moriah, I would explain to him that he still could turn around, could repent of the misunderstanding that he was called to be tried [*forsøges*] in such a conflict, could confess that he lacked the courage, so that God himself would have to take Isaac if he wanted to have him. It is my conviction that such a man is not repudiated, that he can be blessed along with all the others, but not within time. Even in the periods of the greatest faith, would not such a judgment be passed on a man like that? (FT, 32)

But would de Silentio at the last moment seek to wrest the knife out of the deluded man's hand or let a child die so that its deluded father might be confronted with his own delusion? This question is not answered.

What is puzzling is that Kierkegaard in *For Self-Examination* seems to ignore the problem raised by the metaphor of the letter: its invocation of the complex of issues around what Lacan and Derrida, for instance, have called 'the postal system.' The letter's presence is a paradoxical confirmation of the absence of the beloved and all sorts of possibilities of mismatch and error between sender and receiver come into play, the very questions that Kierkegaard explores elsewhere so subtly in his understanding of direct and indirect communication.

That Kierkegaard was not unaware of this dimension of the metaphor is confirmed in a striking paragraph in the section of *Either/Or* volume I, entitled 'Shadowgraphs':

> If a person possessed a letter that he knew or believed contained information about what he had to consider his life's happiness, but the characters were thin and faint and the hand-writing almost illegible, then, presumably with anxiety and agitation, he would read it most passionately again and again and at one moment derive one meaning, at the next moment another, according to how he would explain everything by a word he believed that he had deciphered with certainty, but he would never progress beyond the same uncertainty with which he had begun. He would stare, more and more anxiously, but the more he stared, the less he would see. His eyes would sometimes be filled with tears, but the more frequently this happened to him the less he would see. In the course of time, the writing would become fainter and less legible; finally, the paper itself would crumble away, and he would have nothing left but tear-filled [or 'tear-dimmed'] eyes. (EO1, 190)

Here the reader mourns the incomprehensibility of his letter and paradoxically by his doomed passion for unattainable certainty actually renders it more illegible and himself incapable of reading.

This rather different take on the metaphor makes it all the more intriguing that it is also the prime conceit in Robert Browning's poem 'Fears and Scruples.'[4] Browning's narrator charts the doubts that arise in a friendship that is solely based on a set of old letters. His other friends question the genuineness of the letters and insinuate that the absent friend is playing tricks, watching without communicating, to see how the friend reacts. The poem ends:

> 'Why, that makes your friend a monster!' say you;
>   'Had his house no window? At first nod
> Would you not have hailed him?' Hush, I pray you!
>   What if this friend happened to be—God?

Read in the context of the passage from *Either/Or*, this is Victorian pessimism, mourning the monstrousness of the absent God as the presumed evidence of his existence is questioned by science and biblical higher criticism. Here the letter is not a spur to action, but a sign of absence, to be read with regret or sardonically as a relic of a relationship which is no longer valid, if it ever was. This might make us read Kierkegaard's metaphor rather differently.

Intriguingly, an explicit association of Kierkegaard with this poem of Browning's appears in Jorge Luis Borges' essay 'Kafka and his precursors'. After citing Kierkegaard as a writer of religious parables, Borges outlines Browning's poem. He leaves the question at the end of the poem hanging, because his point is precisely that our answer to it is different from Browning's: 'The poem "Fears and Scruples" by Robert Browning prophesies the work of Kafka, but our reading of Kafka noticeably refines and diverts our reading of the poem. Browning did not read it as we read it now.'[5]

No doubt unknown to Borges, a clue to Browning's own reading of the poem is to be found in a letter of his to W.G. Kingsland:

> Where there is a genuine love of the 'letters' and 'actions' of the invisible 'friend,' however these may be disadvantaged by an inability to meet the objections to their authenticity or historical value urged by 'experts' who assume the privilege of learning over ignorance, it would indeed be a wrong to the wisdom and goodness of the 'friend' if he were supposed capable of overlooking the actual 'love' and only considering the 'ignorance' which, failing to in any degree affect 'love' is really the highest evidence that 'love' exists. So I *meant* whether the result be clear or no.[6]

As an explanation this outdoes Kierkegaard at his most gnarled, and the final sentence is surely a concession to this effect on his reader. What comes through, however, is that where the modern post-Kafkan reader may have assimilated this poem to the ebb-tide of faith in Victorian England, Browning in fact seems to regard the final line as the refutation of the sense of abandonment evident in the rest of the poem. Precisely because the 'friend' is God, the jibes at his failure to communicate cannot stick. We read Browning through Kafkaesque doubt, and not through his own assurance, founded on his faith in God—yet the poem sustains either meaning and we could argue that the crabbedness of Browning's explanation may bespeak more doubt than he explicitly acknowledges. If that is true of Browning, something analogous may be true for Kierkegaard.

This hermeneutical point is borne out in the case of *Fear and Trembling*. If we read that book as a profound exegesis spurred by Kierkegaard's offence at Genesis 22, as I would argue we must, the last sentence of *Problema III* falls into place as the epitome of its fundamental exegetical thesis: 'either there is a paradox that the single individual as the single individual stands in an absolute relation to the absolute, or Abraham is lost' (FT, 120).

De Silentio's arguments throughout the book are designed to clear away any incidental or subsidiary problematic, so as to bring the reader to this stark decision of faith. The question can be rephrased as, 'Do we take it as axiomatic that Abraham is not lost and on what ground?' Unless we do make this claim, there is little point in seeking guidance from the Bible or in putting one's faith in the biblical God. De Silentio affirms that if we cling to Abraham, we must accept the paradox. Conversely, if we assent to the paradox, we can begin to understand, or at least accept, that Abraham is not lost. But any reader, particularly if philosophical or psychological consistency is the axiom for his or her reading, might well come to the conclusion that Abraham *is* lost. Nothing prevents us from reading *Fear and Trembling* in that way.

The issue of how biblical texts are to be read responsibly is dealt with in Tim Polk's *The Biblical Kierkegaard*. There Christian love is identified as the 'rule of faith' by which biblical reading is to be accomplished. However, how is the reader to become educated in that rule? If it is by reading Scripture, is there not a difficulty that, precisely because of the human capacity for sin, our misunderstanding of love may lead us to misread the Scripture that should be instructing us? Polk himself argues that

> Sin is its [sc. theological exegesis's] ultimate antagonist, the largest obstacle in its ground-clearing task of allowing the Word of God to be heard. But because sin is a spiritual condition, it remains highly resistant to exegetical argument and information. That is, Sin can take the argument, appropriate its reason, and marshal the information all to its own purpose and in its own spirit. In fact, in the face of Sin, exegesis itself is powerless; it cannot meet Sin's demand to guarantee the sense it makes. There is a critical point where all it can do is to reaffirm its guiding spirit and re-invoke it.[7]

Moreover, sin can affect our comprehension of love, as Amy Laura Hall tells us:

> The love to which Kierkegaard calls us requires us actively to acknowledge that true love itself is necessarily precarious—requiring

prayers of confession as well as forgiveness. We are to cherish our
loved ones with fear and trembling as the balance wheel for our love,
treading warily with the increasing awareness that works we believe
to be love may instead be occasions of our own self-indulgence or
preservation.[8]

To revert to our core metaphor, the question then becomes: is there
any point in his reading of the letter at which the lover can check himself
and say, 'No, what I read as a clear command is not in accord with love
and so I must not obey it' without risking the rejoinder, 'And who are you
to determine what love might demand?'

It may be that that very uncertainty is the key, however. Gordon
Marino in his article, 'Is Madness Truth, Is Fanaticism Faith?',[9] argues
that fanaticism with its conviction of certainty rules out faith and thereby
demonstrates that its God is an idol: 'No matter what the fanatic thinks
he believes, his God is an impersonal objectified deity. The passion that
might have given rise to an awareness of himself and God as subject
serves only to infuse his object world with an unusual intensity. [38] ...as
madness falls short of truth, fanaticism falls short of faith' [32].

Kierkegaard confirms this at a number of places in the authorship,
and we can cite the following Journal entry:

> The relationship to Christ is this—a person tests for himself whether
> Christ is everything to him, and then says, I put everything into this.
> But I cannot get an immediate certainty about my relationship to
> Christ. I cannot get an immediate certainty about whether I have faith,
> for to have faith is this very dialectical suspension which is continually
> in fear and trembling and yet never despairs; faith is precisely this
> infinite self-concern which keeps one awake in risking everything, this
> self-concern about whether one really has faith—and precisely this
> self-concern is faith. (JP I, 108, §256; IX A 32 n.d. 1848)

This centrality of uncertainty and therefore choice in appropriating the
Bible is explicit in the prayer that opens *For Self Examination*. After
praising God for his concern for human beings, Kierkegaard goes on,
'...finally, you gave him your Word. More you could not do. To force
him to use it, to read it, or to listen to it, to force him to act according
to it, that you could not wish' (FSE, 13).

A God who entrusts revelation to text is a God who risks our
incomprehension. In a fascinating reading by the German theologian
Ida Görres, the manifest examples in the book of Judges of atrocities
committed in God's name demonstrate the peril God faces in his

involvement with humankind. Her work is expounded by Rowan Williams in his discussion of divine risk:

>...to be the 'God of Israel' at that moment [i.e. at the time of the Judges] is to be what legitimates genocide and terror; to be a tribal fetish at the most bloody stage of Israel's development. In being the God of these people, bound in holy alliance with them, God becomes what is not God, becomes a tool of human dominance and violence.[10]

How then can we distinguish God from idol in our interpretation? Can we in any way confront the fanatic? The answer I derive from Kierkegaard, unexpectedly, is to ask the one who acts on the text, do you do this in certainty or in doubt? To act in certainty, paradoxically, is to obey an idol; true faith rests on uncertainty. As Kierkegaard reveals about Abraham, his murder only becomes a sacrifice because he has such love for both Isaac and God. His faith enables that love but also raises the apparent clash of loves to the highest pitch. Faith does not make his act easier by making the outcome unproblematic whatever the discomfort of the process; it makes it infinitely more difficult. Analogously, Christ's divinity did not, as some superficial readings might have it, make his sacrifice on the cross easier, but infinitely harder than it would be for the human being.

The scandal Kierkegaard develops from the gospel is that what we suffer *and the way in which we suffer it* contributes to the suffering of God, which is as much greater than our suffering as is his love greater than ours. If we cannot accept this interpretation as it applies to Abraham, then we will not accept it in the form of Christ. We are caught up not in a reading of 'because' but of 'nevertheless': the reciprocal 'nevertheless' of divine forgiveness which appears in the impossible fact that God humbles himself to ask our forgiveness through the form of the monstrous and unforgivable face of the world. The God of Jesus Christ risks being read as the God who endorses or even demands the acts of violent fanaticism. Maintaining faith in the God of Jesus Christ does not make it easier to reconcile the horror of the human actions taken in God's name with his love. It is living in that very difficulty that constitutes the suffering of faith.

Reading either the Bible or Kierkegaard faithfully might well frighten me, because it shows me that I do not love enough, and that to love more will increase rather than diminish the painful scandal of the text. It is easier to try to set bounds to other people's readings rather than to take on board the way in which the texts are misread as part of their meaning, as part of the generation of the scandal of uncertainty which is the condition of faith.

Notes

1. In the Journals SK expands on this notion as follows:

    > Think of two lovers. The lover has written a letter to the beloved. Would it ever occur to the recipient to be concerned about how other will interpret this letter, or will he not read it all alone?
    >
    > Suppose now that this letter from the lover has the distinctiveness that every human being is the beloved—what then? Is the intention now that they should sit and confer with one another, not to speak of dragging along the scholarly apparatus of countless generations?
    >
    > No the intention is that each individual shall read this letter before God solely as an individual, as the single individual who has received this letter by God or from God!
    >
    > But it was soon forgotten that this letter is from God and entirely forgotten that it is to the single individual. The race has been put in his place. And therefore we have completely lost the impression of the Bible. (JP, 1, 86, §213; X3 A 348 n.d. 1850)

2. Lest it be though that this is simply an isolated case of metaphor gone awry or being deliberately stretched to scandalize, consider this passage from the *Journals*:

    > When, in order to subvert the position that there is an absolute in morality, an appeal is made to variation in custom and use and such shocking examples as savages putting their parents to death, attention is centered merely upon the external. That is to say, if it could be proved that savages maintain that a person ought to hate his parents, it would be quite another matter; but this is not their thought; they believe that one should love them, and the error is only in the way of expressing it. For it is clear that the savages do not intend to harm their parents but to do good to them. (JP I, 398, §889; III A 202 n.d. 1842)

    So if the motivation is love, however misguided, even killing one's parents becomes at least forgivable and presumably within the bounds of the tolerance of the beloved. Motive is all, effects are merely external.

3. This need not entail distorting biblical texts to invent outrageous demands. What could be plainer and more imperative than the commands put in the mouth of Jesus himself in Matthew's gospel about the cutting-off of the hand or foot or the gouging out of the eye that offends us? Granted that this discussion comes in the context of the exceptional love of Abraham for Isaac, and the assertion that only one who is capable of such love can truly be put to the text in this way, the cautions against textual study in *For Self-Examination* make these arguments hard to bring to bear against the fanatic who is convinced of his calling.

4. R. Browning, *The Poems:Volume 2* (ed. J. Pettigrew, supplemented and completed by T.J. Collins; Harmondsworth: Penguin Books, 1981), pp. 446–47. Philip Drew, in his *The Poetry of Browning: A Critical Introduction* (London: Methuen and Co, 1970), could not be more confident of the similarities between Browning and Kierkegaard, writing 'The religious ideas and techniques of demonstration of Browning and Kierkegaard coincide so often that there is no room to comment on each instance. One or two particularly interesting congruences will be specifically mentioned: otherwise this general indication must suffice' (p. 205 n.1). Others, however, see a great difference between Browning's optimism, sometimes dismissed as facile, and Kierkegaard's pessimism, sometimes dismissed as morbid. Where they do approach each other is in their awareness of the problems raised by Higher Criticism, and in their use of complex literary techniques of pseudonymity or the dramatic monologue to enact rather than simply describe the unsettling effects of textuality on the reconstruction of history and the siting of authoritative meaning. The matter is well explored by Anne Hiemstra in her unpublished dissertation, 'Browning: History, Myth and Higher Criticism' (Columbia University, 1996). She summarizes her view of what Browning had learned from his engagement with Higher Criticism as follows: 'He more than any other poet of his era implicitly argued...that understanding the source and nature of both ancient and modern discourse is a way of locating oneself in a human continuum, a way to bridge the gulf many of his Victorian contemporaries claimed separated them from the past' (pp. 284–85). This could be seen as Browning's more amiable version of the communicative basis of Kierkegaard's abolition of Lessing's gulf through the categories of contemporaneity and scandal.

5. 'Kafka and His Precursors,' in Jorge Luis Borges, *Selected Non-fictions*, ed. Eliot Weinberger (trans. Esther Allen, Suzanne Jill Levine and Eliot Weinberger; New York: Viking, 1999), pp. 363–365 (365).

6. Browning, *The Poems*, vol. 2, ed.John Pettigrew, supplemented and completed by Thomas J. Collins (Harmondsworth: Penguin Books, 1981), pp. 1047–48.

7. *The Biblical Kierkegaard* (Macon, GA: Mercer University Press, 1997), p. 142.

8. *Kierkegaard and the Treachery of Love* (Cambridge: Cambridge University Press, 2002), p. 106.

9. *Kierkegaard in the Present Age* (Milwaukee: Marquette University Press, 2001), pp. 28–41.

10. R. Williams, 'God and Risk (2),' in R. Holloway, ed., *The Divine Risk* (London: Darton, Longman and Todd, 1990), p. 15; cp. Ida Friederike Görres, *Broken Lights: Diaries and Letters 1951–59* (trans. B. Waldstein-Wartenberg; Westminster, MA: The Newman Press, 1964), pp. 87–88.

The Lesson of Eternity: The Figure of the Teacher in Kierkegaard's *Philosophical Fragments*

Imagine, if you will, a situation where a school board has decided that the children under their care are in need of special instruction. Naturally, they will consider carefully just what they want the children to learn before they begin to advertise for a teacher. They will want someone who can communicate to the children what it is they need to know, someone who can explain in language the children will understand the workings of a steam engine or the evolution of the pentadactyl limb. Not only that, however. The teacher will have to be able to show the children that they need to learn the subject in the first place. They will need to be persuaded that the knowledge is either useful or enjoyable, or at least that the consequences of not learning it will be rather uncomfortable.

It stands to reason, then, that the teacher must communicate with the children in their own language. Or does it? Take, for instance, the problem of learning a foreign language, say French. The school might imaginatively decide that they will employ a teacher who speaks only French in the classroom. The children may never have met anyone who did not speak their native language before. At first, they will be baffled, but they will quickly learn that if they want to communicate with the teacher, they are going to have to adopt a whole new means of communication. Not only that, they will realise that what they had never questioned as a universal medium of communication, their own language, is in fact a language, one among many.

Of course, the success of the experiment depends entirely on the children's desire to communicate, on their decision to break out of the constraints of the language which, until then, they have seen as entirely sufficient. It may be very hard for the teacher, too, especially if she is bi-lingual and has to suffer the twin frustration of being unable to use the common language she shares with the children to express herself and of finding her beloved second language mangled and abused. She will also need to be willing to run the risk that she and her language may be rejected.

If the board decide to opt for this style of teaching despite these possibilities, then they may choose a candidate who paradoxically seems not to fulfil the fundamental condition of communicating with her pupils. Yet this is precisely because the children are being provoked to question the process of communication itself so as to expand their understanding.

Imagine, then, that instead of being exposed to merely another language the children are being asked to learn to exist. This seems an absurd proposition. Children who do exist can be enough of a handful to teach, and no doubt many a weary teacher has devoutly wished at times that her beloved pupils would cease to exist. These problems are insignificant, though, beside the practical problems of teaching a non-existent class.

Yet this is the task which the pseudonym Johannes Climacus identifies for the Teacher in *Philosophical Fragments*. The whole book can be seen as an extended discussion paper of the qualifications required for a teacher of existence. The recommendation which is put forward has analogies to that of the language teacher who uses the language she is trying to teach as the medium of instruction. In order to teach people to exist, you have first to make them realize that they do not exist, and then hold out before them the actuality of existence in such a way that they grasp it as a realizable possibility for themselves.

Whatever the merits of this proposal, it still seems absurdly paradoxical to expect the teacher to address a non-existent being (which can only even be spoken about in an oxymoron). The only entity that might persuade someone who thinks he exists that in fact he does not would be an entity which could not exist and yet does. This calls into the question the whole understanding of what it might be to exist. Persuaded of this, the hearer might be brought to such a revolution of understanding that he comes to see that he had not existed, as ex hypothesi a non-existent being can no more comprehend his non-existence than he can anything else. The category of non-existence can only be dealt with in retrospect, yet it is one all of us do retrospectively come to grips with in the attempt to contemplate the world before our own birth.[1]

We should recall that, despite the seeming impossibility of this position, Kierkegaard had made considerable study in his youth of the writings of a man who was happy to declare that he had once been dead: the man who wrote, 'I was once alive apart from the law, but when the commandment came, sin revived and I died; the very commandment which promised life proved to be death to me. For sin, finding opportunity in the commandment, deceived me and by it killed me' (Rom 7:9-11). In the letter to the Romans, Paul recalls to his readers the fact that they were all buried with Christ in their baptism, that they have all died to sin (Rom. 6:1-11), and by that same token that they have been given life in Christ. Again, in his letter to the Galatians, he writes: 'For through the law I died to the law, that I might live to God. I have been crucified with Christ; it is no longer I who live, but Christ who lives in me' (Gal. 2:19-20).[2]

Paul writes out of an experience of a new birth, and part of the problem examined in *Philosophical Fragments* is to explore the philosophical consequences of such a claim. What kind of anthropology does it imply, and what is the communicative mechanism by which it works? The teacher who is a 'stumbling block to the Jews and folly to the Gentiles', the teacher who is represented as telling parables in order that the people should not understand,[3] is a figure who raises deep questions about the nature of communication.

The form of Climacus's argument here calls to mind that of St Anselm in his *Cur Deus Homo*. In that work, Anselm demonstrates the fitness of the incarnation by considering the problem of the satisfaction due to God for human sinfulness 'remoto Christo'—as if Christ had not existed.[4] *Philosophical Fragments* can be read as a similar attempt to introduce the figure of the God-man by an exploration of the communicative problem between God and humanity. Given Kierkegaard's account of this communicative problem, only the paradoxical figure of the God-man can effect any form of communication. In a very Anselmian formulation, Climacus writes: 'Faith, then, must constantly cling to the teacher. But in order for the teacher to be able to give the condition, he must be the God, and in order to put the learner in possession of it, he must be man' (PF, 62).

Climacus is not simply producing his specification for the teacher in a vacuum. There are two formidable candidates for this post who set the parameters for the discussion in the *Philosophical Fragments*: the figure of Christ according to Hegel and Kierkegaard's understanding of Christ as the God-man. Both of these are set against another figure who might be thought to be an eminently suitable candidate: Socrates.

To carry our metaphor further, Climacus seeks to show why it is that Socrates not only does not fit the bill, but is wise enough not to apply. Socrates is a teacher of recollection, who brings people to a realization of what is already within them.[5] He is an occasion, a reminder, to those who do exist, but have forgotten it. That is a very different thing from bringing one's pupil's into existence. Socrates, however, knows that this is the highest relation between human beings. One human being can serve as mid-wife to another, but it is for the God alone to give birth (PF, 9–11). Socrates took care never to claim authority. Christ, however, made explicit claims which both Hegel and Kierkegaard see as of primary importance in their discussion of his role.

Though the figure of Socrates is of great importance in the *Philosophical Fragments* as a foil to the Teacher, illuminating that role by contrast, I propose to focus on the two candidates who can be regarded as vying for the post. In particular, how do their claims reflect the perception of the communicative problem of their respective sponsors, Hegel and Kierkegaard?

To begin with, it is important to realize that there are basic areas where Hegel's and Kierkegaard's accounts of Christ agree in the face of many of their contemporaries. Both of them insist that the being of the God-man, his ontological reality, is fundamental to coming to grips with Christianity. The concept of incarnation is the bedrock of both their accounts. Christianity is not simply a matter of a series of timeless moral teachings given by a respected prophet. It is a response to an event and a person. Where the two disagree is on the way in which that incarnation works as a strategy of communication between God and humanity, because they have fundamentally different views on the process of communication.

That difference can be obscured because Kierkegaard makes use of Hegel's terms and concepts to put forward a radically different view of the significance of Christ. It is not fair to represent this as demonstrating that Kierkegaard was ultimately dependent on Hegel. Kierkegaard himself accounts for the lack of Christian terminology in the *Philosophical Fragments* as an attempt to get away from a form of language which has been twisted by its incorporation into the Hegelian system.[6] He is trying to restate the truths of Christianity as he interprets these within a context where the very tools of argument have been appropriated by his opponents. Hegel and the Hegelians purport to have established the meaning of words such as Spirit and reconciliation in a way that finally does justice to the insights contained in them. Rather than abandon this terminology to the Hegelians, Kierkegaard runs the risk of being interpreted as a parasite on their discourse in the attempt to rescue the language that Hegel has, in Kierkegaard's opinion, misappropriated.

Kierkegaard's own situation parallels that of the Teacher is some respects, although it is crucially different in others. He is addressing problems of communication, but has to do this within a system which has already been set up on what he is arguing on fundamentally false principles.

Let us then begin by looking at Hegel's account of Christ, concentrating particularly on the issue of Christ as communicator or teacher, in order to draw out some of the principles in question.

Hegel's Account of Christ as Teacher[7]

For Hegel, the incarnation is the necessary concrete demonstration of the process of reconciliation which constitutes the being of God and defines the meaning of love, a demonstration which brings humankind to the awareness of the eternal truth that this constitutes the nature of humanity as well. It holds up a mirror in which the human individual can finally recognize herself.

By taking on human nature, the Christ demonstrates finally that the divine and human natures are one and the same. For Hegel, God is the process of postulating another and reconciling it to oneself through love, an eternal dynamic which Hegel relates to the Church's doctrine of the trinity. But humanity is not merely an accidental adjunct to this process. As absolute self-consciousness, God postulates finite consciousness in order that he can both know and be known. As Hegel puts it in the 1831 version of his *Lectures on the Philosophy of Religion,*

> Absolute self-consciousness is found only to the extent that it is also [finite] consciousness; it thus splits into two, on the one side the subject remaining wholly and simply present to itself, on the other also subject, but differentiated as finite. Thus God knows himself in humanity, and human beings, to the extent that they know themselves as spirit and in their truth, know themselves as God.[8]

But the problem is that humanity is finite and therefore unaware of its infinite capacity. And yet, humankind does have a consciousness of its insufficiency, a sense of its finiteness which gives an entrée to the idea of the infinite. There is an anguish which results from the awareness of the radical evil of the human being and the infinite demand of the good. What might otherwise be construed as an exoneration of human evil, the human lack of ability to will the good, is in itself the index of just how radical the problem of evil is. Redemption consists in bringing this tension to the highest pitch to allow for a sublation, and ultimately a recognition that precisely this sublation is the determination of the idea of God. The 'otherness' of the human can be subsumed in the reality of God because God is the process of the sublating of otherness, or, in other words, love.

But how is this synthesis to be made apparent to humanity so that this sublation may occur? Somehow God must reveal himself to humanity. That he will do so is, for Hegel, inevitable. It is a necessary consequence of God's being. As God is love, he is ipso facto self-revelatory. This is constitutive of the idea of God as Spirit:

> A spirit that is not revelatory is not spirit. It is said that God created the world and has revealed himself. This is spoken of as something he did once, that will not happen again, and as being the sort of event that may either occur or not occur: God could have revealed himself, he could have created the world or not; his doing so is one of his capricious contingent characteristics, so to speak, and does not belong to the concept of God himself. But it is the essence of God as spirit to be for another; i.e. to reveal himself. He does not create the world once and for all, but is the eternal creator, the eternal act of self-revelation. This actus is what he is: this is his concept, his definition[9]... What indeed does God reveal other than that he is this process of self-revelation?[10]

How, though, is this revelation to be effected? How is humanity to be made aware of its true nature as essentially divine when it labours under the consciousness of its finitude? The truth has, according to Hegel, to appear as certainty, as something that is before us, something immediate and sensible which can be experienced before it is thought. It has to be presented as a brute fact, of the order of the existence of the sun, something that 'has to be put up with because it is there.'[11] For Hegel, this immediate communication can only be through the appearance of a concrete human being in the flesh. This appearance, the incarnation, is a necessary corollary of the nature of the spirit.

The success of the communication requires that 'a human being appears to consciousness as God, and God appears to it as a human being.'[12] Hegel insists on the importance of this appearance as a concrete and specific human individual. He characterizes as 'revolting arrogance' and 'sentimentality'[13] any attempt to decry the need for this sensible presence in the interests of a supposedly higher abstract thought. It may be true that humanity in the universal sense is implicitly to be defined as the unity of God and humanity, but this is not immediately available to consciousness. Hegel calls the concept of the God-man a 'monstrous compound', but concedes its usefulness in making it clear that the otherness, the finitude, of human nature does not damage the fundamental unity of the human and the divine.

Christ, then, appears as an ordinary human being, but a human being whose sole concern is the proclamation of the truth. His office as Teacher is central to this. Hegel takes pains to differentiate Christ's own teaching as recorded in the Gospels from the later doctrine of the Church. Christ's teaching is immediate, appealing to the sensible consciousness through intuition, unlike doctrine, which is conceptual and mediated. It is a teaching which negates the present world, demanding that the whole attention of the hearer is directed to the infinite interest. In its extravagant claims which demand the severance of natural bonds of affection and family loyalty and its bold assertion of the imperative necessity of love and of the search for truth, it has a sweep and an authority which mark it as divine. This teaching is not mediated: 'nothing is said about any mediation through which this elevation [of soul] may come to pass for humanity; rather what is spoken of is this immediate being, this immediate self-transportation into the truth, the kingdom of God.'[14]

Hegel summarizes the demand made by this teaching as the need to 'cast oneself upon the truth.'[15] Such a demand throws attention onto the one who makes it. What is his authority for issuing such a summons? It is clear that Christ here speaks as a prophet rather than as a teacher. 'He is the one who, because his demand is immediate, expresses it immediately from God, and God speaks it through him.'[16] Yet he is essentially human, so that he becomes the revelation of God's divine presence as 'essentially identical with this human being.'

At this point one might ask what is unique in this. What about other great prophetic teachers who have presented their hearers with the immediate demand for personal commitment to the truth? For Hegel, the final determinant of Christ's singular significance is his death and resurrection.[17] In his 1831 lectures, Hegel makes explicit how this is in contrast to Socrates, whose career he sees as similar to Christ's until the point of death.

He grants that there is nothing unique in the fact that Christ dies, nor in the manner of his death as an innocent man cruelly executed. Indeed, Hegel argues that it is precisely the fact that death is the universal demonstration of the finitude of humanity that gives Christ's death its unique significance. Christ's death is the proof that this finitude is to be found in God:

> God has died, God is dead—this is the most frightful of all thoughts, that everything eternal and true is not, that negation itself is found in God. The deepest anguish, the feeling of complete irretrievability,

the annulling of everything that is elevated, are bound up with this thought.[18]

Out of infinite love, God has taken upon himself this ultimately alien finitude.

Yet even here there is a sublation and it is in the light of this that God's involvement with Christ and so with humanity is made manifest. God maintains himself through death and rises again. In this God has demonstrated his reconciliation with the world. It is not a reconciliation that has to be effected in some specific transaction between God and a world that has alienated itself through sin. God is eternally this reconciliation of the other. By the concrete example which Christ's resurrection affords, God has shown that 'even the human is not something alien to him, but rather that this otherness, this self-distinguishing finitude as it is expressed, is a moment in God himself, albeit a disappearing moment.'[19] Christ has made explicit what is implicit in the ontology of every human being, and in the teaching of every religious system. He has demonstrated the essential identity of the human and the divine, in which human individuality becomes a 'disappearing moment' in the wider identity of God.

Hegel makes it clear, however, that this understanding of the death of Christ is only accessible to those who are brought into the community of the Spirit. The Spirit itself is characterized by its work of bringing humankind into community. It is in the community that the consciousness of the reconciling work of Christ can arise. This community, which becomes the Church, sustains itself by offering those who wish to come to the truth a presupposition of the certainty of reconciliation. This presupposition becomes enshrined in the Church's doctrine.

As a result, we can distinguish between three groups of learners in Hegel's account:

1. The contemporaries: those who encounter Christ before his resurrection, who have a presentiment of the reconciling power of God through the direct teaching of Christ.
2. The disciples of the first generation: those who experience the emergence of the Spirit in the formation of the post-resurrection community, and who thus come to a certainty about the nature of Christ as God-man, the representation of the reconciliation of the divine and human.
3. The disciples of the second generation: those who come to know the truth of reconciliation through the teaching of the Church.

The Church presents them with religious truth as an external
certainty with which they must come to terms, which they must
appropriate to themselves.

In all these cases, however, what Christ's hearers must realize is something
that has always been true about their own nature. It is, in Kierkegaardian
terms, a matter of recollection rather than repetition. Ultimately, the
teacher's task is to prompt the learner to realize a truth which has always
been accessible to her, to look again at an aspect of her being which
she has never truly understood. The teacher is the unarguable, pellucid
immediate demonstration of this truth.

Kierkegaard's Account of Christ as Teacher in Relation to Hegel

The depiction of the Teacher in *Philosophical Fragments* stands
in conscious opposition to the Hegelian account. Fundamental to
this opposition is the radically different view of the communicative
transaction involved. Where Hegel sees the figure of Christ as the
crucial immediate communication of a truth intrinsic to the human
condition, the Teacher of *Philosophical Fragments* is the occasion for
scandal and misunderstanding which may bring about the new birth
of the individual. The God-man does not make anything clearer, but is
himself the Absolute Paradox.

For Kierkegaard, the implications of God's loving concern for those
who cannot understand him are quite the opposite to those set out by
Hegel. God's love is what prevents him from communicating directly
with those who are incapable of understanding him.

Climacus uses the parable of the king who loves the servant girl to
make his point (PF, 26–29). The king cannot communicate his love
directly to her because the difference in rank and understanding between
them will cloud the girl's apprehension both of her own worth and of the
king as a man. Such a difference is the case between the God and the
human learner; knowing that the learner has fallen into untruth by his
own fault, the God still loves him. Though it is an option, the God will
not abandon the learner because of his love for him, which yearns to be
reciprocated, yet the God cannot directly communicate with the learner
who has no faculty to understand the God. Through love, the God must
restrain his impulse to declare himself, and that restraint is a source of
grief. Climacus sums this up as follows: 'Who grasps the contradiction
of this sorrow: not to disclose itself is the death of love; to disclose itself
is the death of the beloved' (PF, 30).

The only answer to this contradiction is for the lover to become the equal of the beloved, not by appearing in disguise, but by truly taking on the condition of the lowliest. Otherwise, the lover will deceive the beloved by glossing over the beloved's lack of understanding. Either he will surreptitiously remove the veil over the beloved's eyes in such a way that the beloved is never conscious that such a veil existed, or else, he will allow the beloved to fool himself into thinking that his distorted vision of their relationship represents the true depth of love which should exist between them.

The nature of this communication and its causes and consequences are spelled out in *Practice in Christianity*, in particular in the section on 'The Categories of Offense' (PC, 123–44). Here Kierkegaard writing as Anti-Climacus clarifies the concept of indirect communication as it applies to Christ. Far from being the immediate physical manifestation of the self-revealing God, Christ's human appearance serves in fact as an incognito which ensures his unrecognizability. The spectacle of a human being, indistinguishable from his fellows, who announces himself to be God is one calculated to provoke scandal and offence rather than the immediate acceptance of his claims as the key to human self-understanding. Though the communication may be direct, it contradicts the person of the bearer of that communication who is seen to be human. Such a mismatch between the communication and the communicator faces the hearer with the choice between offence or belief.

This is all in complete contrast to Hegel's account. Kierkegaard insists that there is no possibility of direct communication between the God and a human being in the grip of deception, or, in other words, of sin. While Hegel's Christ comes as the inevitable revelation of a self-revealing spirit in immediate and concrete form to provide a basis of certainty to human self-understanding, Kierkegaard's God-man comes as the representative of a loving God unable to communicate his love to a sin-deadened human being, and thus resorting to a paradoxical communication which may bring the dead to life by revealing the deadly nature of sin.

Yet this leaves us wondering what exactly sin can be if it has so devastating an effect on the communication between God and humanity. Climacus does not specify this in *Philosophical Fragments*. For a fuller exposition of Kierkegaard's understanding of sin, we can turn to his *The Sickness unto Death*, where he defines it as: 'before God or with the conception of God, in despair not to will to be oneself, or in despair to will to be oneself" (SUD, 77). But what is the root of this despair, and how might it act as a barrier to communication?

Kierkegaard relates despair to the notions of possibility and necessity.[20] Both are essential for the actualization of the self. By refusing to acknowledge its necessity, the self can lose itself in a realm of abstract, unrealized, and ultimately unrealizable possibility. On the other hand, the self can also loses its actuality by refusing to acknowledge the transforming power of possibility. Insofar as it loses its grip on one or the other pole of this dialectic, then the self can be said to lose its actuality, or in plain language, not to be.[21]

The relationship between possibility, necessity and actuality is also discussed in the Interlude in *Philosophical Fragments*. Here again we find a radically different account from that found in Hegel. For Hegel, actuality and possibility interact to constitute necessity. By possibility he means what he defines as 'real possibility': the totality of conditions presupposed by a certain actuality. If all these conditions are fulfilled, then the actuality itself will be instanced. The inevitability of this outcome constitutes necessity, but is also the essence of freedom, in that freedom is the untrammelled outworking of the relations of co-implication.

Kierkegaard, on the contrary, regards this as the negation of freedom. He reorientates the whole dialectic.[22] Far from necessity being the union of actuality and possibility, he sees actuality as 'the unity of possibility and necessity' (SUD, 55). His definition of the possible is very different from Hegel's. Rather than possibility preceding actuality in the guise of necessary conditions, possibility is infinite, and to be identified with the future, not the past. *The Sickness unto Death* makes explicit a further implication: 'since everything is possible for God, then God is this— that everything is possible' (SUD, 40). Hegel's God is free because he can manifest his necessity; Kierkegaard's is free because he has infinite possibility.

The role of the teacher, then, is to point to the realizability of possibility in the learner's life. Paradoxically, it is the impossibility of the God-man which is the source of his salvific role. As the concrete instance of the impossible actualized, he bursts the bonds of the necessity that masquerades as possibility in the Hegelian account. As Kierkegaard remarks in *Judge for Yourself!*, considered as mere possibility, Christianity seems easy, attracting the plaudits of the crowd. What an illusion, however, if someone imagines that by instanciating this possibility he would draw even greater acclaim (FSE, 116–17). Actuality is the occasion of offence, not a means of ensuring capitulation to the irresistible evidence of God's nature.

This in turn means that Kierkegaard can regard everyone as standing in an equal relation to the communicator, regardless of the temporal distance between them. Unlike Hegel, with his three classes of believers, Kierkegaard sees everyone as standing in an equal relationship of possible offence at a paradox which is absurd in a way that has no relationship to the historical context in which it occurs, rather as the square root of two is an irrational number. Whether a contemporary or a follower at any remove, it is the hearer's reaction of offence or faith to the paradox embodied in Jesus Christ that is important.

Kierkegaard protests vehemently at the idea that for subsequent generations Christianity becomes a doctrine which must be agreed to. He agrees with Hegel that this idea arises as an inevitable development given the human condition, but unlike Hegel, he sees it as one to be deplored and resisted at every level. If the content of Christianity is reduced to a body of knowledge which can be assented to, then the essential recreative movement of faith has been lost. What is more, the person of the teacher loses its significance; knowledge is knowledge, independent of its source.

Rather than confronting the problem of existence, this attitude compounds it by assimilating the paradox of the God-man to the etiolated life of illusion which passes for existence. It is as if the teacher of a foreign language were to assimilate its pronunciation and its cultural references entirely to his own, through coming to his knowledge of it not from the immediate circumstance of communication, but by memorizing a grammar book. Perhaps such a teacher can persuade children to parrot the phrases of the language, but will not expand their possibilities of communication, and so the parameters of their own existence.

To find an account of how Kierkegaard conceives the educative process, we can turn to an astonishing passage in *Practice in Christianity* (PC, 174–79). Here Anti-Climacus explains how to introduce the story of Christ to a child 'who is not warped by having learnt by rote a simple school assignment about Jesus Christ's suffering and death' (PC, 174). Anti-Climacus envisages showing the child a picture book which contains among other pictures of heroes an illustration of a crucified man. He traces the child's reaction from discomfort to indignation at God's permitting it to happen, and then to a desire to avenge this death. But as the child matures, it becomes a desire to share in that suffering.

It is the concrete image of the crucified Christ place in the context of the triumphs of human heroes that is the key to this process, not rote learning of catechisms and creeds. Nor is it the glorious outcome of the resurrection from which Kierkegaard starts, as that can only have meaning in the light of being seized by the innocent suffering of the figure on the cross. The child is confronted with an impossible possibility, the cruelty inflicted on the best of men the paradox of suffering, and the alarming confession of the child's confidant: 'At that moment, the adult stands there as an accuser who accuses himself and the whole human race!' (PC, 176).

It is in this sense that the summary of the message that Climacus provides as all that would have been necessary for the contemporary generation to relay has its power: 'We have believed that in such and such a year the god appeared in the humble form of a servant, lived and taught as a servant and then died' (PF, 104). This is the impossible possibility in its starkest form. It is the paradox that cannot even be engaged with; it can only have been engaged with.

To ask, then, what the teacher can do for me is, to return to our initial scenario, as if the pupil were to persist in asking the teacher in English for an explanation of what she is doing speaking this gibberish. Explanations can only be given if the child enters into the world of this new language, tentatively exploring and building a capability. In itself, as this is confirmed by the encouragement of the teacher, it becomes its own explanation. By entering into the process, the benefits of entering upon it make themselves manifest in the expansion of the world through the increased possibilities of communication, possibilities which may allow the pupil to change, to 'come to be', to grasp the lesson of eternity.

Notes

1. 'In the moment, a person becomes aware that he was born for his previous state, to which he is not to appeal, was indeed one of "not to be."[sic] In the moment, he becomes aware of the rebirth, for his previous state was indeed one of "not to be." If his previous state had been one of "to be," then under no circumstances would the moment have acquired distinctive significance for him, as explained above' (PF, 21).

2. See also Col. 2:11-14; 3:3-4; Eph. 2:1-7.

3. Mk 4:10-12; Mt. 13:10-13; Lk. 8:9-10.

4. See the Preface to *Cur Deus Homo*: 'In accordance with the subject-matter with which it deals I entitled [this work] Why God became a man; and I divided it into two short books. The first of these contains the answers of believers to the objections of unbelievers who repudiate the Christian faith because they regard it as incompatible of reason. And this book goes on to prove by rational necessity—Christ being removed from sight, as if there had never been anything known about Him—that no man can possibly be saved

without Him' ('Why God became a Man,' in *Anselm of Canterbury*, Vol. III [ed. and trans. J. Hopkins and H. Richardson; Toronto: Edwin Mellen Press, 1976], pp. 39–137 [43]).

5. Kierkegaard, in a note in *Concluding Unscientific Postscript* (CUP1, 184–85), acknowledges that a distinction should be made between Plato and Socrates on this point. However, Socrates in *Philosophical Fragments* represents a position, and indeed represents the Hegelian reading of Socrates, rather than offering a rigorous analysis of the Greek philosopher.

6. 'Just as a toothless old man is reduced to mumbling through the gums, so modern discourse about Christianity has lost the rigor that can only come from an energetically sustained terminology, and the whole is reduced to a toothless twaddle' (CUP1, 325).

7. This account of Hegel's teaching draws mainly on his *Lectures on the Philosophy of Religion* in the edition edited by P.C. Hodgson (3 vols.; Berkeley, CA: University of California Press, 1985). This is not a claim that Kierkegaard was directly influenced by these lectures, but rather an attempt to set Kierkegaard's account in the context of an approach which has fundamental differences and yet intriguing similarities to his own, and which, at whatever level of direct or mediated influence, was a powerful force in the theological climate in which he worked.

8. Hegel, *Lectures*, I, p. 465.

9. Hegel, *Lectures*, III, p. 170 (emphasis in orig.).

10. Hegel, *Lectures*, III, p. 22.

11. Hegel, *Lectures*, III, p. 336.

12. Hegel, *Lectures*, III, p. 313.

13. Hegel, *Lectures*, III, p. 134.

14. Hegel, *Lectures*, III, p. 319.

15. Hegel, *Lectures*, III, p. 320.

16. Hegel, *Lectures*, III, p. 320.

17. 'The history of [Christ's] teaching, life, death and resurrection [has] taken place; thus this history exists for the community, and it is strictly adequate to the idea. <[It is] not just teaching, a [merely] intellectual foundation.> This is the crucial point on which everything depends, this is the verification, the absolute proof' (Hegel, *Lectures*, III, p. 145).

18. Hegel, *Lectures*, III, p. 323 (emphasis in orig.).

19. Hegel, *Lectures*, III, p. 327.

20. See here especially SUD, 35–42.

21. The well known opening paragraph of *The Sickness unto Death* (SUD, 13), where Kierkegaard concludes that the human self is not yet a self, illustrates this paradox. Insofar as the self is not yet itself, it does not exist.

22. He takes issue with Aristotle's discussion of the inter-relationship of these three terms in his *De Interpretatione* (see *The Works of Aristotle*, Vol. 1 [ed. W.D. Ross; Oxford: Clarendon Press, 1926]) on the grounds that Aristotle makes a fundamental error in describing what is necessary as possible. Aristotle's argument is that if what is necessary has happened, that shows that it must have been possible that it would happen. This, however, involves him in distinguishing different senses of the concept 'possible'. If we mean by describing an event as possible that it could have happened or not, then

this cannot apply to necessary events by definition. They could not fail to occur. Hence Aristotle adopts a definition of possibility which lies behind Hegel's discussion; what is possible for a subject depends on what it has the intrinsic capacity to become. Kierkegaard, however, refuses this argument. The necessary is just that: necessary; talk of possibility and actuality has no meaning in this context as the necessary is absolutely different from both (PF, 74–5).

CITIES OF THE DEAD: THE RELATION OF PERSON AND *POLIS* IN KIERKEGAARD'S *WORKS OF LOVE*

Anyone who evinces an interest in Kierkegaard's view of human society and how his distinctive views of the nature and duties of the human individual are to be expressed in community is likely to be directed to his self-styled 'Christian Deliberations' in *Works of Love*. There we find that Kierkegaard recommends those who are overwhelmed by the scope of the subject to look to a brief summary. He directs the reader to resort to the dead as the best way to gain a handle on life. He goes on to explain that in order to understand the more specific but central question of love and its place in human relationships, we should remain with the dead. There we will find the key to the problem: 'The work of love in recollecting one who is dead is…a work of the most unselfish, the freest, the most faithful love. Therefore go out and practice it; recollect the one who is dead and just in this way learn to love the living unselfishly, freely, faithfully' (WL, 358).

Thus Kierkegaard sets up the criterion by which human community is to be judged. It is by our love for the dead that our true calibre as members of community will be revealed. At best, this seems a deeply unconventional if not perverse point of view. To begin with, it seems that a very one-sided relationship is being promoted. It is surely axiomatic that any concept of human community must advocate a mutual commitment if it is to survive. Yet Kierkegaard' s emphasis here, as in all his writings, seems to be overwhelmingly on the duties, responsibilities and, indeed, the pains of the lover, not on the responsibilities of being loved. Can we envisage a community where each member conceives it solely to be his or her duty to love and where none is responsive to the love of others? In the flippant terms of the old parody of English manners, surely it would be a community where people would perish of hunger in the doorways to restaurants, each being determined to defer to his or her neighbours, with the consequence that no one would ever be able to enter. Would not this be an ultimately sterile and self-centred exercise in compassionate individualism? If none is able or willing graciously to receive love, then in what sense can loving occur and in what sense can we speak of community?

Quite apart from these questions, there is a darker side to Kierkegaard's encomium of the dead. This can be brought into focus by referring to Lionel Dahmer's account of his struggle to come to terms with the unspeakable crimes of his son Jeffrey, the serial killer.[1] Lionel Dahmer seeks to explain his son's almost incredible record of murder, necrophilia and cannibalism as a product of his inability to make human contact with another person, which was compounded with an overwhelming terror of abandonment. Only when dead would people make no demands; only when dead would they remain with him. In Jeffrey Dahmer's nightmarish vision of the world, only the dead were safe to love because they would not desert him. An awful but strict logic propelled Dahmer to the ultimate solution of cannibalism, where the assimilation of the object of desire is complete. In this context, it becomes an urgent question as to whether Kierkegaard's advocacy of 'love for the dead' does not carry within it at least the seeds of this appalling conclusion.

Furthermore, we might argue that even the premises of Kierkegaard's case are flawed. His insistence that the love of the dead is free because the dead make no claim on us seems to come oddly from a man who lived his life in the shadow of the melancholy of his own father. As George Steiner puts it in discussing Kierkegaard's fascination with the figure of Antigone, 'Antigone's tortured relation with her father, the devouring immanence of the dead father in the living child, exactly mirrors Kierkegaard's image of his own circumstances.'[2] So much for the undemanding dead. Dead devouring the living, the living devouring the dead; this seems infertile ground for a study of human community.

Yet just such appalling instances of human interaction in community are graphically depicted in the biblical tradition. Deuteronomy 28 catalogues the disasters that will come on the people as a result of their disobedience, with this promise:

> ...when you are shut up in all your towns throughout the land that the Lord your God has assigned to you, you shall eat your own issue, the flesh of your sons and daughters that the Lord your God has assigned to you, because of the desperate straits to which your enemy shall reduce you. He who is most tender and fastidious among you shall be too mean to his brother and the wife of his bosom and the children he has spared to share with any of them the flesh of the children that he eats. (Deut. 28:52-55)

This prophecy is all too graphically enacted in the siege of Samaria in 2 Kings 6. Such mutual devouring of living and dead serves as the ultimate sign of the condition which human society manifests in the absence of obedience to the divine.

Strong meat—but I put it in this stark way because it reflects my own immediate reaction to Kierkegaard's call to love the dead. Surely what he is saying is scandalous and inimical to any true human community. Yet it is in wrestling with this grotesque picture of human relationships that we will find what Kierkegaard has to say about the matter of human communities in the light of biblical and other models. Despite my initial aversion, I shall argue that Kierkegaard's account of the work of remembering the dead is a profound reflection on person and *polis* in Christian terms. Its offensiveness is part and parcel with the ultimate offence of the Christian message. This points up the fact that yet again Kierkegaard is, for my money, one of the few authors who are strong enough misreaders, in Harold Bloom's terms, to come to grips with the scandal of the biblical tradition.

What, then, does it mean for the structure of human society to love the dead? In seeking to tease out the radical social understanding which is implied in this phrase of Kierkegaard's, I found my thoughts crystallizing around the consideration of five cities: Thebes, Copenhagen, Sodom, Eusapia and the New Jerusalem. The city, as we shall see, represents the pinnacle of ordered human sociality. It is not insignificant that Deuteronomy sets its vision of cannibalistic carnage amongst people 'shut up in towns'. Kierkegaard was himself a man of the city in a very particular way, and it is in a consideration of his thought in relation to the city, the *polis*, that its political dimension can best be explored.

Thebes

Let us begin, then, in Thebes with Antigone, such an important figure to Kierkegaard. As recounted in Sophocles' eponymous play,[3] her story is one of devotion to her dead brother Polyneices which leads her to defy the decree of the tyrant, Creon, in order to ensure his decent burial. Her defiance brings about her own death and the death of Creon's son and mother. Antigone's fatal loyalty lays bare the interpenetration of the living and the dead in the polity of the city of Thebes.

The city of Thebes, as with any city, sets bounds between living and the dead in the effort to ensure its own survival. It is a city of the living which owes its identity and sense of continuity in the face of death to the stories of its noble dead. The tales of its great founders live on after their death and so does the city they founded, undergirding its claim to set death at defiance. But death is also ambiguously present in the maintenance of the authority of its tyrant, Creon. He seeks to preserve the life of the city by holding the threat of death over the rebellious. The city can retain its integrity by removing those who rebel to the realms of the dead. But it must still attempt to maintain a differentiation here. The *polis* owes its existence to the honoured dead and can incorporate them in its memory, but the rebellious must be excluded from the city of the dead itself by the refusal of burial. So Creon orders that the body of the traitor Polyneices should remain unburied.

The dead, however, reveal the limits of the power of the *polis*. The dead are both totally at the mercy of the tyrant in that their bodies are open to every degradation, and yet ultimately beyond his grasp. The distinction between rebel and hero which death was supposed to mark suddenly becomes impossible to maintain when both are reduced to corpses.

What the play reveals is that the dead hold the reins in the foundation and maintenance of the city and that the living become caught up in this sphere at their peril. Here we can find a parallel in the argument of Zygmunt Bauman in his *Mortality, Immortality and Other Life Strategies*.[4] According to Bauman, culture is the testimony to the human achievement of constructing meaning in the face of death. Bauman's case is that 'the perception of death makes life meaningfulness possible—nay unavoidable, precisely because it makes life first empty of meaning and thus leaves it to humans to conjure up any meaning that could fill the void.'[5] The meaning which they conjure up is enshrined in culture. Culture is thus rooted in the fact of death and the avoidance of that fact. It exists to conceal the absurdity of human existence in the face of death.

This is the insight which Hegel[6] develops when he discusses the role of the family as a mediator between the dead individual and the state. The duty of the family is to hold the dead man in memory so that he does not fall into the universal of nature but retains a place in the universality of the state. This thought can be traced down through Heidegger to Derrida, who in his *Aporias* argues that politics is always founded on a space of mourning.[7] The political is about managing the memory and influence of the dead. So, too, the city, as the site of culture and its most elaborate artefact.

Such a relationship between the city and death imbues the biblical treatment of this theme. It is Cain, the first murderer, who founds the first city (Gen. 4:17), the first delimited bulwark of culture against nature and the first community which will outlive the death of its founders. It is not an accident, then, that Deuteronomy sets its grim vision of cannibalistic carnage amongst the people 'shut up in towns'. This biblical link between the city and murder, indeed fratricide, is developed by Augustine in his *City of God*.[8] In drawing the contrast between the earthly city and the heavenly city, he traces the earthly city to Cain. It was founded in fratricide and it is both bounded by and dependent upon death. It is engaged in constant strife, internally and externally in the hope of ensuring its survival. In a sense, its *raison d'être* is its struggle to survive. Without threat, it would not exist. All its victories, however, are ultimately meaningless because 'they bring death with them or are doomed to death'.[9] Augustine draws the parallel with the founding myth of Rome, which grows out of the fratricidal struggle between Romulus and Remus, making the point that such associations between murder and the city are widespread in legend and story.

Throughout the biblical texts, the epitome of cities in this respect are Sodom and Gomorrah. These cities are repeatedly held up as an archetype of the wickedness and weakness of human societies. It is important to realise that these archetypal cities do manifest human solidarity. In Genesis 19, all the men act in concert with a common purpose when they turn up outside Lot's door to ravish his guests, but this is a solidarity of rapine and violence. Culture has allowed the flourishing of a society which is no longer constrained by nature and the wider laws of hospitality that treat all men as neighbours.

The city, then, as the embodiment of culture is an aspiration, a defiance of death, but is founded on death. This account of the city explains the source of Antigone's threatening power in the eyes of the tyrant Creon. She, a living woman, has given herself to the dead, to the world where a uniformity of rights is axiomatic. As Steiner puts it,

> Antigone's exaltation of the ethical and visceral demands of death carries all before it. It is not only that Hades requires equal rites/ rights for all, whatever the discriminations grossly made by mundane politics... It is that 'loving care, the loving humaneness of mortal solidarity' or *philia*, while bridging the ultimately trivial gap between life and death, has its foundations in the realm of eternity. It is *philia* which ensures the salutary pressure of transcendence on the living.[10]

The relevance of this discussion to our investigation of Kierkegaard's social thinking becomes clear when in repudiation of this pressure of transcendence, Creon explicitly uses the Kierkegaardian phrase we are exploring. He tells Antigone that she should 'go down below and love—if love you must—love the dead' (ll. 591-93). His command shows that this sort of love is something that the living *polis* cannot sustain. Love of the dead is the prerogative of the dead. For Creon, *philia*, human solidarity, stops short at death, at least in part because it is a solidarity of the living *against* the dead. The boundaries are not to be blurred.

How telling, then, that it is the same Creon, stunned by being told that his son has followed Antigone into death through love and that his wife has killed herself in grief at the news, who cries out 'I died once, now you kill me again and again' (l. 1416). Creon himself articulates the fact that he, the living tyrant, embodies death. The bounds between the living and the dead are not ones that he can draw or bounds that run where he would wish them to be. He himself is within the realm of the dead, but dying repeatedly.

Eusapia

The effacing of these boundaries is elegantly displayed in Italo Calvino's poetic masterpiece, *Invisible Cities*.[11] The city of Eusapia is one of several cities of the dead described in this fictional travelogue. It is a city whose inhabitants have built below ground a replica of their city, peopled by the dried corpses of the dead. The copy is not exact, however; many people opt for a change of career when they are dead. So, Calvino says, the numbers of big game hunters and mezzo-sopranos are more than the living city ever contained. The conveying and arranging of the corpses is the job of a hooded brotherhood who, it is said, perform the same function once they themselves are dead. At this point a qualm may come over the reader, to be borne out by the end of the story. It is said that these brothers find that, slowly, the dead make innovations in their city which, when they hear of them, the inhabitants above ground eagerly copy. Indeed, rumour has it that this is no new phenomenon. It is said that it was the dead who built the upper Eusapia in imitation of their own city. And further, 'They say that in the twin cities there is no longer any way of knowing who is alive and who is dead.'[12]

Copenhagen

A city where we cannot distinguish between the living and the dead is a picture that Kierkegaard uses for his own city of Copenhagen. We may remember the term that is used for the secret society to which the papers in the first part of *Either/Or* are addressed, the 'Symparanekromenoi':

those in fellowship in death whom, in a journal entry, Kierkegaard calls his ideal audience. But what would it be to live in such a society?

The voices of just such a city are represented in the work of a writer who followed Kierkegaard in his use of multiple voices: the Portuguese poet, Fernando Pessoa. The diary of his 'semi-heteronym', Bernardo Soares, published under the title *The Book of Disquiet*, contains this highly pertinent passage:

> We are death. This thing we think of as life is only the sleep of real life, the death of what we truly are. The dead are born, they do not die. These worlds have become reversed for us. When we think we are alive, we are dead; we live even while we lie dying...

> Living in itself is dying because every new day we enjoy is another day of our lives lost...

> Never to find God, never to know even if God exists! To pass from world to world to world, from incarnation to incarnation, nursed always by the same illusion, cosseted always by the same errors!

> Never to find truth or peace! Never to know union with God! Never to be completely at peace, but instead always to be troubled by the suggestion of what peace is and by our desire for it![13]

Here Soares is giving voice to the view of those who live in despair, who see themselves as perpetually dying yet unable to die, perpetually unable to find union with God. Here, truly, the dead are speaking. For Kierkegaard, too, despair is to be perpetually dying, to die and yet not to die, to die death. 'Life is death we're lengthy at', wrote Emily Dickinson, in her own gnomic summary of this insight.[14]

Lazarus

Such neat oxymorons are all very well, but can they be given any substance? This is precisely the problem that Kierkegaard confronts in his reading of the story of Lazarus which forms the starting point of his *The Sickness unto Death*. Taking wing, as so often, from a seeming contradiction in the biblical text, Kierkegaard argues that Christ's words about Lazarus, that his sickness is not 'unto death', must sit strangely with Lazarus's subsequent demise unless we can distinguish the sickness unto death from actual death. The mere physical death of Lazarus, tragedy though that is, is not to be confused with the seemingly worse possibility of the sickness unto death. 'Christianly understood, then, not even death is "the sickness unto death"' (SUD, 7).

The sickness unto death is to be perpetually dying and yet not able to die, and is also named despair. Kierkegaard goes so far as to say that death is indeed the expression for the state of the deepest Christian wretchedness. (SUD, 6) As despair, so Kierkegaard claims, is universal, so all of us must be dwellers in cities of the perpetually dying.[15]

If this is so, we may revisit the question with which we began this investigation and in a sense turn it on its head. If death is equated with despair and the human condition is to be in despair, then we are all dead. The question then becomes not why we should love the dead rather than the living. Rather, it is this: who else is there to love *but* the dead, our *symparanekromenoi*? Kierkegaard's point is not to advocate a flight from the hurly-burly of the city to the silent and sterile solitude of a country churchyard, but to direct our gaze below the frantic attempt of the city to manage and ward off death and instead to the reality of the dead souls around us.

The problem that now faces us is *how* we are to love the dead and what the nature of that relationship may be. Antigone stands here, too, as witness to the dangers of transgressing these bounds. Creon's fatal error is to overreach himself in daring to interfere in the economy of the dead and in his attempt to import to it distinctions which belong only to the society of the living. Antigone, for her part, brings about her own doom and the death of her lover by removing herself from human society through her conscious option for the dead. Her flaw is seen when she turns this love of the dead against the living, most notably in her furious repudiation of her sister. As Ismene pleads to share her fate, Antigone lays claim to her own death:

> Never share my dying,
> Don't lay claim to what you never touched.
> My death will be enough. (ll. 615-7)

Ismene has chosen life, Antigone death, and so Ismene has forfeited her sister's love. Antigone allows her love for the dead to eliminate her care for the living. The solitude of death becomes for her the spur to a denial of human love and solidarity in death. Steiner's claim that '*philia* transcends the ultimately trivial gap of life and death' founders here. Whatever that gap is, it is not trivial, and Antigone finds herself on one side of it, isolated from her living companions.

Death is profoundly solitary. We can only die our own death, and in its grip we pass beyond the claims and possibilities of the human. Death does, as Bauman argues, put a question mark to the whole concept of human sociality. If this ultimate act is solitary, if it removes us from the responsiveness and responsibility which characterize human social being, then perhaps it does reveal that social interaction as a charade. Yet death is also profoundly social. In a characteristically controversial reversal of the intuitive, Bataille argues in his *Eroticism* that it is sex which divides us as it sets us in the position of being insurmountably alien to one another. Death, however, the great leveller, is the one universal human experience. Such solidarity as we have is in the common life of the grave.[16]

Insofar as human society is a mask, a way of covering and excluding death, but itself founded on the inevitabilities of death, neither the biblical tradition nor Kierkegaard can condone it. Society's view of love as reciprocity is exposed as a false levelling out of human aspiration and existence in an unholy compact with death. Antigone reveals this but provides no answer because she refuses the sociality of death. Antigone's love of the dead is simply a negation of the *polis* which offers no possibility of its transformation.

What alternative, then, can Kierkegaard offer? For Kierkegaard, the love for the dead is of no value except insofar as it informs our love for the living. He provides his own counter to the spell of the dead in his insistence that we are 'to love the man we see' (WL, 154). In loving the individual, actual, man, we must not slip in an imagined concept of how we believe or might wish that this man should be. Kierkegaard draws here the distinction between the love for the dead and the love for the yet unborn. The parent may love the unseen child but knows that it represents potential, the potential for reciprocal love, whereas the dead man bears no possibility. He is changeless and complete.

This is crucial, it seems to me, to understanding this strange passage. Kierkegaard demands that the dead be loved *as* the dead, and remembered as such. The dead are not to be loved as if they were alive, nor are they to be confounded with, or to usurp, the living. To remember the dead, Kierkegaard warns, is not at all the same as being unable to forget them. That is to remain in thrall to the dead as they once were. No, they must be loved *as they now are*. This discipline may then enable us to love those who share with us the life of the human *polis* as they now are. Love for the physically dead teaches us how to love those who are spiritually dead. It also teaches us a signal lesson in the love of the self. If salvation depends on dying to the self, then love of the self must be love of the dead. Only if we are able to love ourselves as dead can we claim a Christian self-love.

But to see and know the dead *as they are* is precisely what human culture evades. What is necessary, Kierkegaard asserts, is not to evade death, but truly to undergo it. For Kierkegaard, the human problem is not how to gain eternal life. Eternity is at the heart of who we are, and is the source of our anguish. The problem that we have is our inability to die. That problem is overcome in Christ. His victory for us is that he underwent death, took death upon himself in its entirety, thus enabling the believer truly to die with him rather than to be condemned to an eternity of dying.

As usual, Kierkegaard's argument proceeds by paradox. It is precisely because death is the antithesis of the social, the seeming end of love, the ultimate solitude, the quintessentially human, that it can be confounded by the miracle that God died for us, and with us. Kierkegaard must ruthlessly expose any attempt to allay the pangs of death in order to establish the full enormity and wonder of the claim that it is precisely there that God meets us. In that supreme moment of solitude, where even Jesus cried out in abandonment on the cross, we are caught up together into the loving society of the life of God. To take on this truth in actuality beggars all the sophisticated tools of language and culture, of communication and social interaction. If it seems an absurd, incoherent and frankly inhuman account, then Kierkegaard can only say that it would do, given that it is the very categories of rationality, coherence and humanity that have to be put to death.

This emphasis on the scandal of the death of Christ may be the reason that in the famous summary of the god's life among us in *Philosophical Fragments*—'We have believed that in such and such a year the god appeared in the humble form of a servant, lived and taught among us and then died' (PF, 104)—the resurrection does not appear. In itself, the idea of resurrection is by no means a unique Christian insight. After all, it is the business of gods to live eternally, to leap triumphant from the grasp of death. Jesus' resurrection only acquires its special status in the context of the death not of a god, but of God.

This central moment in Kierkegaard's thought is both closely related to and profoundly different from Hegel's trope of the death of God. For Hegel, God reveals that he has taken on and sublimated the ultimate constitutive fact of humanity. God manifests that death is as much a part of his being as of ours and so negates the gap between human and divine. For Kierkegaard, on the contrary, death is not constitutive of human being; it is not even a human possibility. Only God can die. His death is the ultimate sign of the 'infinite qualitative difference' between the divine and the human. Christ's work of salvation is the conferring of that possibility of death, and therefore of resurrection, on humanity.

This insistence on the saving power of Christ's death seems to be a perfectly responsible reading of Paul. Consider Rom. 6:3-5:

> Do you not know that all of us who were baptised into union with Christ Jesus were baptised into his death? Well then, by virtue of undergoing baptism into death we were buried with him, in order that, as Christ was raised from the dead by the Father's glorious power, we, too, might live and move in a new kind of existence. And indeed if through a death after the likeness of his death we have become one with him, a resurrection after the likeness of his resurrection will likewise be ours.[17]

We, 'the very men who were lying dead by reason of their offences' (Eph. 2:5), are offered life through undergoing true death with Christ. Kierkegaard's insistence on this paradox seems to me simply to be taking such passages seriously. But such an insistence must mean that the city, that compromise with death, is to be utterly swept away and renewed in the resurrection. The new Jerusalem, the city founded not on human mutuality but God's love, is to take its place. In the meantime, however, the Christian is enjoined to love his neighbour, to love him as he is, even if he is, as he must be, one of the dead who inhabit this city of the dead.

But we still must ask the question which struck us first in this discussion. Does this analysis leave any room for the human joy of reciprocity in love? Kierkegaard seems at times to argue that the desire for mutuality, the need to be loved, is revealed as a product of, not a cure for, alienation and despair. Hence the superiority of the love for the dead which cannot depend on mutuality. Put so starkly his view may seem to many simply repellent, to others possibly rather magnificent but frighteningly impersonal. Divine love seems to overwhelm merely human ties.

It is undeniable that this seems to be the bias of *Works of Love*. There is, however, one passage in the book where Kierkegaard does develop the idea of the need to be loved (see WL, 155–57). Once again, his discussion is rooted in his puzzling over an enigmatic biblical passage. At the end of John's Gospel (John 21:15 ff.), Jesus asks Peter three times if he loves him. It is a plea not only for love, but to be the particular love: Jesus asks not just whether Peter loves him but, 'Do you love me more than these?' Three times Peter responds, 'Yes, Lord you know that I love you.'

In Kierkegaard's discussion, he supposes that Peter can only have taken this repetition as a covert reproach to his love. If the one who, as

Peter says, knows everything asks three times, what does he know about the quality of Peter's love? Are Peter's protestations in fact covering something which the one who can read all hearts sees all too well? Should Peter then doubt the adequacy of his own love?

This is not in the end the interpretation that Kierkegaard invites us to place on the story. He argues that it bespeaks Jesus' need for assurance. One of the glories of human love is that it takes the beloved's assurance as the highest guarantee of love. Such a dependence on another's assurance rather than direct knowledge is a distinction of human love that omniscience cannot know. Jesus, then, is speaking out of a *kenosis* of his knowledge of Peter's heart. His relationship to Peter is revealed as one not based on an omniscient certainty of love, but the truly human and therefore divine vulnerability and joy of trust in the affirmations of the beloved.

This passage is rather undeveloped in *Works of Love* and the discussion quickly turns elsewhere. But there is at least a glimpse here of a vulnerability in Jesus which is in Kierkegaard's world a mark of the divine and an opening to the reciprocity of the divine community. It is as divine to rely on the assurance of being loved as to love.

We might even venture beyond Kierkegaard here and wonder if another, not necessarily contradictory, reading of Peter's experience of the repeated questioning might not point to a dawning realization in Peter that indeed Christ, who does know everything, also knows, better than poor fickle Peter himself, the depth of Peter's love and that Peter can and must make that affirmation out of a depth he has not yet fathomed himself. It is out of this relationship, of course, between Peter and Jesus, and between Peter and the sheep to be fed, that the new society of the Church is being founded. Kierkegaard does not choose to pursue this line of thought, but it is in this new social context of the relationship between God and humanity that the social ethic of the *Works of Love* is embedded.

If there is a problem with Kierkegaard's account of community, it is not his alone. He seems to me in the end to be giving as clear an account of the implicit dynamics of the biblical paradoxes of community and death as one has a right to expect. It is in the universal experience of the singularity of death grounded in the death made available in Christ that human love and solidarity have their foundation. The new Jerusalem, the city where mourning is done with, the city peopled by the dead raised in Christ, is where true community and the true *polis* can be established.

Earlier I quoted Emily Dickinson's inimitable summary of the human condition as follows: 'Life is death we're lengthy at.'[18] We may now add her completion of the aphorism: 'death the hinge to life.' In the seemingly extraordinary injunction to love the dead, Kierkegaard leads us to think through the nature of death, love and the life eternal, of person and of *polis*, in the face of the collapse of the culture which not only fills out these symbols for us but gave them to us in the first place. He urges us to take the risk of dismantling culture in Bauman's sense, of being reduced to meaninglessness, of facing death. Only once confronted by the vanity of the human attempt to impose meaning on death can we hope to be transformed into what God means by us.

Notes

1. Leo Dahmer, *A Father's Story: One Man's Anguish at Confronting the Evil in his Son* (London: Little, Brown & Co, 1994).
2. George Steiner, *Antigones* (Oxford: Oxford University Press, 1984), p. 62.
3. Sophocles, *Antigone*, in *The Three Theban Plays* (trans. R. Fagles; Harmondsworth: Penguin, 1984), pp. 35–128. Subsequent references are to line numbers in this edition.
4. Zygmunt Bauman, *Mortality, Immortality and Other Life Strategies* (Cambridge: Polity Press, 1992).
5. Bauman, *Mortality*, p. 32, n. 23.
6. See G.F. Hegel, *The Phenomenology of Spirit* (trans A.V. Miller; Oxford: Clarendon Press, 1977), pp. 270–71.
7. See J. Derrida, *Aporias* (trans T.Dutoit; Stanford: Stanford University Press, 1993), p. 61: 'In an economic, elliptic, hence dogmatic way, I would say that there is no politics without an organization of the time and space of mourning, without a topolitology of the sepulcher, without an anamnesic and thematic relation to the spirit as ghost [*revenant*], without an open hospitality to the guest as *ghost* [in English in the original]...'
8. Augustine, *City of God* (trans. H. Bettenson; Harmondsworth: Penguin, 1972).
9. Augustine, *City of God*, 599.
10. Steiner, *Antigones*, p. 265.
11. I. Calvino, *Invisible Cities* (trans. W.Weaver; London: Pan Books [Picador], 1979). For Eusapia, see pp. 88–89.
12. Calvino, *Invisible Cities*, p. 89.
13. Fernando Pessoa, *The Book of Disquiet* (London: Serpents Tail, 1994), p. 182.
14. Emily Dickinson, *Selected Letters* (ed. T.H. Johnson; Cambridge, MA: Belknap Press, 1990), p. 183.
15. Remarkably similar insights are expressed by Jean-Luc Nancy in the following paragraph from his *The Inoperative Community* (ed. P.Connor; Minneapolis: Minnesota University Press, 1991), p. 13: 'Now the community of human immanence, man made equal to himself or to God, to nature and to his own

works, is one such community of death—or of the dead. The fully realized person of individualistic or communistic humanism is the dead person.'

16. George Bataille, *Eroticism* (trans. M. Dalwood; London: Marion Boyars, 1987), pp. 94ff.

17. The translation used is H.W. Cassirer, *God's New Covenant* (Grand Rapids: Eerdmans, 1989).

18. Dickinson, *Selected Letters*, p. 183.

Adam's *Angest*: The Language of Myth and the Myth of Language

Begrebet Angest was characterized by Walter Lowrie, its first English translator, as a 'tormenting' book[1] and it continues to intrigue, puzzle and frustrate readers from a wide variety of academic disciplines. Of these, the study of the Hebrew Bible might not seem the one most likely to shed light on its riddles, although any student of the Hebrew Bible can offer long experience of bafflement in the face of impenetrable texts whose background and authorship is a matter of speculation and which have been argued over vehemently.

Yet, whatever else he was, Kierkegaard was an engaged reader of the Bible, struggling throughout his life with the recalcitrant texts of the Scriptures. The more I read his works, the more it seems to me that much of what is most original in his writings arises from his wrestling with biblical texts and his attempts to see the sense in what seem to be contradictory or simply incoherent passages of the Scriptures. The sacrifice of Isaac, the odd ending of Job, the problem that Jesus says of Lazarus that his sickness is 'not unto death', the logical absurdity of issuing a commandment to love one's neighbour: each of these exegetical cruces is the seed and backbone, to mix my metaphors, of a major work. This is in addition to his copious production of avowedly exegetical *Upbuilding Discourses* and the explicit discussions of biblical exegesis which form major portions of several works.

Biblical exegesis is also part of the argument of *Begrebet Angest* and I want to suggest that it is more important than has often been acknowledged. It is here that the student of the Hebrew Bible may have some insights to offer. This is not simply a question of the content of the biblical passages cited and the exegesis which is offered. The readings of the Bible in *Begrebet Angest* may give indications as to how this text itself is to be read. One way in which a text may give clues to the reading strategies that may be appropriate to interpreting it is by offering what might be called 'internal models of text reception.' The text displays strategies of reading in its reading of antecedent texts. In so complex a text as *Begrebet Angest*, we need all the help we can get with reading.

So my contention in this essay will be that some of the tangles of *Begrebet Angest* can be loosened, if not unknotted, by considering the biblical sources of the work. In particular, I want to suggest that there is a scriptural source for some of the work's most particular insights: the Letter of James. In the brief compass of this essay, I shall concentrate on one aspect of this: the interpretation in *Begrebet Angest* of the fall of Adam and Eve in terms of the relationship between *angest* and language. This seems to me to reflect Kierkegaard's reading of Genesis 2 and 3 through the lens of James, and itself mirrors and shapes the relationship between reader and text.[2]

It is not surprising, one might think, that the events and characters in the narrative of the Garden of Eden are the main biblical resource in *Begrebet Angest* as a discourse on hereditary sin. However, as an interpretation of the Hebrew Bible this connection is not so obvious. The Jewish tradition, in particular, has not seen it necessary to interpret the story in Genesis 2–3 in these terms. Subsequent human beings may have to live with the consequences of Adam and Eve's actions and are all too likely to repeat them, but they sin on their own behalf, so to speak. Indeed, it is noteworthy that Adam, Eve and Eden are scarcely mentioned in the rest of the Hebrew Bible. Nor do they appear in the Gospels except in genealogies. It is Paul who introduces the typological link between Adam and Christ as the 'last Adam', and who makes it clear that every human being is tainted by Adam's sin and subjected to death.[3] It is not until Augustine that we see the full development of the teaching that human beings not only inherit a propensity to sin, but also a measure of Adam's guilt for that first sin. I mention this simply to make the point that the exegesis of Genesis 2–3 in itself does not inevitably lead to a notion of inherited sin and therefore to alert us to the fact that Kierkegaard's appeal to these texts is set in a theological context.

Begrebet Angest itself contains a stern warning on the misuse of the Bible in this connection where the analogy is drawn with the technique of the Persian king Cambyses who set the sacred animals of the Egyptians before his army as a defence against Egyptian attack (CA, 40). In the same way, Haufniensis argues, too often the classical biblical passages are set out and an argument constructed in a way which defends the interpreter from having to address the existential question of sin.[4] The exercise becomes a matter of clever juggling with the text. We find an extended version of this analogy in a letter to P.W. Lund, written in 1835, where Kierkegaard writes,

> ...the rationalists behave like Cambyses, who in his campaign against Egypt dispatched the sacred chickens and cats in front of his army, but they are prepared, like the Roman Consul, to throw the sacred chickens overboard when they refuse to eat. The fallacy is that when they are in agreement with Scripture, they use it as a basis, but otherwise not. (LD, 46)

Kierkegaard here gives us a standard by which to measure the responsible use of the Bible thereby opening himself to the question as to whether it is only the rationalists who fall foul of this pertinent criticism.

In the light of this, then, how does Haufniensis deal with Genesis 2–3? There is no sustained verse-by-verse exegesis of the passage in *Begrebet Angest*; instead, Haufniensis turns to it when he wishes to defend some particular theological or psychological interpretation. A key text for him here is the divine prohibition: 'You may freely eat of every tree of the garden; but of the fruit of the tree of the knowledge of good and evil, you shall *not* eat' (Gen. 2:16-17). What is striking about the complex discussion of the reception of the prohibition which ensues in *Begrebet Angest* is the central role this reading gives to one of Kierkegaard's enduring preoccupations, the problem of communication. When God prohibits Adam from eating the fruit of the tree of the knowledge of good and evil, Haufniensis asks how Adam will comprehend this. The answer is that he cannot, but that the very statement of the prohibition awakens 'the anxious possibility of being able' (CA, 44). The same applies *a fortiori* to the word of judgment that completes the verse: '...for in the day that you eat of it you shall die' (Gen. 2:17). Again, how can Adam understand what it is to die? But this word, and the tone in which it is spoken introduces a new possibility to Adam, one he cannot grasp, which awakens in him not a fear of death but 'the ambiguity of anxiety' (CA, 45).

Adam's predicament is a version of the problem which underlies *Philosophical Fragments*: how can one learn a new truth? Either one understands it already, in which case one is not learning it, or else one cannot understand it. But here it is not simply the definition of a noun which is puzzling. Adam is exposed to a new form of grammar. It has long been remarked that the prohibition against eating the fruit is the first use of the negative in speech in Genesis, and therefore, in terms of the biblical narrative, the first use ever. Before this incident, speech has gone uncontradicted. When God says, 'Let there be light', there is light;

when Adam names the beasts, what he calls them *is* their name. Word and world correspond. The prohibition and the warning of punishment alter this. God's speech here is the first to introduce language as the instrument of the counterfactual. Through the serpent's duplicitous language, then, innocence awakes to possibility, the notion that things could be other than they are.

So far Haufniensis has offered a reading of the biblical text but now he admits that he is about to depart from it. In the first place, he is unhappy with the idea that the prohibition stems from a voice from without and is addressed to Adam by another. On this matter he is quite prepared to criticize and in effect to rewrite Genesis: 'The imperfection in the [Genesis] narrative—how could it have occurred to anyone to say to Adam what he essentially could not understand—is eliminated if we bear in mind that the speaker is language, and also that it is Adam himself who speaks' (CA, 47). Though this solution to the problem is obscure even by Haufniensis's standards, it is clear at least that language and the problem of communication are brought to the forefront. But is Haufniensis not now open to the very charge that he brought against the proponents of rationalism above, of 'flinging the sacred chickens overboard', disregarding biblical evidence because it does not suit a particular view he has of the genesis of *angest*?

Worse is to come in this regard in his treatment of the serpent. 'I freely admit my inability to connect any definite thought with the serpent', he writes, notoriously (CA, 48). Haufniensis's problem with the serpent is that it has tempted writers to be clever, but more particularly that it represents an external temptation and one which he, though not Genesis, relates to the divine voice. Here again externality is unacceptable to Haufniensis. But by side-stepping the serpent, is he not riding roughshod over the biblical text once more? How can this be defended exegetically?

Haufniensis's first line of defence is the ancient one of turning to another biblical verse to clarify a difficulty. In this case he invokes the epistle of James to make the counter-claim that 'God tempts no one'. The passage from which this crucial quotation comes, Jas 1:13-15, is worth citing in full:

> Let no one say when he is tempted, 'I am tempted by God'; for God cannot be tempted with evil and he himself tempts no one; but each person is tempted when he is lured and enticed by his own desire. Then desire when it has conceived gives birth to sin; and sin when it is full-grown brings forth death.[5]

Given the lack of respect for James in Lutheran exegesis—Luther famously dismissed it as 'a right strawy epistle' because it did not, to his eyes, preach the saving grace of Christ—it is noteworthy that here a passage from that epistle is being used to correct a passage from Genesis.[6] This reflects the abiding interest in James in Kierkegaard's authorship. My argument here is that this one direct citation is the tip of the iceberg in regard to the influence of James on *Begrebet Angest*, and that James provides a hermeneutical key to the reading of Genesis 2–3 for Haufniensis—and Kierkegaard.

The importance of James for Kierkegaard can hardly be over-estimated. In his journal he recalls preaching on what he calls 'my first, my favourite, text: James 1' (JP, 6769), and later writes, 'If a person were permitted to distinguish among Biblical texts, I could call this text [Jas 1:17-21] my first love, to which one generally ("always") returns at some time: and I could call this text my only love—to which one returns again and again and again and "always"' (JP, 6965). This is a suppressed portion of the dedication of the final discourse on 'The Unchangeableness of God'. Some of the imagery and the emotional intensity of the passage may be partly explained by a journal entry where Kierkegaard records the importance of this text in his relations with Regina Olsen: 'The first religious impression she had of me is connected with this text, and it is one I have strongly emphasized' (JP, 6800). The connection with Regina both reflects and enhances its importance for Kierkegaard.

His published works bear out the extent and duration of this interest. Three of the *Eighteen Upbuilding Discourses*, all originally published in 1843, are based on Jas 1:17-22: the second of the *Two Upbuilding Discourses* and the third and fourth of the *Four Upbuilding Discourses*. This is a notable concentration among his earlier works, but there is also a fourth discourse on the same text based on the sermon alluded to in the journal entry above, preached on 18 May, 1851 (MT, 263–82). As the last discourse he published (it appeared in August 1855), this has a particular poignancy.

These discourses, however, are only part of Kierkegaard's writing on James. Two other significant works arise from his intense engagement with it. The first part of *For Self-Examination*, 'What is Required in Order to Look at Oneself with True Blessing in the Mirror of the Word?', is a discourse to which we return in the conclusion to this essay. The other work which is an extended meditation on a passage from James is Part One of *Upbuilding Discourses in Various Spirits*, published separately in Douglas Steere's English translation under the title *Purity of Heart*

Is to Will One Thing,[7] a title which itself is a paraphrase of Jas 4:8. That verse also contains the concept which becomes the kernel of the entire discourse when James refers to sinners as 'you double-minded ones' [δίψυχοι], picking up the term from Jas 1:8. Teasing out the implications of 'double-mindedness' gives the discourse its structure.

The way in which James is used in this discourse raises an important point. Although Kierkegaard quite openly points to a particular verse as his point of departure, the explicit references to James such as an index would cite are actually relatively few in the main body of the discourse. Nevertheless, the reader who has James in mind finds a constant engagement with concepts and vocabulary drawn from the letter. The same is true, I contend, for portions, at least, of *Begrebet Angest.*[8]

We have already seen, for instance, Haufniensis's direct and unambiguous use of James to counter the suggestion that an external tempter is responsible for Adam's lapse. James, however, can also be shown to underlie Haufniensis's second line of defence over his questioning of the role of the serpent, which is his resort to the category of *myth*. Here things become more rather than less unclear as Haufniensis is notably ambivalent over the use of this term in relation to Genesis 2 and 3. To begin with, he enjoins us in our approach to this narrative to 'attempt to dismiss the fixed idea that it is a myth' (CA, 46). Two paragraphs later, in apparent contrast, he is happy to say of the seduction of Eve by the serpent that 'Even though one may call this a myth, it neither disturbs thought nor confuses the concept, as does myth of the understanding. The myth allows something that is inward to take place outwardly.'[9]

What is going on here? A little earlier in the text, Haufniensis sets out a more general proposition:

> The Genesis story of the first sin, especially in our day, has been regarded somewhat carelessly as a myth. There is good reason why it has, because what has been substituted in its place was precisely a myth, and a poor one at that. When the understanding takes to the mythical, the outcome is seldom more than small talk. (CA, 32)

The substituted 'myth', it turns out, is a way of dealing with the offence the biblical narrative has caused. The 'myth of the understanding', or the re-telling of the story to fit more understandable categories, explains the circle of the leap as a straight line, smoothing out difficulties. This kind of myth is a hermeneutic device to deflect offence. But is Haufniensis not guilty of the same kind of 'smoothing out' of the problem of the serpent? Why is he willing to accept the designation of *this* element of the biblical story as myth?

An intriguing and suppressed sentence from an earlier draft of *Begrebet Angest* adds to our understanding of the part the serpent plays in this text: 'If anyone wishing to instruct me should say, "Consistent with the preceding you, of course, could say, 'It [the serpent] is language,'" I would reply, "I did not say that"' (CA, 185). Such an identification of the serpent with language is understandable as a logical development of the earlier claim we quoted above that in the temptation scene 'the speaker is language'.[10] The difficulty in interpreting this suppressed fragment is discerning what Kierkegaard's own attitude to such an identification may be. Is he dismissing the idea that the serpent is language, or more teasingly, refusing to be tied down to this statement, which is not at all the same as denying it? Indeed, if the suggested statement is true, if language itself is the deceitful serpent, what would any such disclaimer be worth?

If nothing else, however, this suppressed sentence shows that such an identification has occurred to Kierkegaard himself. I want to suggest here that Kierkegaard's reading of James may have been one source for this interpretation. The deceptiveness of language is a *Leitmotif* for the epistle.[11] As just one instance of this, the text from James that Haufniensis quotes in *Begrebet Angest* in its original context itself involves forbidden speech: 'Let no one *say* when he is tempted, "I am tempted by God."'

James's fiercest warning of the dangers of speech comes in the denunciation of the tongue in 3:6: 'The tongue is a disorderly evil, replete with deadly poison,' he writes; it is 'a fire, an unrighteous world among our members,' something which 'sets on fire the cycle of nature and is set on fire by hell', metaphors which certainly evoke the demonic. Whenever James speaks of the tongue, however, the Greek word he uses (γλῶσσα) can equally well be translated 'language'. The phrase 'the tongue is a disorderly evil, replete with deadly poison' (Jas 3:8) could equally well be rendered as '*language* is a disorderly evil, replete with deadly poison.'

Moreover, it has been suggested that the words 'deadly poison' may be a distant allusion to the poisonous tongue of the serpent in Eden.[12] Now, I do not claim that James originally intended to connect language and the serpent, nor indeed that this is ultimately a tenable translation in the context. The point is that the allusion is one that has a resonance with the association of language and the serpent in *Begrebet Angest*. Any reader of James in the Greek is bound to spend time working over this verse as the whole passage is a notorious crux. For an imaginative exegete such as Kierkegaard, James offers one source for the connection between the serpent and language which he coyly raises, half-dismisses and then suppresses in the text of *Begrebet Angest*.

This hypothesis of the influence of James may seem a large claim to base on one brief allusion. However, a second juxtaposition of James and the serpent seems more than a coincidence. The one other place that a discussion of the serpent appears in Kierkegaard's authorship is in the first of the two 'Upbuilding Discourses' on Jas 1:17-24 published in *Four Upbuilding Discourses* of 1843 (the year preceding the publication of *Begrebet Angest*; EUD, 125–40). The first few pages of this discourse offer an imaginative recreation of what the world would have been like had Adam not sinned, which contrasts with Haufniensis's dismissal in *Begrebet Angest* of any such speculation as a waste of time (CA, 36).[13] How, then, does Kierkegaard handle the serpent in this reconstruction? The key term here is 'deception': '…the serpent deceived Eve (Gen 3:13) and thus by way of a deception the knowledge [of good and evil] came into the world as a deception' (EUD, 126). The consequence of deception is doubt, a doubt which separates the giver of all good gifts from the gift. For, Kierkegaard asks, how can we recognize the source of all good if we do not know what the good is, and how can we recognize what is good without knowing its source? The severance itself arose from deception.

In this discourse, it is doubt which is the inherited flaw that no man can overcome of himself, because doubt cannot cast out doubt; any human answer to the question of doubt is only a more brilliant and so more dangerous deception. What saves us is faith, faith in the unchangeableness of God, who, as James writes, 'brought us forth by the word of truth, that we should be a first fruit of his creation' (Jas 1:13). Kierkegaard stresses here the gift of the condition of truth, which puts doubt in its place. 'False doubt doubts everything except itself; with the help of faith, the doubt that saves doubts only itself' (EUD, 37).

On the face of it, there are several differences between these accounts of the temptation. Here no question over the externality of prohibition and temptation is raised, and the concept of *Angest* itself is not mentioned. Its place is taken by doubt. Nor is there a question over the place of the serpent. Yet there are important similarities also. The crucial aspect of their relationship comes through in Paul Ricoeur's remarks on the serpent's speech in his essay on 'Thinking Creation':

> …the temptation episode…stems from the questioning of the prohibition as a structuring component of the created order. Did God say? Posing this question ends the unquestioned confidence in this prohibition as one of life's conditions, that had made it seem self-evident as the plants

of the garden. The era of suspicion is opened, a fault line is introduced
into the most fundamental condition of language, namely, the relation
of trust, what linguists call the sincerity clause.[14]

This seems not far from the argument of the *Upbuilding Discourse*. The
serpent—Paul Beauchamp calls it 'le serpent herméneute'[15]—is the first
practitioner in the Hebrew Bible of the art of interpretation. The reader
has read what God said in the prohibition. By raising the question, 'Did
God say …?', the serpent asks Eve, and thereby the reader, to consider
what was *unsaid* and to ask what motivation lay behind God's speech.

The common point between the discussion of the prohibition in
Begrebet Angest and Ricoeur's version is that in both 'an era of suspicion'
is inaugurated. Where *Begrebet Angest* differs is that the 'era of suspicion'
is moved back even further. The prohibition itself reveals the gap
between language and reality. The relation of trust as the 'fundamental
condition of language' is shown to be a more problematic issue. The
need for trust, and the possibility of suspicion, is intrinsic to the nature
of language itself, not a consequence of its misuse.[16] James knows this
and it is summed up in that odd disclaimed equation, 'It [the serpent] is
language.'

This understanding of language also lies behind Haufniensis's
ambiguity over the use of the word 'myth'. In a journal entry, Kierkegaard
offers a definition of mythology which, intriguingly, uses grammatical
metaphors to explain its characteristics and its shortcomings:

> Mythology is the compacting (suppressed being) of eternity (the eternal
> idea)… Just as the poetic is the subjunctive but does not claim to be
> more (poetic actuality), *mythology, on the other hand, is a hypothetical
> statement in the indicative*…and lies in the very middle of the conflict
> between them, because the ideal, losing its gravity, is compacted in
> earthly form. (JP, 2799; my emphasis)

These rather odd metaphors drawn from the technical language of verbal
moods are illuminated by a remarkable passage in *Johannes Climacus*
on the effect of the discovery of grammar on the young Johannes as he
studies at school. This comes just after the well known description of the
imaginary walks through Copenhagen taken by Johannes and his father.
One phrase in this account stands out in this as we ponder the Genesis
story: 'For Johannes, it was *as if* the world came into existence during the
conversation, *as if* his father *were* our Lord…' (JC, 120).

The father, like God, speaks the world into existence. The difference
between God and Johannes's father is encapsulated in the all-important
qualification of the repeated 'as if' and its attendant subjunctive. The

significance of this becomes clearer when we read on to discover that
Johannes's sense of the creative scope of language was, we are assured,
only reinforced by his introduction to Latin and Greek grammar. The
authority and dignity of Latin grammar was a revelation, but even more
so was his study of Greek:

> The Greek teacher presented grammar in a more philosophical way.
> When it was explained to Johannes that the accusative case, for example,
> is an extension in time and space, that the preposition does not govern
> the case but the relation does, everything expanded before him. The
> prepositions vanished: the extension in time and space became like an
> enormous empty picture for intuition. (JC, 121)

The revelatory effect of the grammar of verbal moods is the subject of a
cluster of journal entries in 1837:

> A remarkable transition occurs when one begins to study the grammar
> of the indicative and the subjunctive, because here for the first time
> one becomes conscious that everything depends upon how something
> is thought, consequently how thinking in its absoluteness supersedes
> an apparent reality [*Realitet*]. (JP, 2309)

Kierkegaard defines the difference between the two moods as follows:
'The indicative thinks something as actuality [*Virkeligt*] (the identity of
thinking and actuality). The subjunctive thinks something as thinkable'
(JP, 2310).

Language becomes a space within which intuition can construct
meaning out of possibility. Just before this passage, a striking simile has
been used to describe the sensation caused by the abrupt shifting of an
argument by a well chosen remark. The effect on the beholder is like
the sudden gleam of a shark's belly as it turns upside down in the act of
snatching its prey. Something similar happens with the subjunctive: '...
he saw how one word could change a whole sentence, how a subjunctive
in the middle of an indicative sentence could throw a different light on
the whole' (JC, 122).

This gives some background, then, to Kierkegaard's definition of
mythology as a 'hypothetical statement in the indicative' and gives some
clue as to why he so often objects to the mythical. The mythical is not a
synonym for the fanciful or the poetic. On the contrary, it historicizes a
poetic idea, one that demands the subjective investment of the listener.
It reduces the subjunctive to a hypothetical indicative and so can all too
easily act as a way of evading that subjective engagement. It evades the
possibility of the terrifying yet beautiful gleam of the shark's belly. The

amazon.co.uk

Thank you for shopping at Amazon.co.uk!

Invoice for
Your order of 25 January, 2013
Order ID 202-3387132-8630757
Invoice number DnCmNrfOR
Invoice date 25 January, 2013

Billing Address
Dr James I Ewing
Goldenhill Resource Centre
199 Dumbarton Road
CLYDEBANK, Dunbartonshire G81 4XJ
United Kingdom

Dr James I Ewing
Goldenhill Resource Centre
199 Dumbarton Road
CLYDEBANK, Dunbartonshire G81 4XJ
United Kingdom

100 A2

Qty.	Item	Our Price (excl. VAT)	VAT Rate	Total Price
1	**The Joy of Kierkegaard: Essays on Kierkegaard as a Biblical Reader (BibleWorld)** Paperback. Hugh S. Pyper. 1845532724 (** P-1-B157B420 **)	£16.99	0%	£16.99

Shipping charges		£0.00
Subtotal (excl. VAT) 0%		£16.99
Total VAT		£0.00
Total		**£16.99**

Conversion rate - £1.00 : EUR 1.19

This shipment completes your order.

You can always check the status of your orders or change your account details from the "Your Account" link at the top of each page on our site.

Thinking of returning an item? PLEASE USE OUR ON-LINE RETURNS SUPPORT CENTRE.
Our Returns Support Centre (www.amazon.co.uk/returns-support) will guide you through our Returns Policy and provide you with a printable personalised return label. Please have your order number ready (you can find it next to your order summary, above). Our Returns Policy does not affect your statutory rights.

Amazon EU S.à r.l, 5 Rue Plaetis, L-2338, Luxembourg
VAT number : GB727255821

Please note - this is not a returns address - for returns - please see above for details of our online returns centre

0/DCCjN8MR/-1 of 1-//2ND_LETTER/econ-uk/8326100/0128-17:45/0125-14:23 Pack Type : A2

corollary of this is that by designating a seemingly 'indicative' statement as a myth, we give ourselves permission to regard it as a 'subjunctive' and to interpret its oddities as poetic possibility. Yet that can be another form of evasion. The mere manipulation of verbal moods does not ensure the reader's engagement. Language in any form is a symptom of the problem, not a solution.[17]

George Steiner, who discusses this aspect of language at length, sums up his thought on the matter in the following aphorism: *'Language is the main instrument of man's refusal to accept the world as it is.'*[18] He sees falsehood and counterfactuality as the characteristic element of human language:

> It is unlikely that man, as we know him, would have survived without the fictive, counter-factual, anti determinist means of language, without the semantic capacity, generated and stored in the 'superfluous' zones of the cortex, to conceive of, to articulate possibilities beyond the treadmill of organic decay and death. It is in this respect that human tongues, with their conspicuous consumption of subjunctive, future and optative forms are a decisive evolutionary advantage. Through them we proceed in a substantive illusion of freedom.[19]

Mark C. Taylor makes an explicit link between Kierkegaard's discussion of possibility and his understanding of language. Language allows the human to transcend the immediate by introducing possibility. An alternative state of affairs can be described. This applies within the realm of the subject as well. The child becomes able to articulate a distinction between 'what one is' and 'what one might be', between actuality and possibility.[20] By verbalizing possibilities of becoming, the child invents for himself a future. Taylor summarizes his view of Kierkegaard's understanding of language as follows:

> Language is the organ of possibility. To articulate something in verbal form is to establish a possibility which might be enacted. Because he sees the self in terms of the free realization of possibilities, the ability to use language is a necessary condition of human self hood. To be unable to use language is to have no future.[21]

What Taylor neglects is the inherent ambiguity of any statement of a possibility. Stating one possibility involves stating many. The nature of language and its slippage over reality means that it creates all sorts of possibilities. The importance of language, then, is the facility it affords of saying what is not the case, or what is not yet the case, which affords the only way in which change may occur. This is what gives the human capacity to manipulate the future, to propose, choose between, and then attempt to realize, different possibilities.

Kierkegaard explicitly discusses the duplicity of language in a journal entry which is a draft for *Johannes Climacus*. He sees a conflict between the immediacy of sense perception and the ideality of language. Language introduces the possibility of error and therefore of doubt:

> As long as I am defined as merely a sensory being, everything is true; as soon as I want to express sensation, contradiction is present. To take a very simple example, there is contradiction in my merely wanting to see a repetition in sense perception. For example, if I have seen an egg and then see something that resembles an egg and trace what I am seeing now to what I have seen, then what I have seen is defined ideally, because my having seen it in recollection is a qualification of ideality—it no longer exists. Indeed, even if I place the two objects side by side, the ideality is in the consciousness because ideality is the relation I establish between them. (JC, 251)

Language is inextricably implicated in the genesis of doubt, and therefore of anxiety. This is the implication of a gnomic passage from *Johannes Climacus*:

> Immediacy is reality, language is ideality, consciousness is contradiction [*Modsigelse*]. The moment I make a statement about reality, contradiction is present. For what I say is ideality.
>
> The possibility of doubt, then, lies in consciousness, whose nature is a contradiction that is produced by a duplexity [*Dupplicitet*] and this itself produces a duplexity. (JC, 108)

It is in acknowledgment of this duplicity that Haufiniensis argues that we should resist reading Adam as a myth but at the same time adopt a mythical reading of the serpent. The reason for this differentiation is best explained through the central metaphor for text and interpretation in James: the mirror. In *For Self-Examination*, Kierkegaard explores this metaphor at length in relation to the reading of Scripture. James 1:23-24 condemns the man who does not act on his belief as one who looks in the mirror of the word and then forgets what he was like.

In his discourse on this passage, Kierkegaard insists that we must behold *ourselves* in the mirror. The seemingly obvious criticism that this encouragement to see oneself in the text sounds like a license for subjective eisegesis is entirely beside the point. Mirrors are not blank canvases for us to draw on. They do not let us see anything we like: they show us as much of the truth about ourselves as we are able to bear. Reflections are also ontologically ambivalent. We can say of our reflection 'That's me' and 'That's not me' with equal validity. They are 'real' but not locatable—neither simply 'subjunctive' nor 'indicative'. They are not 'in' the mirror, but only appear when we are in the correct position to behold them.

Begrebet Angest is not itself the mirror; that is the prerogative of the biblical text of Genesis and James, underpinned by the unchangeableness of God, which is the assurance that Kierkegaard constantly returns to James to find. In this metaphorical context, I suggest that *Begrebet Angest* is best understood as a textbook on optics, no more and no less. It ironically teases—or, to use Lowrie's word, torments—those who imagine that to understand optics is the same as being able to see, let alone the same as seeing. It sets out to be 'psychologically orienting [*paapegende*]'. It orients us by helping us to know where to stand in order to see our reflection and explains to us some of the anomalies of the reflection. A manual of optics will explain, at least to some degree, why our reflection seems different from us—why the ring on our left finger is on the reflection's right, for instance, or why, to return to our subject, the world of the text contains a talking serpent.

An extension of the metaphor of the mirror may help to clarify how this impinges on Haufniensis's hermeneutic. Haufniensis can be seen as arguing for this metaphor of the text as mirror against two other possible metaphors: the text as *window* and the text as *picture*. To read Genesis 2–3 as a 'window' means to be concerned to find its historic core, what the text really represents beyond itself in the actual world. This may be interesting to the curious, but it tends to lead to rationalism, the need to trim the text to the world of actuality, and inevitably places Adam 'out there', outside the window, distanced by 4,000 years, as Haufniensis points out. This historical approach can be a defence against engagement with the text.

By the same token, to see the text as a picture can also deflect us from engagement with it. The concept of myth is one that allows us to read the seemingly objective, 'the indicative' as the poetic, 'the subjunctive'. Part of the problem with the idea of myth for Haufniensis is that simply to read the text as a poetic production may allow the reader to take an unhelpfully aesthetic view of the story and to debate the processes of its production or its meaning as abstraction, once again without personally engaging with it. To deny Adam's historicity by reading him as myth, as an aesthetic possibility, allows us to avoid confronting our own ineluctable sense of being embedded in sin.

The serpent is a rather different case. To attempt to see the serpent as history, rather than myth, examining it through the window of the text, will land us in an endless and distracting series of arguments over its actuality because of its internal paradoxes—a talking serpent endowed with comprehension and legs is trivially paradoxical. Here the concept of myth allows us to lift our attention from the snake and focus it on Adam. The serpent *is* the problem of language and its interpretation, the creative potential of counterfactuality which opens the way to deception and the dizziness of possibility.

To ask whether Adam is myth or history deflects us from seeing what in us is mirrored in Adam. Haufniensis's elaborate and not always clear arguments that Adam represents both the individual and the race are an attempt to achieve the seemingly impossible task of making what seems to be the unique features of Adam's existence actually the point at which he resembles every subsequent human being. It is by seeing ourselves in the text, by acknowledging the way in which Adam mirrors us, that we are confronted with what it is for each one of us to be a sinful son or daughter of Adam. In the prohibition and temptation, that first engagement with the counterfactuality of language, its promise of possibility, Adam, exposed to the first hermeneut, the serpent, mirrors every subsequent human being's anxious relationship to the word, and so raises the choice between uncommitted possibility and the reality of commitment, between suspicious doubt and faith.

Notes

1. *The Concept of Dread* (trans. W. Lowrie; Oxford: Oxford University Press, 1944), p. ix.
2. If space allowed, it would be interesting to explore how James' own account of a middle term between temptation and sin affects the concept of *angest* itself. Jas 1:14 reads, '...each person is tempted when he is lured and enticed by his own desire. Then desire when it has conceived gives birth to sin; and sin when it is full-grown brings forth death.' Desire here becomes the neutral middle ground, and temptation, as Haufniensis never tires of insisting, is described as an internal process. It is one's own desire which lures and entices one. Yet this is not sin; sin arises when desire conceives. The link to death is also pertinent, especially in exploring the crucial relationship between *Begrebet Angest* and *The Sickness unto Death*, as indeed is the link to sexuality.

   There is also a fruitful line of inquiry in turning to James to explore the association between *angest*, language, and the demonic as Haufniensis discusses it in section IV 2 of *Begrebet Angest*. James rounds on those who protest their faith without works (Jas 2:1): 'You believe that God is one: you do well. Even the demons believe—and shudder.' The demonic shudder of fear is suggestive of the anxiety over, or fear of, the good, which is Haufniensis's prime definition of the demonic. Either of these topics could engender another essay.

3. See particularly Rom. 5:12-14; 1 Cor. 15:22.

4. In Bruce Kirmmse's *Encounters with Kierkegaard: A Life as Seen by His Contemporaries* (Princeton: Princeton University Press, 1996), p. 20, a reminiscence by Kierkegaard's fellow student Vilhelm Birkedal is recorded, in which he cites Kierkegaard as using the analogy with Cambyses specifically against his teacher H.N. Clausen's work on dogmatics. The extent to which *Begrebet Angest* draws on and reacts against Clausen's teaching on the concept of original sin would repay further study, although in the note to this entry Kirmmse does question the reliability of Birkedal's ascription (*Encounters with Kierkegaard*, p. 275).

5. The importance of this text to Kierkegaard himself is attested by a journal entry (JP, 4001), significantly dated Christmas Eve, 1838, where he reflects on the consolation both that God tempts no one, and that God is not tempted by anyone.

6. For a further discussion of Kierkegaard's defence of James against Luther, see 'The Apostle, the Genius and the Monkey: Reflections on Kierkegaard's "Mirror of the Word"' in this volume.

7. *Purity of Heart Is to Will One Thing: Spiritual Preparation for Confession* (trans. with an introductory essay by Douglas V. Steere; New York: Harper and Row, 1948).

8. For a rather differently focused but interesting discussion of Kierkegaard's debt to James, see Timothy H. Polk, *The Biblical Kierkegaard: Reading by the Rule of Faith* (Macon, GA: Mercer University Press, 1997), p. 119.

9. For an interesting resume of earlier reading of this text by biblical scholars who use the concept of myth, see John Rogerson's *Myth in Old Testament Interpretation* (BZAW, 134; Berlin: De Gruyter, 1974). Rogerson summarizes the view of the pioneering higher critic Johannes Eichhorn in an article on Gen. 2 and 3 published in 1779. Eichhorn sees the elements of the story as historical events mythologically interpreted. Having eaten poisonous fruit which they saw a serpent had consumed unharmed, Adam and Eve became aware of their physical passions and left the garden in fright after a storm which they interpreted as the wrath of God. The mythical elements were the conversation with the serpent and God. Rogerson points out that, for Eichhorn, the conversation with the serpent echoed the woman's own thoughts while the conversations with God were misinterpretations of awe-inspiring natural events. Eichhorn later offered a more philosophical interpretation of the fall in terms of a myth of the Golden Age. A similar interpretation can be found in the works of Gabler, and in G.L. Bauer, and seems to have been at least acknowledged by Kierkegaard's teacher, H.N. Clausen.

10. This gives another twist to the connection intriguingly worked through by Roger Poole, who argues that the serpent dissipates into textual sibilance: 'The text is about the hiss' (*Kierkegaard, the Indirect Communication* [Charlottesville: University Press of Virginia, 1993], p. 107).

11. As early as Jas 1:5 we find that the encouragement to ask God for wisdom is tied to the warning that the asking must be accompanied by faith, and not be

double-minded. In 1: 9-10, there is an injunction to boast, but a seemingly perverse boast. The humble are to boast of their exaltation, the rich of their humiliation. False speech is warned against throughout the epistle. We should be 'quick to hear, slow to speech', James advises (1:19). No one is truly religious who does not 'bridle his tongue' (2:26). Failure to do so 'deceives his heart'. In ch. 2, those who are guilty of the partiality between rich and poor which James denounces demonstrate this by *saying* different things to visitors to their assembly depending on their clothing. Throughout the epistle, the index of a person's disposition is their speech. To say to a poor brother, 'Go in peace, be warmed and filled' without acting is profitless. The speech condemns the one who utters it and shows not their faith, but the deadness of their faith if it does not issue in works. Blessing and cursing come forth from the same source, and this is unsustainable, according to James. Speaking evil against a brother entails setting oneself up as a judge—who are you to do this? asks James. We are not to become teachers lightly precisely because we make mistakes in what we say. To make no mistakes in what we say means that we are perfect. It is not accidental that James is explicit in his condemnation above all of the oath: '...let your yes be yes and your no be no, that you may not come under condemnation' (5:12). The oath is the paradigm case of the way in which language itself escapes from the intention of the speaker, binding her to an unforeseeable future, and opening her to condemnation.

Not all speech is condemned in James, of course. James is aware of the ambivalence of language. The prophets spoke of the Lord and the power of Elijah's prayer for rain as a sign of the effectiveness of rightly directed speech. This validates James' admonitions that we should confess, and pray, and sing praise. However, the clear condemnation of the tongue brings it into the sphere of sinfulness. This linguistic emphasis in James has not, to my knowledge, been much remarked by scholars of the letter. It may be an instance where Kierkegaard's peculiar sensitivity to the theological significance of issues of communication has alerted him to an aspect of the text which biblical scholarship more generally might do well to explore further.

12. Ralph P. Martin in his *James* (Word Biblical Commentary, 48; Waco: Word Books, 1988) cites J.B. Mayor in his *The Epistle of St. James. The Greek Text with Introduction, Notes and Comments* (Grand Rapids: Zondervan, 1951 [1897]) as seeing 'a reference to the serpent in Eden' in the use of the word 'deadly poison' (p. 118), but goes on to remark that this may be too specific an interpretation. In fact, Mayor merely cites a use in an apocryphal text of a cognate word for 'poisonous' in connection with the serpent of Genesis. Notwithstanding this, Martin himself can stand witness that this allusion is not wholly unattested. The point could be strengthened by recalling that Jas 3:7 lists the whole range of wild beasts, birds, reptiles and sea creatures and declares that they are, or will be, tamed by man. This inevitably brings the creation story of Genesis, and especially Gen. 1:26, to the reader's mind and the allusion to reptiles has its own resonance. We may then be led to recall that the snake in Gen. 3 seems to be the one beast clearly not subordinate to human will.

13. Introducing the briefest of allusions along these lines in *The Concept of Anxiety*, he excuses himself by admitting that this is 'to speak foolishly and by way of accommodation' (CA, 93).

14. Paul Ricoeur, 'Thinking Creation', in André LaCocque and Paul Ricoeur, *Thinking Biblically: Exegetical and Hermeneutical Studies* (trans. David Pellauer; Chicago: University of Chicago Press, 1998), pp. 31–67, 42–43.

15. Cited by Ricoeur in 'Thinking Creation', p. 42 n. 19.

16. In his later writings, Kierkegaard comes close to condemning language as intrinsically an evil, rather than simply a temptation to abuse. In the journal entry headed, 'If only Man could not Talk!' (JP, 2337), he writes of the immediacy of a deer's drive in the mating season. 'If it could talk, we would perhaps hear some rubbish about its being motivated by a sense of duty, that out of duty to society and the race it wants to propagate the species, plus the fact that it is performing the greatest service etc...language, the gift of speech, engulfs the human race in such a cloud of drivel and twaddle that it becomes its ruination.'

    An even more direct condemnation comes in JP, 2334: 'There is much talk nowadays about flesh and blood being man's enemy, but I am more and more inclined to look upon language, the ability to speak, as a still more dangerous or as an at least equally dangerous enemy of every man.' Language as serpent: language as the enemy of man. There are places, however, in *Begrebet Angest*, where Kierkegaard sees language as salvific, especially in his discussion of the demonic. One characteristic of the demonic is that it is that which is made to speak against its will, and the act of speech becomes in itself a counter to the 'inclosing reserve' of the demonic (see, for instance, CA, 129).

17. Again, if space permitted, it would be possible to develop the argument that it is in this turn to communication rather than ontology that James has offered Kierkegaard a counter to the Pauline, or more pertinently, Augustinian account of original sin. It is the human being considered as a node of a web of language, not as a discrete entity, which is implicated in sin. The fact of being embedded in language is the point at which the individual and the race coalesce. Language only works because it is shared, but at the same time, it only has meaning because there are differences between individuals who communicate. Kierkegaard makes this point in his rather cryptic discussion of the origin of language in *Begrebet Angest*. Having raised the problem of Adam's comprehension, he adds this footnote:

    > If one were to say further that it then becomes a question of how the first man learnt to speak, I would answer that this was very true, but also that the question lies beyond the scope of the present investigation. However, this must not be understood in the manner of modern philosophy as though my reply were evasive, suggesting that I *could* answer the question in another place. But this much is certain, that it will not do to represent man himself as the inventor of language. (CA, 47 n.**)

    In an earlier draft he appended with approval this wry quotation: '...or, as Professor Madvig has expressed [with profound irony] so superbly in a prospectus, that men reached an agreement on what language they would speak' (CA, 186). Men, Adam and all his descendants, come into language as a given, just as they come into anxiety as a given.

18. George Steiner, *After Babel: Aspects of Language and Translation* (Oxford: Oxford University Press, 3rd edn, 1998), p. 228.

19. Steiner, *After Babel*, p. 238.

20. Mark C. Taylor, *Kierkegaard's Pseudonymous Authorship: A Study of Time and the Self* (Princeton: Princeton University Press, 1975), p. 77.

21. Taylor, *Kierkegaard's Pseudonymous Authorship*, p. 78.

BEYOND A JOKE: KIERKEGAARD'S *CONCLUDING UNSCIENTIFIC POSTSCRIPT* AS A COMIC BOOK

'I am not a religious person but simply and solely a humorist.' (CUP1, 501)

Concluding Unscientific Postscript is a joke. That, in a nutshell, is the thesis which I wish to put forward here. It presents itself as a joke and it is only by taking its character as such entirely seriously that we can deal in earnest with its message. It is no secret that irony, humour and the comic are featured throughout the book as matters of discussion and have important theoretical status as transitional modes between the stages of existence. The tone of the writing itself is by turns playful, satirical, ironic and mock serious. It is not these features which I propose to deal with directly here, however. Rather, I wish to call attention to the overall structure and presentation of the work. It is at this level, not in the components of its argument and rhetoric, that we shall see that the work is a joke, and, furthermore, that it could be nothing else if it was to be adequate to the task it sets out to perform.

Such a claim is not original. The point is well made by Andrew Burgess in his exhaustive investigation of the category of the comic in Kierkegaard's authorship.[1] He summarizes the findings of his computer-assisted analysis by pointing out the pervasiveness of the theme of the comic throughout most of the authorship, but finds it in particular at those points where the structure of the authorship is discussed. He sees the whole authorship as essentially comic, regarding that category as the most useful of those which Kierkegaard addresses precisely because it is concerned with communication. What is found funny depends on the culture, the values and even the maturity of the listener. This orientation to the listener is what makes the category of the comic so useful to Kierkegaard.

Burgess goes on to relate this specifically to the *Concluding Unscientific Postscript*:

> Even such a massive philosophical piece is written from the standpoint
> of the subject—specifically, the subject who is wondering about the
> problem of becoming Christian. It comes as no surprise, then, that
> an everyday conception of the comic fits the pattern of the *Postscript*
> without modification when it is used to describe what the *Postscript* is
> doing…at the right time, *Postscript* may be a colossal joke.[2]

It is this claim which it is the purpose of this essay to develop.

To plead such a case calls for doughty advocates. In the brief compass
of this discussion, two will furnish us with the bulk of our support. Firstly
we shall turn to Gérard Genette, who in his book *Seuils*[3] has undertaken
a witty and comprehensive analysis of what he terms the 'paratext'. This
he defines as 'that by which the text makes itself a book, and offers itself
as such to its readers, and more generally to the public'.[4] The term covers
title, dedication, editorial matter, prefaces, footnotes, epigraphs: all the
attendant matter of the text. It can, of course, itself be part of the fiction
it accompanies. Sir Walter Scott's elaborate devices of fictional editors
and correspondents to whom the text is addressed form an instance of
this. Yet the point is that, fictional or not, these devices serve to entice,
to orientate or indeed to disorientate the reader.

It is in these supplements that we may find what a Freudian might term
'the return of the repressed', where things are said which are excluded
from the main text and yet have to be stated, matters which the author
may be uneasy about which cannot quite be hidden. As with a conjuror's
feint, the device of the preface, the appendix, the footnote, may be used
to distract the audience's attention from the real sleight of hand of his
or her discourse. As we marvel at the illusion that the text produces,
the mundane mechanism at work may be hidden in the margins of our
perception.

Kierkegaard's work shows more than an awareness of this principle.
Indeed, at the end of the *Postscript* we find it spelled out that if a man
loudly proclaims his opinion, the ironist will find, not in what is 'written
in large letters' but in a subordinate clause, or a 'hinting little predicate'
(CUP1, 615) the evidence that the good man is not of this opinion.

This hint itself confirms *Concluding Unscientific Postscript* as a
prime site for the investigation of the paratextual. It is self-confessedly a
supplementary text. It presents itself as a 'Postscript', as an addendum, to
the *Philosophical Fragments*. This presentation, already clear in the title,
is developed further in the attendant texts to the book. It has a cluster
of these, like the moons round a planet: a 'Preface', an 'Introduction', and
a two part appendix, consisting of 'An Understanding with the Reader'

and 'A First and Last Explanation'. This 'concluding postscript' itself concludes with not one but two postscripts and we will see later how inconclusive these are.

The title of a book is for Genette the first and all-important means of attracting the reader. Kierkegaard's title *Afsluttende uvidenskabelig Efterskrift* is what Genette terms a *rhematic* rather than a *thematic* title.[5] By this is meant that it is related to the form rather than the content of the book, informing the reader what it is and how it says it rather than what its contents are. Once again, the validity of focusing on the structure of the book is confirmed. As an enticement to the casual reader, however, this title verges on the self-defeating. What interest it does raise is perhaps its very quaintness, raising the possibility of self-parody.[6]

Furthermore, all the terms of this title are susceptible to various translations. *Afsluttende* carries the same ambiguity as the English 'Concluding'—it can refer to that which brings something to an end in formal terms, but also to the drawing of conclusions, the provision of a solution to a problem. *Uvidenskabelig*, is not simply 'unscientific', but covers a much wider range which in the context might bear the translations 'unsystematic' or 'unscholarly'. The verb *efterskrive* in Danish carries not just the etymologically straightforward connotation of 'after-writing' (post-scriptum) but the derived meaning of 'forgery' or 'counterfeit'. 'Final unscholarly forgery' may be a forced translation, but it emphasizes the point that none of the terms present the contents in a positive light.

Of course these three words do not comprise the whole title. The full title explains that this is the postscript to the *Philosophical Fragments*. Immediately the casual reader is put off by the hint that she or he had better read that work first. Quite apart from that implication, this brings us to a series of questions over the consequences of describing any work as a 'Postscript'.

Genette discusses postscripts under the title of *postfaces*.[7] He characterizes them as the point at which an author may say to his reader, 'Now you know as much as I do, let's chat'. He points out that they lack two vital functions of a preface. Coming after the work, they cannot serve 'to gain or to guide the reader', as Genette puts it, to tell him or her why and how to read the text. The postface can only hope to have either a curative or a corrective function. A whole work set up as a 'postscript' then seems to hold out relatively little prospect of enlightenment to its readers as it can only serve to regulate their reading of another prior work.

If Genette's generalizations hold out no great hopes for such a work, the internal account of the genesis of this specific postscript is, if anything, less encouraging. In the 'Introduction', it is explained that the *Postscript* is the fruit of a casual promise of a sequel to *Philosophical Fragments*, although indeed a promise which the writer had already matter in hand to fulfil.[8] As such, the sequel is a work which, so Climacus argues, 'every young graduate in theology' (CUP1, 10) will be capable of writing. When Climacus praises *Philosophical Fragments* for not following the 'feminine practice of saying the most important thing in a postscript' (CUP1, 11), he again by implication seems to reduce the importance of the *Postscript*. Even the length of the book seems to be an arbitrary and therefore not particularly significant matter. In one sense, the book could be of minimal length as it does not develop the thought. In another it could be an endless supplement as it is presented as the accumulation of historical detail around the issue. The whole book, then, could be seen as a potentially infinite accumulation of learned footnotes, where the real issue is ultimately not enhanced but submerged in the mass of material, where the footnotes, so to speak, occupy the place of the text and relegate the question to be addressed to the margins.

How much harder, we might ask, could an author try to put a reader off reading his book? The answer turns out to be: quite a lot. The introduction then moves into a warning against the power of the introduction. We are presented with the examples of the orator, who bedazzles his hearer with the power of his eloquence without ever dealing with the issue, the systematician, who promises that all will become clear at the end, but who also confesses the end has not yet been reached, and the scholar who confuses a striving toward perfection with a striving toward the issue (CUP1, 12). An introduction which warns against introductions is an archetypally self-consuming text.

Finally, however, Johannes Climacus presents the issue to be dealt with in the *Postscript*: the question as to how he, Johannes Climacus, is to share in the happiness that Christianity presents:

> I, Johannes Climacus, born and bred in this city and now thirty years old, an ordinary human being like most folk, assume that a highest good, called an eternal happiness, awaits me just as it awaits a housemaid and a professor. I have heard that Christianity is one's prerequisite for this good. I now ask how I may enter into relation to this doctrine. (CUP1, 15–16)

To present the question in this way is not immodesty, he claims, but 'merely a kind of lunacy' (CUP1, 17). Presumably, then, the ensuing book is the product of an act of lunacy. Again, this is not obviously a selling point. Here at last, however, we have some prospect of interest. We are offered a question and thereby enticed with the implicit promise of an answer. The quest for this answer may sustain us through the bulk of the book's argument.

What then are the reader's feelings when finally the first postscript to the *Postscript*, 'An Understanding with the Reader,' is reached (CUP1, 617)? In this 'Understanding' Climacus admits, before the accusation can be made, that this whole book has been superfluous. Moreover, he asks that no one bother to appeal to it, because it contains a notice of its revocation: 'What I write contains the notice that everything is to be understood in such a way as it is revoked' (CUP1, 619).

This remark might justify the fact that so far our discussion has hardly touched upon the main text of the *Postscript*. Johannes Climacus has pulled the rug from under the reader's feet and has told us not to bother citing the text. What kind of a trick is this? The reader who has diligently waded through the text, and few readers will not find it quite hard going at times, is entitled to feel a little cheated. Where is the answer to the question that Climacus posed which induced us to devote our attention to reading this text?

One reader who clearly reflects this sense of being deceived by the *Postscript* is Derrida. He cites the paratextual apparatus of *Concluding Unscientific Postscript* in a long footnote to his characteristically vertiginous essay on the paratextual which itself forms a self-consuming preface to the collection *Dissemination*.[9] With the *Postscript* very much in the wings, he writes of the claim inherent in a postface to provide the truth of the preceding discourse. He then turns to the status of a pretended postscript: 'The *simulacrum* of a postface would therefore consist of feigning the final revelation of the meaning or functioning of a given stretch of language.'[10] But there is a further twist when such a simulacrum is play-acted. 'While pretending to turn around and look backward, one is also in fact starting again, adding an extra text, complicating the scene, opening up within the labyrinth a supplementary digression, which is also a false mirror that pushes the labyrinth's infinity back forever in mimed, that is endless, speculation.'[11] If this is so, then such a feigned 'concluding postscript' is an oxymoron. Far from concluding the discourse, it opens up an endless speculation.

Whatever its general validity, this reads as a fairly straightforward account of what seems to be going on in *Concluding Unscientific Postscript*. The *Postscript* purports to tie the themes of the *Philosophical Fragments* to the historical and then all responsibility is disclaimed. The 'First and Last Understanding', at least at first sight, serves to reveal not the meaning but the meaninglessness of the foregoing text.

We might well feel inclined to echo the words of Lewis Carroll's Alice at this point. Excited by the prospect of a riddle when the Mad Hatter asks her, 'Why is a raven like a writing desk?', Alice is exasperated when eventually the Hatter and the March Hare confess blithely that they have not the slightest idea of the answer: 'Alice sighed wearily. "I do think you might do something better with the time," she said, "than waste it in asking riddles that have no answers."'[12]

Indeed, but it precisely at this point that another line of attack on this problem may prove fruitful. Just this problem of why anyone would waste time on such a pursuit is taken up by Sigmund Freud, the second of our champions. In a footnote added in 1912 to his *Jokes and Their Relation to the Unconscious*, he tells the story of a man at dinner who dips his hands in mayonnaise, runs them through his hair and then, seeming to notice his mistake, remarks to his neighbour, 'I'm sorry, I thought it was spinach.'[13] Why would anyone make such an absurd and meaningless remark?

Rather startlingly, a remarkably similar story is to be found in an inordinately long footnote in *Concluding Unscientific Postscript* (CUP1, 514–19). Climacus gives a series of random examples to demonstrate his contention that the comic is present wherever there is contradiction and where one justifiably avoids the pain of the contradiction because it is inessential. Amongst these examples is the rather odd incident of an absent-minded man who reaches his hand into a spinach casserole and then, realising his mistake, excuses himself by saying, 'Oh, I thought it was caviar' (CUP1, 516).

How intriguing, given what we have been saying about the importance of the marginal, that both these writers have hit upon a very similar joke and that both have thought fit to place it in a footnote; in Freud's case, in a footnote to a footnote. What grist to the mill of a deconstructive critic for whom, as Christopher Norris writes,

> ...it is often in the margins or obscure minor passages of a text—in the footnotes, perhaps, or a casual parenthesis—that its strains and contradictions stand most clearly revealed... The very fact that they bear a problematic relation to the rest of an author's work—or beyond

that to the ruling assumptions of philosophic discourse—may have caused them to be tucked away out of sight in a footnote or simply passed over by commentators in search of more enduring truths. It is precisely by seizing on such uncanonical texts, passages or details that deconstruction seeks to resist the homogenising pressure of received ideas.[14]

What, then, do the two make of this story? In Freud's account, this exchange counts as 'idiocy masquerading as a joke.'[15] Climacus, in a wonderfully Kierkegaardian phrase, regards it as absent-mindedness 'raised to the second power' (CUP1, 516 n.). Their contrasted reactions make the point that the same comic narrative affects different hearers rather differently. Freud reads it as a deliberate, and indeed somewhat malevolent, attempt to discomfit the hearer, whereas Climacus sees it as a rather endearingly compounded form of distraction.

The matter of the reception of such tales will occupy us further, but for the present let us remain with the problem of the motivation of the teller. Freud gives what could well stand as two separate accounts of the pleasure afforded to the teller. Firstly, this mechanism allows the pleasure of spouting nonsense to be liberated. Secondly, the teller gains pleasure from misleading and annoying his listener, who can salvage some satisfaction from resolving to tell the story in his turn. Here we find two fundamental principles of Freud's analysis of the function of jokes. The pleasure of jokes consists in the lifting of inhibitions, either inhibitions which enforce the 'proper' use of language or inhibitions about the subjects which can be spoken of. Freud tends to focus on puns and other plays on words where he sees a principle of economy at work. At a purely verbal level, by making one lexical item perform several semantic functions, the joke economizes on effort, and the excess energy is liberated in the form of laughter. At the level of meaning, the joke may allow an 'economy of affect.' In other words, serious and troubling matters are spoken of in a way which deflects attention from their emotional import, again liberating emotional energy in the form of laughter. Puzzling over the verbal conundrum to find the 'thought content' of the joke deflects attention from the emotional content.

Samuel Weber,[16] however, homes in on this particular story which Freud appends as a footnote to a footnote with deconstructive zeal. Why does Freud feel he has to supplement his text with this absurd story? Weber's answer is that in such nonsense-jokes there is *no* thought content. The joke works, if it does, by refusing the attempt to sort out a sensible meaning from the verbal play. Freud, Weber argues, was driven to add this supplementary footnote because this strange form of joke, a joke which is playing with the conventions of joking, threatened to undermine the elaborate account of humour that Freud propounded.

Weber uses the term 'shaggy dog story' to describe this form of humour. He seems to be focusing on the refusal of the traditional shaggy dog story to offer the kind of neat condensation of language in a 'punch line' that is the promise of the standard joke. This is only part of the story, however. The art of the shaggy dog story is not simply that it is a meta-joke, a joke on the conventions of joking, but also that it parodies narrative conventions.

Freud makes much, as we have seen, of the importance of condensation and economy in the joke work: brevity is the soul of wit. The shaggy dog story, on the other hand, makes a virtue of its ability to spin out the thread of the listener's attention to the greatest length possible with the least expenditure of material. It is narrative at its most ductile. If we follow the line of Peter Brooks in his *Reading for the Plot*,[17] the listener's engagement in any narrative depends both on the promise of closure and on the deferral of that closure. Narrative happens in the space between the promise and the fulfilment. But this is true not only of narrative but of any sustained utterance.

In such terms, *Concluding Unscientific Postscript* can be seen as a prime example of a shaggy dog story, indeed a St Bernard amongst such stories. It does not have a conventional plot, perhaps, but it is set up as providing the answer to the question Climacus has posed himself. Even the simple promise to answer a question sets up a tension of expectation and fulfilment, in itself sufficiently engaging to underpin countless quiz shows on television, all the more so when the reward of the question answered is coupled to the offer of a cruise to the Bahamas. The joke, or what is set up as a joke, operates in the same way, offering not only the promise of closure, but the additional reward of laughter, of the pleasure of the effects that Freud enumerates in his consideration of humour. A comic narrative can then be spun out perilously far because the reward at the end is not simply the answer to a question but also the catharsis of laughter.

The shaggy dog story gains its effect from its ability to hold the listener's attention with the promise of such a reward which at the end it withholds, leaving the listener with a banal denouement. The genre, however, would not survive long if the only reward was for the teller to pull a fast one on the listener and for the listener perhaps to join ruefully in the laughter as he realizes that he has been fooled. The listener may well be aware that this is the game and be intrigued by watching the teller's skill in spinning out the story, by a sense of complicity in the overturning of a convention and even by the skill in which false clues are laid which lead to the bathetic climax. The stories need be neither the rather malicious assault on the listener that Freud seems to envisage, nor simply a product of absent-mindedness, as in Kierkegaard's reading.

It seems to me that *Concluding Unscientific Postscript* is quite consciously set up as a philosophical/theological shaggy dog story, something that promises a conclusion which it then withdraws but which offers another sort of reward to its readers—the incidental rewards of watching the master strategist at work, the rewards of humour, but also a supplementary pleasure, something that takes it beyond a joke.

As such, however, is it not simply a hypersubtle and highly artificial device, remote from any serious engagement with philosophical issues and a mere irresponsible game with language? I believe that the opposite is the case. Both Freud and Kierkegaard offer support to the view that in fact a text such as the *Postscript* offers a clear view of how the comic is not a parasitic form of language and discourse but a window into the intrinsic limitations and possibilities of what language can do. The comic, Climacus argues, is all pervasive. 'On the whole,' he writes, 'the comic is everywhere' (CUP1, 462)—although we should not miss the hint of contradiction and the comic in the juxtaposition of 'on the whole' and 'everywhere.' Nevertheless, such a statement surely argues for caution in designating the comic as in any sense parasitic on language.

This insight is borne out by Freud's account of the aetiology of the comic.[18] He argues that the first function of speech is pleasure. The child gains physical satisfaction from trying out her developing speech organs and from the aural stimulation of chiming sounds and the effort of mimicry. The notion of responsible speech, of answering or posing a question which could be answered, one form of speech production which seems to entail another, is a derived state. The comic for Freud gains its place in adult discourse because it allows for the temporary lifting of the inhibitions which adult responsibility places upon us. In this sense, the 'serious' use of language is derived from the playful.

The change that comes about in the development from childhood is also discussed in the unfinished work *Johannes Climacus*. There is consciousness in the child, but doubt is outside it, Kierkegaard reports Climacus as arguing. This means that for the child, who is immediacy, everything is true, but at the same moment, everything is untrue. Immediacy cancels the question of truth. As soon as the question of truth arises, so does untruth. Indeed, so Climacus argues, it is untruth that makes it possible for consciousness to be brought into relation with something else. For Climacus, the agency by which this is brought about is language. This is spelt out rather cryptically at the beginning of the second part of *Johannes Climacus*, where Johannes is confronted with the question as to whether mediacy or immediacy comes first. Which is parasitic on the other? This he dismisses as a non-question, as by the time that consciousness is in place to ask the question, the two are mutually coimplicated. 'Immediacy is reality, language is ideality, consciousness is contradiction. The moment I make a statement about reality, contradiction is present, for what I say is ideality' (JC, 168). If contradiction is present, then so is the potential for the comic as Climacus defines the comic as an apprehension of contradiction.

The heart of language is contradiction: saying against. We speak not to mimic a static world but to bring about change in a world in flux. What we say always 'speaks against' a situation, always counters another and encounters another. Both comedy and tragedy arise from this opposition of language and world. How many of the great tragedies turn upon a vow, a promise, an oracle or prophecy which lures the hero into an inexorable and crushing collision between word and world. The tragic hero despairs of the way out of this contradiction and dies. The comic, however, holds to the way out—the clever parry of the quip, the verbal feint, the disguise adopted and then shed. The union of tragic and comic is in this fundamental characteristic of language, in the fundamental structure of communication. Neither comic nor tragic is a parasitic or derived function of language. Rather it is the neat formulations of the systematists and the polite platitudes of social discourse which are the parasites on language which leach it of its passion.

So both Freud and Kierkegaard can be adduced as witnesses to the fundamental role of the comic in language. That being said, Freud's principal concern in his book on jokes is to account for the fact that jokes have to be told. Given the function of the comic in language and the apprehension of the comic in contradiction, we have yet to account for the need to tell a joke to another party in order to make that person laugh. What lies behind this apparent compulsion to communicate? Ordinarily, those who tell jokes do not laugh at their own witticism and so this need to repeat the joke is not a simple need for the teller to experience again the pleasure of the catharsis the joke offers. What kind of transaction, then, is involved here? In terms of the *Concluding*

Unscientific Postscript, what leads to the writing of the work? Why does this joke need to be told?

The title of the chapter where Freud's discussion is to be found itself bears out this aspect of the question: 'The Motives of Jokes—Jokes as a Social Process.'[19] Freud insists on the transactional nature of humour. The joke in the end depends on the hearer, what Freud calls the 'third person.' The 'second person', which need not be a person, is the subject of the joke. As his analysis progresses, Freud gives increasing weight to this audience. In the end, it is the listener who makes or breaks the joke. A joke, he says, is a 'double-dealing rascal which serves two masters at once.'[20] Everything in jokes that is aimed at gaining pleasure is calculated with an eye to the third person, to the audience, as though there were internal and insurmountable obstacles in the way of that pleasure in the first person. He concludes that we are compelled to tell a joke to another person precisely *because* we are unable to laugh at it ourselves.[21] It is the hearer's laughter which liberates the teller.

It is not ultimately in the control of the teller of the joke whether the listener will laugh. Jokes, indeed provide a fascinating case of the negotiation of authority in language. Laughter is to an extent involuntary and a good comedian can reduce us to a state of 'helpless' laughter. However, the same comedian may well 'die' in front of a different audience which sees no reason to laugh or may be offended rather than amused by his or her material. So, paradoxically, the comedian makes the audience laugh but cannot *make* them laugh. She or he is more than the simple occasion for laughter—she or he has an intention of causing laughter and a repertoire of techniques to draw on—but the teller cannot guarantee success.

We have already quoted Burgess on the importance of the joke as the epitome of communication for Kierkegaard. A quotation from *Stages on Life's Way* makes this point succinctly: 'To believe the ideality on the word of another is like laughing at a joke not because one has understood it but because someone else has said it was funny. In that case, the joke can really be omitted for the person who laughs on the basis of belief and respect; he is able to laugh with equal *Emphasis* [significance]' (SLW, 438–39). Here Kierkegaard uses the example of the jest as the clearest instance of the role of the subjective in the receipt of communication. It also neatly reveals the essential fallacy of Climacus's strategy in the *Postscript* and therefore the necessity of its revocation. Why do we read the *Postscript* if it is not in some sense to believe on the word of another? The joke has to be made so that the effect of omitting it can be made clear. The truly comic is not the contradiction between Climacus's aims and the impossibility of their achievement, but between the infinite and the finite, between the ideal and the actual.

The fact that the work which promises to answer Climacus's question turns out to have been a joke is not simply the result of an elaborate evasion of Climacus's question. The question posed by Climacus is such that it could only lead to an absurd answer and a revocation. Superficially, it may seem plausible, even important, but it is an impossible formulation. Climacus defends his question on the grounds that, unlike the dry objectivity of the systematicians who only ask what Christianity is, his concern is with the central issue of the subjectivity of Christianity. If that is his aim, then his question rests on assumptions as absurd as the explanation that accounts for dipping one's hand in spinach by explaining that one thought it was caviare. He wants to know how he can gain the goods of Christianity without gaining the goods, or in other words, how he can receive the benefits of the transformation wrought by Christianity without being himself transformed. Johannes Climacus is to undergo the transformation of Christianity, but somewhere the old Johannes must persist in order to be able to act as reporter and commentator on the process.

There is no way in which the question as to how to gain the goods of Christianity can be posed as such an item of discussion. It is not possible on Climacus's own account to inspect the life of the religious as it consists in hiddenness. One might as well ask why a raven is like a writing desk. Unless one knows the answer, there is little point in posing the riddle. As *Philosophical Fragments* points out, the answer is a matter of infinite interest, not simply a piece of knowledge to catalogue alongside others. There is no way in which the question as posed could be intelligibly answered. That is the basic point which the elaborate devices of the *Postscript* are designed to bring home to the reader, who, if he or she is intrigued by the title of the book, may well be the kind of interested but detached, humorous individual who takes the absurdity of Climacus's question seriously. As we have seen, the title itself together with the other paratextual features make the book attractive to those who share delight in the subversive power of language, in the clever manipulation of literary conventions, in a sense of irony. A particular readership has been winnowed out, a readership which is in sympathy with Johannes Climacus and who may well fall into the same kind of absurdity to which he is prone.

This absurdity, however, cannot be communicated directly. The obstacle to plain speech here is not simply an inhibition, an imposition of the ego on the unconscious as Freud would have it, but the category of the absurd. Humour and the comic are the results of the realization of the contradiction, the incommensurability between the finite and the infinite, the human and the divine, made concrete in the figure of the God-man. Where Freud accounts for humour and the role of the jest in terms of an interplay between different aspects of the individual human mind mediated through communication, Kierkegaard's thinking starts from the possibility of communication and an account of human being which sees it as characterized by its relation to the eternal and the infinite.

Burgess points out, however, that the danger in designating the authorship as comic is that it all too easily lays one open to the very trap that Kierkegaard was so concerned to point out and which the *Corsair* epitomized: a too easy definition of the comic. Kierkegaard's papers reveal that the *Concluding Unscientific Postscript* was intended originally literally to conclude the authorship (JP, 5873). In this work, he had gone as far as he could to lead the reader to the brink of the religious, trusting to the reader's apprehension of the true comic which embraces both jest and earnestness.

Arguably, it was the realization of the error of this presupposition which prompted him to continue his writing in a new way, discarding the devices of pseudonymity and indirection. It was immediately after the publication of *Concluding Unscientific Postscript* that he became embroiled with the satirical magazine, the *Corsair*. In response to the ridicule that he was subjected to as a result of this affair, with heavy irony Kierkegaard records his former opinion that the most difficult task is 'to deal with the comic in fear and trembling.' As such, it follows that only a few are truly capable of the comic. Now he is told that things are the other way round. Everyone else in Denmark is capable of the comic and he stands out by his renunciation of any reputation for the comic (COR, 179). 'As a matter of fact, everybody in Copenhagen but me understands the comic' (COR, 188), he concludes sourly.

The key to the comic is contradiction, but this is also the condition for the tragic. The difference, according to Climacus, is that the comic vision always has its eye on the way out. '*The tragic is suffering contradiction and the comic is painless contradiction*' (CUP1, 514). It knows there is an escape from the contradiction whereas the tragic vision does not and therefore despairs over the way out. The illegitimate comic, however, consists in holding to an illusory way out, either a fantastic resolution of the contradiction, or a failure to appreciate the nature of the contradiction. The trouble with a comic book is that it may encourage people in an illegitimate apprehension of the comic.

In the end, the reader always has a way out of a book: he or she can simply stop reading it. In this sense, it is possible to read *Concluding Unscientific Postscript* as purely a comic book, one that provides its own way out, in its reiterated insistence that it is not even worth reading. We might even share Freud's verdict of such a production and see it as 'idiocy masquerading as a joke.' We can shut the book—and go home. A book can only ever be an occasion, a transaction. *Concluding Unscientific Postscript* is thus not unique in this. It shares this characteristic in common with all books. To pretend otherwise would involve a contradiction between what the book claimed and what it could do, in itself enough to qualify it as a joke. What it does evince is a particular self-conscious reduplication of the joke which can recall us from our absent-mindedness.

Yet it may be that the book itself becomes the occasion that brings us face to face with the contradiction at the heart of our very notion of our selves. In that sense, it may prompt us to go beyond the joke. The religious is something beyond both the comic and the tragic. Abraham, for instance, acts in the hope of a resolution of the dilemma of losing his son or obeying God in the knowledge that there is, humanly speaking, no way out. That sense cannot be communicated, but only lived. As soon as religiousness manifests itself, it becomes legitimate material for the comic. Climacus indicates that on the level of the apparent, the humorous is the highest state in that it sees clearly the contraction between the inner and the outer, but the truly religious category is defended 'by the comic against the comic' (CUP1, 522). Religiousness escapes the comic by incorporating it and so as a higher principle is defended against it. Because religiousness is hidden, it cannot come into contradiction with anything and therefore is immune from the comic.

The nearness of the existing humorist and the religious is to be seen in their common awareness that suffering is not an accident of existence but something that stands in relation to existing. The humorist is aware of this, but makes the 'deceptive turn' by revoking everything in jest. 'He touches the secret of existence in the pain but then he goes home again' (CUP1, 447). 'The ironist levels everything on the basis of abstract humanity; the humorist on the basis of the abstract relation with God, inasmuch as he does not enter into the relationship with God. It is precisely there that he parries with a jest' (CUP1, 448 n.).

The humorist is quoted as refusing to attempt to answer the riddle of existence as in the end, the one who proposed it will answer it anyway. Climacus uses the simile of the riddle printed in a daily paper with the answer printed the next day, accompanied by the name of an old maid who had guessed the riddle. But as the answer is printed, the humorist argues, she only anticipates common knowledge by one day (CUP1, 451). Of course, the fallacy in this is to assume that the important thing is to add the answer to the riddle to one's stock of knowledge. The important thing, surely, is not what the answer is, but arriving at the answer, even if that answer is no answer. Kierkegaard offers the reader the opportunity to enact that experience.

The ideal reader to whom Climacus addresses himself in the 'Understanding' will understand that 'to write a book and to revoke it is not the same as refraining from writing it' (CUP 1, 621). To elaborate a theory of humour, as the *Postscript* does, is one thing, but it is another to see the joke. When the book is revoked, the theory of humour still stands, for those who have the leisure to be interested in things, and a very illuminating theory it is. But as an answer to Climacus's question, it only goes to show that the question could not be asked, and so therfore, the whole enterprise has to be erased. Yet, as in mathematics, arriving at an absurd answer which needs to be rubbed out may not solve the immediate question, but may well be an important moment in learning to see how the problem is to be tackled. It may also be an important lesson in persistence and serious engagement.

The humorist, says Climacus, knows the depth of suffering—and then goes home. The religious consciousness, however, has no home to go to. There is still a barrier between the humorist's consciousness of the contradiction and his or her sense of that consciousness. For the religious, that contradiction is constitutive of the consciousness that is aware of it.

Thus there is no place for the religious to evade the contradiction which the humorist knows but does not yet live. There is no way to evade being posed the riddle which only God can answer. The humorist may close the book and walk away. The religious reader is left living the unanswered riddle.

Notes

1. Andrew J. Burgess, 'A Word-Experiment on the Category of the Comic', in Robert L. Perkins (ed.), *International Kierkegaard Commentary: The Corsair Affair* (Macon, GA: Mercer University Press, 1990), pp. 85–121.
2. Burgess, 'Word Experiment', pp. 118, 119.
3. Gérard Genette, *Seuils* (Paris: Éditions du Seuil, 1987).
4. Genette, *Seuils*, p. 7.
5. Genette, *Seuils*, p. 82.
6. In the 'Editor's Preface' to David Swenson's translation of the work, Walter Lowrie recounts Swenson's tale that 'attracted by the quaint name of a book *Concluding Unscientific Postscript to the Philosophical Fragments*' he took the book home and 'read it all that night and all the next day, with the profoundest emotion' (*Concluding Unscientific Postscript* [trans. David F. Swenson and Walter Lowrie; Princeton: Princeton University Press, 1941], p. xi).
7. Genette, *Seuils*, p. 219.
8. The promise occurs in this remark near the end of *Philosophical Fragments*: '...in the next section of this pamphlet, if I ever do write it, I intend to call the matter by its proper name and clothe the issue in its historical costume' (PF, 109).
9. Jacques Derrida, *Dissemination* (trans. Barbara Johnson; London: The Athlone Press, 1981), pp. 1–51.
10. Derrida, *Dissemination*, p. 27 n. 27.
11. Derrida, *Dissemination*, p. 28 n. 27
12. Lewis Carroll, *Alice's Adventures in Wonderland* and *Through the Looking Glass*, (Harmondsworth: Puffin, 1962), p. 96.
13. Sigmund Freud, *Jokes and Their Relation to the Unconscious*, vol. 6 in *Pelican Freud Library* (trans. James Strachey; Harmondsworth: Penguin, 1976), p. 190 n. 1.
14. Christopher Norris, *Derrida* (London: Fontana, 1987), p. 134.
15. Freud, *Jokes*, p. 190 n. 1.
16. Samuel Weber, *The Legend of Freud* (Minneapolis: University of Minnesota Press, 1982), pp. 113–14.
17. Peter Brooks, *Reading for the Plot: Design and Intention in Narrative* (Cambridge, MA: Harvard University Press, 1992). See especially chapter 4, 'Freud's Masterplot: A Model for Narrative'.
18. Freud, *Jokes*, pp. 174–75.
19. Freud, *Jokes*, pp. 191–211.
20. Freud, *Jokes*, p. 208.
21. Freud, *Jokes*, p. 209.

'Sarah Is the Hero': Kierkegaard's Reading of Tobit in *Fear and Trembling*

'Perhaps the most extreme misreading of the book of Tobit is Søren Kierkegaard's deliberately "imaginary" reading.' So claims David McCracken in his stimulating article 'Narration and Comedy in the Book of Tobit.'[1] Such a remark throws down a challenge which is hard to resist. It would be fascinating, if unfair, to take this as an incentive to trawl the literature for more extreme misreadings. In any case, to pinpoint definitively the 'most extreme' would require us to subject the notion of misreading to more scrutiny that it could perhaps bear. We can more profitably ask what leads McCracken to read Kierkegaard this way and how such disagreements over what constitutes a misreading may illuminate our reading of Tobit.

As the title of his paper indicates, McCracken reads Tobit as a comedy. By contrast, Kierkegaard, or, more accurately, his pseudonym Johannes de Silentio,[2] devotes four pages of *Fear and Trembling*, his astonishing attempt to work out the consequences of Abraham's sacrifice of Isaac, to a discussion of the plight of Sarah and writes, 'I have read about many griefs, but I doubt that there is to be found a grief as profound as the one in this girl's life' (FT, 102). It is de Silentio's insistence that Sarah is a tragic figure that seems to be at the root of McCracken's accusation of misreading. 'No reader is likely to be in tears,' claims McCracken, while reading Sarah's story.[3]

How are we to adjudicate between these two positions? Humour, after all, is in the eye of the beholder. Events a reader finds amusing may not amuse the characters, as indeed McCracken concedes when he writes that the assurance of a happy outcome 'does not preclude the tears of the characters.'[4] Graham Greene's short story, 'A Shocking Accident,' illustrates the real point at issue well. The story turns on the varied reactions of the characters and the reader to the fact that the narrator's father was killed when a pig fell on him from a balcony in Naples. As a boy and young man, the narrator learns to dread telling the story because of the laughter, outright or suppressed, that it provokes. When he brings his new fiancée home to meet his aunt, the aunt insists on telling the story, and his heart sinks. 'And then the miracle happened. Sally did not laugh. Sally sat with open eyes of horror while his aunt told her story and at the end, "How horrible," Sally said. "It makes you think, doesn't it? Happening like that. Out of a clear sky."'⁵

Greene's story is itself a comedy in the classic sense. It moves from disruption to a positive resolution and ends in a marriage. He has made comedy out of the mismatch between the comic and tragic apprehensions of a story. It is certainly a tragic story for the father and for the orphaned boy, made all the more poignant by the ridicule it attracts.

What clinches the narrator's feeling that Sally is the girl for him is that she goes on to ask the same question that he had asked his headmaster when the news of his father's death was broken to him: 'What happened to the pig?' It is a tragedy for the pig, too, although the headmaster took his question as a sign of heartlessness and the reader may find it hard not to smile. Who best reads the incident of the father's death? Who gets to say how we 'ought' to read it and by what moral criteria? Who is misreading the story? Who, then, is misreading Tobit?

To answer this question, we need to delve further into the presuppositions and purposes behind these readings of the book. Intriguingly, it turns out that there is a common precursor for both readings in Luther's preface to Tobit in his Bible of 1534.⁶ 'A fine, delightful, devout comedy' is Luther's description of the book which he summarizes as being about the problems of the harmony of the home. It culminates, as comedies so often do, in a happy marriage. It instils the hope which should encourage married couples to endure hardships and difficulties with patience. Luther is agnostic as to whether the events of the book really happened. Tobit, like Judith, may be a 'holy history' or else an invention, a 'beautiful and instructive fiction or drama'; either way, he concludes, it is worth reading. The idea of the book as drama is expanded upon when Luther makes the suggestion that the Greek version of Tobit might have at one time been written as a play, taking as evidence its use of dialogue and the first-person narration in the outer chapters, which was later recast as a narrative. Indeed, he goes as far as to hypothesize that the Jewish community had a custom of presenting plays at their festivals to entertain and instruct the young and that it was from this source that the Greeks learned the art of drama. If this were true, although all historical evidence would suggest it is not, Tobit would be not just any comedy, but the prototype of the whole tradition of comedy in the classical world.

McCracken's reading follows similar lines, although he makes no reference to Luther. In his view the book is comedy in so far as it leads to a happy ending for all concerned, and the suffering that occurs is relieved as part of a more general restoration of all good people. In addition, many of the details and episodes in the story are ludicrous: the means by which Tobit is blinded and the fish entrails which are supposed to be the cure, for example. McCracken's most original point is that the narrative structure itself is comic. One important aspect of this is the change between first- and third-person narration in the book which McCracken sees as involving a radical change in point of view. The limited first-person narrative of the outer chapters is replaced by a truly omniscient third-person narrator. In McCracken's view, this change makes manifest the comic limitations of Tobit's perspective.

He also points out the discrepancy between 'Tobit-as-character' and 'Tobit-as-narrator', picking up in a different way on the change of narrative voice that Luther notes. The Tobit who tells the story is the older Tobit who has been cured of his blindness and has received back his son and new daughter-in-law. He paints a picture of his younger self as a fallible character, one who mistakenly accuses his own wife of stealing and then complains of being the victim of unjust insults when she responds vigorously to this groundless charge. Yet even the later Tobit proves to be fallible and not, as he presents himself, a unique paragon of faithfulness. McCracken makes much of the contradiction between Tobit-as-narrator's claim in 1:6 that he alone went often to the festivals in Jerusalem and his acknowledgment in 5:13 that Hananiah and Nathan, sons of Shemaliah, used to go with him. As with Elijah on Horeb, his claims to be the only faithful member of his generation turn out to be exaggerated. McCracken points out his emphasis on his particular tribe and insistence on marriage within this narrow grouping.

At this point, it is appropriate to introduce another reading to the discussion. In his article, 'Tobit: A Comedy in Error?', which is a direct response to McCracken, J.R.C. Cousland takes issue with many of his contentions.[7] McCracken is now the misreader. Cousland argues that Tobit is not an intentionally comic book and that many of the details that strike the modern reader as humorously incongruous would not have seemed so to its ancient readers. In particular, he reads the third-person narrator as confirming Tobit's self-evaluation rather than contradicting it. On the point of the contradiction between 5:13 and 1:6, he argues that

McCracken misses the force of the word 'often' in 1:6. Tobit's claim that he was the only one who went 'often' to Jerusalem does not imply that no one else ever went.[8]

This is a fair point, but Cousland is on more shaky ground when he argues that Tobit was justified in feeling aggrieved at Anna's reproaches when it is he who falsely accused her of theft. The justification is that by taking on work at all she was humiliating her husband 'even if she was technically in the right about the goat.' Cousland cites Sir. 25:22 in defence of this view. This may not satisfy a modern readership, he concedes, but an ancient readership would have taken Tobit's point.

I am not sure how we know that. 'Technically right' is right in this case and Tobit is wrong. This rather strained argument becomes understandable in the light of Cousland's more general statement that if Tobit is seen even partially as a figure of fun, his status as an exemplar is devalued. To preserve the serious message of the book, Tobit must be taken as a moral, if not infallible, guide. The problem here is this: is this ethical criterion for preferring certain readings intrinsic to the book, or is it rather a product of its canonization? If the latter, then Cousland and McCracken are not asking quite the same question. There is a difference in asking how can a particular book be read and how should it be read, both in the answer that may be given, but also in what counts as a valid methodology. One might agree with Cousland on his readings of some details without thereby affirming his overall stance.

Cousland does concede that the narrative contains what he calls 'outlandish circumstances.'[9] He sees these as part of the narrator's attempt to depict a kind of dystopia, but for purposes which are not comic. The point is to set the scene for a divine restoration of an ordered world. In this connection he makes the interesting observation that Sarah's plight is an inversion of Gen. 1:28, the injunction to be fruitful and multiply. Not only does Sarah fail to add humans to the earth, she substracts them. Instead of life, she brings death. Cousland also detects echoes of Gen. 6:1-4 with Asmodeus taking the part of one of the Watchers who lust after daughters of men, although again the effect is to prevent rather than to further procreation.

Details apart, Cousland and McCracken are closer than might appear. Cousland ends by acknowledging that Tobit is not a work of unremitting high seriousness. Its irony may make the reader smile and its exoticism has charm. McCracken, on the other hand, is far from dismissing the suffering in the story. His view is summed up as follows: 'The author's comic view requires that the suffering be serious but not so serious or pathetic that the affliction eclipses the joy of God's order.'[10] Both of them are responsible enough readers to allow that the text itself resists the broader interpretative stance each wishes to take towards it.

Already, however, this would seem to reduce the force of McCracken's critique of Kierkegaard. Johannes de Silentio does not deny its comedy as he notes the 'almost unavoidable' comic effect of the seven husbands, which puts him in mind of 'a student who failed his examination seven times' (FT, 102).[11] In the context of Tobit, however, this heightens the danger to Tobias and brings to the fore his status as an only son. What he is interested in, though, is to understand Sarah's situation before she is aware of the possibility of a cure. Kierkegaard does not attempt to give an overall reading of the book. He focuses entirely on Sarah. The reasons for this, and the reason he is drawn to this episode in the first place are in themselves intriguing and do raise some important questions about the book.

Just as McCracken's characterization of Tobit as comedy can be traced to Luther's preface, so can Kierkegaard's concentration on Sarah. The importance of the feminine element in Tobit is something Luther emphasizes in his *Table Talk*, where he sums the book up as a comedy dealing with women, which is an exemplum of domestic economy.[12] In the preface itself, Luther singles Sarah out and gives the derivation of her name from the Hebrew for a champion or a victor: 'one who comes out on top' as his translator Bachmann has it, as close as we may expect to finding her called a hero.

What influence might these remarks of Luther's have had on Kierkegaard's reading of the book? Kierkegaard was brought up and educated in a Lutheran context, although he had a complex relationship to Luther. In the discourse, 'What Is Required in Order to Look at Oneself with True Blessing in the Mirror of the Word?', which forms the first part of *For Self-Examination*, he performs the interesting rhetorical feat of enlisting Luther's support for his promotion of the Letter of James, which Luther had notoriously described as a 'right strawy epistle.'[13] In this essay at least, Kierkegaard shows his knowledge of Luther's biblical writings but is also prepared to challenge him.

In the case of Tobit, Kierkegaard makes no direct reference to Luther's reading in either his published or unpublished works. What his journals do contain, however, are selections from Tobit in a context which suggests, at least to their editors, that they relate to lectures given in 1839 by H.N. Clausen, the remarkable biblical scholar who was professor of New Testament at Copenhagen at the time and with whom Kierkegaard studied.[14] The evidence is tantalizingly brief and incomplete, but it is at the very least plausible that Clausen would have alluded to Luther's preface in the course of his comments on Tobit, and more than likely that Kierkegaard would have looked at it in his own reading.

However Kierkegaard came across Luther's views, the theme of perseverance in marriage could hardly have failed to struck a chord with him in his own struggles over his engagement to Regina Olsen. The idea that Sarah rather than Tobias is the hero may also be one that he could have picked up from Luther.

The importance of this for Kierkegaard should not be underestimated even though Sarah occupies only four pages in his huge output. On the face of it, this might suggest that his interest in her was slight and passing, hardly worth much further examination. Those four pages, however, contain the following sentence, in de Silentio's voice: 'She is the one I want to approach as I have never approached any girl, or been tempted in thought to approach anyone of whom I have read' (FT, 104). There could hardly be a stronger expression of interest or of Sarah's importance as a character. She takes precedence over all women, real or imagined. De Silentio adds a passing remark that he admires her more than Tobias loved her.

What is it that is so heroic about Sarah, then? De Silentio sees Sarah's tragedy in her being deprived of the ability to give herself in love. This is an infinitely greater cause for grief than the merely contingent sorrow of a young girl who has not yet found love. For de Silentio, Sarah is unique in the deprivation she suffers, a fact made the more tragic in that she is innocent. It is not that she is psychologically incapable of love or indifferent to it but she knows she is doomed to bring death on any man she loves. She is, as Kierkegaard rather brutally puts it, 'a botched job', a 'damaged specimen of humanity from birth' (FT, 104), but through no fault of her own.

As so often in Kierkegaard's works, it is an irresistible temptation to find an analogy here with his understanding of his relationship with his one-time fiancée Regina Olsen, although it should be remembered that it remains a potentially misleading temptation. In his *Journals*, Kierkegaard records that his decision to induce Regina to break their engagement arose from his sense that he was so infected with melancholy that he could not ask Regina to share his life. The sense of some intrinsic flaw that debars one from the possibility of love, of being a 'damaged specimen' is something that he certainly shared with Sarah.[15]

What he admires in Sarah, what makes him see her as a truly heroic character, is her courage and her love of God that allows her to ask for and accept help even when she is a damaged specimen. A man could not do this, de Silentio is sure. No man could have the humility to bear Tobias's sympathy and his courageous self-sacrifice as she does. This is why de Silentio sees Sarah as the heroine, rather than Tobias. To the poetic sensibility, Tobias is the hero for risking death for his betrothed. For de Silentio, it is Sarah's humble acceptance of the fact that Tobias is willing to make such a sacrifice that is the truly courageous act.

Yet is this not itself a poetic romanticization of Sarah's circumstances, a piece of psychological and spiritual eisegesis on Kierkegaard's part? Here, an understanding of the dilemma in which all the characters find themselves is in order. Underlying the story are assumptions that are bound up in the general understanding of marriage and procreation in ancient Israel, compounded by the more particular constraints of the Law, which are best understood by the similarities and differences between Sarah's case and that of another woman who lost more than one husband, Tamar in Genesis 38.

In that chapter, Tamar is married to the patriarch Judah's son Er who is killed by the Lord because of his wickedness. Under the levirate law as set out in Deut. 25: 5-10, Tamar as his widow has a legal right to be married to his brother Onan, but he refuses to impregnate her as any child would be accounted an heir to his dead brother rather than as his own. The Lord then punishes Onan with death, leaving Judah with only one son left. Judah's dilemma is that Tamar is entitled to marry this son, and indeed has no other obvious option. All Judah knows, however, not being privy to the Lord's designs, is that through association with this woman two of his sons have died childless. Can he risk his only surviving son? His death will bring Judah's own line to an end as Judah's wife has already died. Judah opts to withhold him from Tamar and his choice is to some extent vindicated by a later rabbinic ruling which Frank Zimmerman helpfully cites in relation to Sarah:

> In the later rabbinic thought, a woman who had buried three husbands was called a *qatlanit* as if there were something in her that was man-killing. Cf. Yeb. 64b: 'If a woman is married to one husband and he dies; to a second, and he dies; she should not be married to a third. Such is the opinion of R. Judah. R. Simon ben Gamaliel avers, "She may be married to a third, but not married to a fourth." R. Huna declares, "The source is the cause" i.e. such is the nature of this woman. R. Ashi says, "It is her evil fortune."'[16]

Sarah, under this ruling, is indisputably a *qatlanit* (literally, a 'killer') and by the time Tobias arrives on the scene has had more than her share of husbands.[17] The statements of R. Huna and R. Ashi would justify the assumption that, even if she is technically an innocent party (and the maidservants doubt even that), responsibility if not blame for the deaths rests with her. Something in her nature, some ill fortune, brings this dreadful situation about. Indeed, Asmodeus could be seen as a personification of the deadly power of which the *qatlanit* is innocent and unconscious, but which is bound up with her most intimate being.

Zimmermann puts Sarah's resulting predicament succinctly:

> We now see the poignancy of Sarah's plight. Her past seems black without redemption and her future without hope. She has killed off seven husbands, and there is no surviving levir (apparently) to marry her. As she puts it herself, her father has neither close brother or relative for whom she should keep herself as a wife (6.15)... Were she to be married to another man aside from Tobias, she would be guilty of *zenunim*, a violation of the law of Moses and punishable by death.[18]

The levirate law itself is intrinsically unsettling, as Dvore Weisberg has pointed out.[19] It exists in order to ensure that the line of the dead can continue, but at the same time it can threaten the continuation of the line of the living. For this reason, in Weisberg's view, it is met with male reluctance whenever it is invoked. Even the programmatic statement of the law in Deut. 25:5-6 immediately goes on to give the sanctions which a woman can apply to a man who refuses to perform the duty, which indicates that such refusals can be expected. Her recourse is to pull off his sandal and spit in his face, but the lasting sanction is that the man's own line becomes a source of perpetual disgrace. Instead of being remembered with reverence, his line will be known as the 'house of him who had his sandal pulled off' (Deut. 25:10). Boaz, who may seem to be the exception in his willingness to marry the widow Ruth to maintain the inheritance of her dead husband Mahlon, can rely on the reluctance of her unnamed nearer kinsman to undertake this marriage, even at the cost of losing the chance to redeem some of Naomi's land. His plea is that it will 'damage his own inheritance' (Ruth 4:6).

From Tobias's or Tobit's point of view, the danger is real and the potential sacrifice is great. Tobias is the only son of elderly parents and the tragedy of his death would be compounded as it would bring Tobit's line to an end. It would be understandable if Tobit were to react in the same way as Judah. Of course he is not available to be consulted. On the other hand, his absence, together with his age and his continuing marriage, means that the solution found by Tamar is not open to Sarah and so the moral pressure on Tobias is all the stronger.

Sarah's tragedy is a product of a legal and social system designed to contain the tension generated by male anxieties over procreation. Levirate marriage is a way of ensuring the reproductive rights of dead men and their living widows. It brings the inextricable but repressed connection between sex and death into the open. In a society where procreation is understood as the carrying forward of the male line, legitimate sons are necessary for a man's survival, but by the same token a reminder that he himself is mortal. There is no explicit description of how the processes of conception and childbirth in ancient Israel are understood, but what clues there are point to a the common view in the ancient world that the male seed is the carrier of life and the woman provides the 'field' in which that seed is planted. Much of the legal material that deals with sex is understandable under this model. The seed itself becomes holy, and therefore can convey uncleanness. Any activity involving that seed that does not take into account its sacred purpose as the conveyor of life is forbidden.

Again, the physiology of sex is not described in detail anywhere in the Hebrew Bible, but there are almost inevitable conclusions that those who understand the process in this way will be led to. The biblical traditions are clear that life is situated somehow in the blood. Male seed is the quintessence of that life-giving fluid. Men are the carriers of this life-giving substance. This means both that they are deserving of respect and that they are open to particular sorts of danger. If seed is precious then it stands to reason that there are those who will steal it. In particular, the demonic world has an interest in this potent and life-giving substance. Legends abound of succubi, demonic female figures who need human seed to bring to material life their demonic offspring, but the other side of this is the impotent anger and envy of male demonic figures who are denied this quasi-divine power.

Sarah is Judah's nightmare, every Israelite male's nightmare, and her own nightmare. In the world of the text, de Silentio's sympathy for her as the unhappiest of women is not a romantic exaggeration, but a sober description of her state in her own eyes and the eyes of her community. That this is embedded in a comic narrative does not detract from that reality. It is not a misreading of Sarah but one borne out by the intertextual allusions of the book.

In the light of this, McCracken's charge against Kierkegaard is hard to sustain. As we have seen, both he and Cousland from their different positions end up with the paradox of a comedy that encompasses genuine suffering and grief and the problem of reading such a book. Kierkegaard's reading seems to me defensible, and, to put it cautiously, no more of a misreading than either McCracken or Cousland's.

Kierkegaard, I would claim, is not only exonerated from the accusation of an extreme misreading, but also provides us elsewhere in his works with a particularly powerful analysis of the causes of just this tension between readings of a book like Tobit. In the *Concluding Unscientific Postscript*, ascribed to the pseudonym Johannes Climacus, there is a typically telling but condensed footnote that describes the difference between the ironist and the humorist. When confronted with human expressions of pain, 'Irony would promptly be distinguishable by its not expressing the pain but teasingly replying with the aid of the abstract dialectic, which protests the excessiveness that is in the unfortunate person's cry of pain' (CUP, 448). In other words, irony shields itself from pain by placing individual misfortune into an abstract picture where it becomes easy to depict the individual as almost comically unaware of where he fits in the great scheme of things. So you lost your beloved—so do millions every day.

Climacus goes on to contrast this with the humorist who is

> inclined to think that it [sc. the cry of pain] is too little, and the humorist's indirect expression for suffering is also much stronger than any direct expression. The ironist levels everything on the basis of abstract humanity; the humorist on the basis of the abstract relationship with God, inasmuch as he does not enter into the relationship with God. It is precisely there that he parries with a jest. (CUP, 448)

In that sense, de Silentio has a humorist's relationship to Sarah. He understands the nature of her anguish, and indeed states it in extreme terms that far outrun the rather more matter-of-fact if still poignant description of her state in Tobit itself, but it is precisely on the faith in God that she represents that he 'parries with a jest' and excuses himself. Just the absurdity of the cure with fish-gall would lead the humorist to a rather patronizing smile at the desperation and concreteness of immediate suffering which puts its faith in what seems so trivial and even absurd a cure, with perhaps a touch of envy at so simple and naïve a faith.

If we wish to find a biblical parallel, we could turn to 2 Kings 5 and the reaction of the Syrian general Namaan to Elisha's prescription for his leprosy. Furious and insulted at the apparent triviality of being asked to bathe in the Jordan seven times, he stalks off and refuses the cure.

It is his servants who make the point, 'If the prophet asked you to do something difficult, would you not do it? How much more when he has only said to you "Bathe and be clean"?' (5:13). It is of a piece with the context of the Elisha cycle that there is humour and bathos in this scene; the image in 5:14 of the mighty general's flesh being restored to that of 'a little boy' points out the healing but also the humbling of the man who has such pride in his own status, riches and homeland.

For all the humorist's seriousness with which de Silentio treats Sarah's situation, there is a lighter side manifested in Kierkegaard's treatment of Tobit. The story of Sarah is set alongside other secular literary works: the tale of Agnes and the merman, Shakespeare's Richard the Third and the legend of Faust in his treatment of what he calls 'Problema III' in *Fear and Trembling*. The reason he is reading the story at all is that it offers another aestheic example in his wider investigation of the question: 'Was it ethically defensible of Abraham to conceal his purpose from Sarah, from Eleazar, from Isaac?' He does not appeal to it as Scripture at any point. Yet the point at issue is a profoundly religious one.

The relationship between the religious and the comic is most clearly set out by Kierkegaard's pseudonym Johannes Climacus:

> The religious person is one who has discovered the comic on the greatest scale and yet he does not consider the comic as the highest, because the religious is the purest pathos. But if he looks upon the comic as the highest, then his comic is *eo ipso* lower, because the comic is always based on a contradiction, and if the comic itself is the highest, it lacks the contradiction in which the comic exists and in which it makes a showing, that is why it holds true without exception that the more competently a person exists, the more he will discover the comic. (CUP, 462)

To discover the comic in a religious work such as Tobit, then, is not to trivialize it. It is the mark of a religious sensibility, and insofar as both reader and writer take seriously the religious, the comic will come to the fore in the writing. To see the comic as the point, however, is not only a misreading of its religious power, but actually reduces the comic force of the book. Taking the comic seriously means it must not be taken too seriously. McCracken and Cousland are aware of the tightrope to be walked between jest and earnest, but, I would argue, fall on either side of it; McCracken overemphasizes the jest, whereas Cousland is too earnest.

What is at issue here is a problem that Kierkegaard knew well and which he analyses as subtly as anyone; the mismatch between what is written and what is read, between utterance and reception. In his account of indirect communication, he takes as a prime example the ambiguity between jest and earnest. There is nothing intrinsic to any statement that makes it incontestably one or the other. Indeed, humour is the prime showcase of the problems of intention in language.[20] A comedian can intend to make us laugh and we can be perfectly aware of that without feeling in the least amused, while being convulsed with laughter at an unintentional blunder. Yet that response itself is not entirely voluntary: no one can guarantee to make us laugh, but we can certainly be made to laugh despite our best efforts. The response to the comic complicates the distinction between voluntary and involuntary.

That is why the comic appears in Kierkegaard's account of the three stages of life, the aesthetic, the ethical and the religious. How these stages should be interpreted and how far Kierkegaard himself was committed to this schema are much-debated questions which cannot be settled here. The point is that for Kierkegaard the comic is the transition between the ethical and the religious.

What this implies is that the comic is a way of comprehending the world, not a distinguishable element within it. This comic view should not be understood as failing to take things seriously. That particular error would be one that the aesthete might fall into. On the contrary, the comic is a step beyond the high seriousness of the ethical approach that takes the world and its woes entirely seriously, but also takes too seriously any one individual's capacity to be responsible for the world. In the ethical stage, a laudable sense of responsibility fails to be tempered by humility and risks becoming absurd itself. The humorist knows how incommensurate his own powers are in the face of the ills of the world. For Kierkegaard, the religious response means learning to rely on God's power and re-establishing one's engagement with the world in a completely new way. The humorist does not make this move as he fails to see the possibility of a new kind of earnestness that never loses the sense of absurdity but is not disempowered by it. In Kierkegaard's telling phrase, he 'closes the book and goes home.'

In this sense, the debate over whether Tobit is comic or not can be taken as a testimony to its subtlety as a communication. How we respond to Tobit says more about us as readers than it does about the intentions of its writer. Writers can write better than they know, as well as worse and they can certainly be comic without meaning to be. To rule out the comic in Tobit simply because the book has acquired scriptural status is certainly an extrinsic and restricted reading, one towards which

Cousland veers, as it would be to use the possibility of a comic reading to deny scriptural status to the book. Any book that addresses human existence is bound to contain the absurd and the painful. Whether we laugh or cry, or whether we ought to laugh or cry, are questions the text may pose us as readers. The answers, however, as Kierkegaard will never let us forget, are ours and so is the responsibility.

Notes

1. David McCracken, 'Narration and Comedy in the Book of Tobit', *Journal of Biblical Literature* 114 (1995), pp. 401–418 (401). McCracken's verdict is the more surprising in view of the fact that he is also the author of *The Scandal of the Gospels: Jesus, Story and Offense* (Oxford: Oxford University Press, 1994), a remarkable, perceptive and too little known book which draws explicitly and insightfully on Kierkegaard's hermeneutics of scandal.
2. The implications of Kierkegaard's use of pseudonyms and particularly the question of how far their opinions reflect those of Kierkegaard himself are the subject of a voluminous literature in Kierkegaard studies. I adopt the pragmatic approach of attributing quotations to the pseudonym while taking it that any opinion expressed by the pseudonym has at least occurred to Kierkegaard, even if it may not represent his settled view on the matter.
3. McCracken, 'Narration and Comedy', p. 402.
4. McCracken, 'Narration and Comedy', p. 402.
5. Graham Greene, *Collected Stories* (London: The Bodley Head and William Heinemann, 1972), pp. 110–117 (117).
6. Martin Luther, 'Preface to the Book of Tobit [1534]', in *Luther's Works. XXXV. Words and Sacraments I* (ed. and trans. E. Theodore Bachmann; Philadelphia: Muhlenberg Press, 1960), pp. 345–47 (345).
7. J.R.C. Cousland, 'Tobit: A Comedy in Error?', *Catholic Biblical Quarterly* 65 (2001), pp. 535–53.
8. Cousland, 'Tobit', p. 542.
9. Cousland, 'Tobit', p. 548.
10. McCracken, 'Narration and Comedy', p. 418.
11. To give him his due, McCracken also notes this sentence. Another group of readers who may be responding, but in a very different way, to the incongruity of the 'seven' husbands are the Sadducees in Mk 12:18-23. P.G. Bolt argues persuasively that the story of Sarah is a good candidate as a source for the case they present as a *reductio ad absurdum* of any doctrine of resurrection (P.G. Bolt, 'What Were the Sadducees Reading? An Enquiry into the Literary Background of Mark 12:18-23', *Tyndale Bulletin* 45 [1994], pp. 369–94).
12. 'Iudith videtur mihi esse tragoedia, in qua finis describitur tyrannorum, Tobias vero comoedia, quae de mulieribus loquitur; illa est exemplum politicum, his est exemplum oeconomicum.' *Dr Martin Luthers Werke Kritische Gesamtausgabe: Tischreden 1–6*, vol. 1 (Weimar: Hermann Böhlhaus Nachfolger, 1912), § 697, p. 338.

13. *For Self-Examination/Judge for Yourself!* [KW XXI] (ed.and trans. H.V. and Edna H. Hong; Princeton: Princeton University Press, 1990), pp. 7–52. For a further discussion of Kierkegaard's argument and its consequences, see 'The Apostle, the Genius and the Monkey: Reflections on Kierkegaard's "The Mirror of the Word,"' in this volume.

14. See JP, 5419, which lists the books and the associated note 556: 'Presumably related to H.N. Clausen's lectures during the academic year 1839–40'.

15. As an example, in one of the many journal entries dealing with the reasons for his rupture with Regina he writes, 'There is—and this is the good and the bad about me—something spectral about me, something which no one can endure who has to see me every day and have a real relationship with me' (JP, 6488). For a succinct account of the circumstances surrounding Kierkegaard's relationship to Regina, see the section headed 'Regina' in Walter Lowrie, *A Short Life of Kierkegaard* (Princeton: Princeton University Press, 1942), pp. 135–43, and also Kierkegaard's extended journal entry on the topic (JP, 6772).

16. Frank Zimmermann, *The Book of Tobit* (New York: Harper and Brothers, 1958), pp. 62–63.

17. It is impossible to know whether the author of Tobit was aware of legal material cognate to the rabbinic teachings, but the intertextual links between Genesis and Tobit are extensive and not limited to this chapter (see on this, George W.E. Nickelsburg, 'Tobit, Genesis and the *Odyssey*: A Complex Web of Intertextuality,' in D. R. MacDonald [ed.], *Mimesis and Intertextuality in Antiquity and Christianity* [Harrisburg, PA: Trinity Press International, 2001], pp. 41–55). In addition, one wonders if the story of Judah and Tamar may lie behind the disagreement between R. Judah and R. Simon. Under Rabbi Judah's ruling, Judah is justified in withholding his third son from Tamar, as Tamar has had the two husbands she is entitled to. This exonerates him from some of the guilt of needlessly creating the dilemma Tamar finds herself in, but it raises the problem of Judah's own commerce with Tamar and the status of the twin sons subsequently born to her who are vital in the genealogy of David. We are not told that Judah married Tamar (indeed, Gen. 38:26 states flatly that 'he did not lie with her again'), but the children are acknowledged as being Judah's sons in 1 Chron. 2:3. In that sense he takes his place as Tamar's third husband. Rabbi Simon would seem to allow for this. The fact that the two rulings sit in tension reflects the intrinsic moral ambiguity of the story and Judah's ambiguous status as husband and not-husband. It may also be that the two statements of R. Huna and R. Asha reflect a disagreement about how far the woman is ontologically culpable, so to speak. Is she the source of the fault, as R. Huna claims, intrinsically a *qatlanit* with no other option, or is she a victim herself: the innocent sufferer from an evil fortune, as R. Ashi suggests, which could have turned out differently? The difference is subtle but real. For a discussion of the legal conundrums in this area, especially in the light of prohibitions against sexual relations between father-in-law and daughter-in-law such as Lev. 20:12, see E.M. Menn, *Judah and Tamar (Genesis 38) in Ancient Jewish Exegesis* (Leiden: Brill, 1997), specifically the section on 'Levirate Law and Incest', pp. 55–64.

18. Zimmermann, *Tobit*, p. 83.

19. D. Weisberg, 'The Widow of Our Discontent: Levirate Marriage in Israel and the Bible,' *JSOT* 28 (2004), pp. 403–429.

20. A more extended and illuminating examination of these points is to be found in John Lippitt's *Humour and Irony in Kierkegaard's Thought* (Basingstoke: MacMillan, 2000), particularly in the discussion of the joke as the paradigm case of 'seeing as' on p. 111.

How Edifying Is Upbuilding? Paul and Kierkegaard in Dialogue

Kierkegaard's various series of what he called 'Upbuilding Discourses' form a significant part of his authorship and one which he took very seriously. Later readers, however, seduced by the literary and philosophical virtuosity of his pseudonymous words, have tended to neglect them, a balance which is now, happily, to some extent being redressed.[1]

In this paper, my aim is to open up questions rather than to provide answers. I want to concentrate on the title itself: *Upbuilding Discourses*. My main question is: why does Kierkegaard opt for this particular designation for this part of his authorship and what are the implications of this? I want to suggest that the root of this choice of title lies in his engagement with St Paul and that Paul is a more significant, and unsettling, presence in these works than is at first apparent—as he is, I would contend, in the authorship as a whole. In these early discourses, Paul acts as Kierkegaard's prime example of the upbuilding, but in a way that Paul might well have taken issue with.

It is surprising, even astonishing, how little work there has been on Kierkegaard's relationship to Paul, an observation also made by Lori Unger Brandt in her contribution on Paul to the *Kierkegaard Sources and Resources* volume on the New Testament.[2] Her article is easily the most comprehensive treatment of this important relationship that has been produced to date. In terms of the *Upbuilding Discourses*, the exception to this neglect is Andrew Burgess's study of the claim in *Concluding Unscientific Postscript* of a progressive approach to the humorous throughout the eighteen discourses which he tests against the shifting engagement with Paul in the discourses, but with an eye to the deployment of humour, rather than to the meaning of upbuilding.[3]

Brandt's article does not deal specifically with the notion of upbuilding, either. It also seems to me to underplay the tensions in Kierkegaard's relationship to Paul and in particular his conflicted understanding of

Paul's apostolicity and authority. How far Kierkegaard, despite his protests, allowed himself to hear the unsettling whispers of the little bird 'comparison' in relation to Paul is an intriguing and illuminating question, but one that it would be a temptation rather than a necessity to explore at this juncture. I will say, though, that there is certainly enough material for more than one doctoral thesis on this relationship, if anyone is searching for a topic, and its pertinence is increasing in these days of 'Paul among the Philosophers' and the combined Pauline and Kierkegaardian interests of Badiou, Žižek, Caputo and others.

Paul's explicit presence in *EUD* is not hard to demonstrate. Several of the discourses are based on Pauline texts and in three of them Paul appears as a character: 'Strengthening in the Inner Being', 'The Expectancy of Eternal Salvation' and, in particular, 'The Thorn in the Flesh'. This latter deals in a very direct way with Paul and upbuilding and so will be the focus of my attention in the second part of this chapter. Yet I hope that the questions this may raise have a bearing on the *Upbuilding Discourses* as a whole, even where Paul is not explicitly mentioned, through the mere fact that they are labelled 'upbuilding' discourses.

'Upbuilding' or 'Edifying Discourses' is, after all, an unusual designation for a book. For what it is worth, extensive research suggests that the expression *Opbyggelige Taler* only appears on one other occasion in the title of a work in the catalogue of the Royal Library in Copenhagen.[4] This discovery rather surprised me as I had imagined that Kierkegaard was picking up a title that might be familiar to a pious Danish readership and that would set his work within a recognizable tradition. As far as I can tell, and here is at least one of these hostages to fortune, that is not the case.

George Pattison does make the point that Bishop Mynster uses the phrase 'Opbyggelige Taler' in his 'Remarks Concerning the Art of Preaching' of 1810 to describe the nature of the contemporary sermon, though he leaves open the question of any direct influence of Mynster's text on Kierkegaard.[5] While not a coinage on Kierkegaard's part, then, his use of the phrase as a book title appears to be distinctive, and therefore already is at work to select the readership of these volumes.

This makes it all the more intriguing that he should choose this designation. As Johannes Climacus rather patronizingly comments in *Concluding Unscientific Postscript*, 'Magister Kierkegaard most likely knew what he was doing when he called the upbuilding discourses *Upbuilding Discourses*' (CUP, 272). Climacus calls attention to the abstention from any Christian dogmatic categories, but also notes the pervasiveness of humour, ultimately in the lack of the imperative of decision. Andrew Burgess, as we noted above, has discussed humour and Paul in the discourses, but we need to remember that Climacus is himself a self-confessed humorist. As such, he may be all too ready to see the jest in the earnest and may be guilty of underestimating the earnestness of a jest, so we need to check his explanation against the evidence.

Anyone familiar with the *Eighteen Upbuilding Discourses* will know that Kierkegaard prefaces each of the constituent volumes of the collection with a sort of explanation of the title, although, as is the way with his explanations, this raises at least as many questions as it answers. He explains each time that these pieces are 'discourses', not 'sermons', because the author 'does not have authority to *preach*' and that they are 'upbuilding discourses', not 'discourses for upbuilding', because 'the speaker by no means claims to be a *teacher*' [*som derfor kalden* »*Taler*« *ikke Prædikener, fordi dens Forfatter ikke har Myndighed til at prædike*; »*oppbygelige Taler*« *ikke Taler til Opbyggelse, fordi den Talende ingenlunde fordrer at være Lærer*]. What strikes me is that, although he gives an explicit, if not entirely transparent, account of why he chooses the word 'discourse' over 'sermon', turning on the issue of authority, he precisely does not explain here what we are to understand by 'upbuilding', apart from making a point of distinguishing between what is 'upbuilding' and what is '*for* upbuilding', a distinction that has proved more puzzling than illuminating to many commentators.

In order to pin this term down, then, we need to look elsewhere for explanations, both in Kierkegaard's other works and also in his sources. Where does the term 'opbyggelige' come from?

Paul and Upbuilding

The answer, I think, is that Kierkegaard would have found the word *opbyggelig* in his Danish Bible and particularly in Paul's letters. Whatever later associations the term had gathered, this is the source, and one with which Kierkegaard was intimately familiar. What follows may involve a little more New Testament exegesis than may be comfortable for most philosophers, but it certainly would not be alien to Kierkegaard. Those who have read the Danish or English versions of the SKS edition of the journals will know the time and energy Kierkegaard devoted to poring over the Greek text of Paul's letters to produce his own Latin translations and his sensitivity to the nuances of their language.

The Greek word that is translated by *ophygge* and its derivatives is οἰκοδομέω, a verb which combines the root οἰκος (house) with the root δεμω (to build) but which as a compound is a fairly standard verb in Greek used for the erection of a building. It is found in both the Septuagint and New Testament, but has a distinctive Pauline usage.[6]

What is interesting is that it turns out to be used in ways that might seem incompatible. Some enduring controversies in Pauline studies depend on the conflicting translations of this word. The ambivalence this brings to the Pauline texts is intriguing. For this point, as for a number of elements in the following discussion, I am indebted to the work of a former doctoral student of mine, Bart Woodhouse.

Paul offers an aphorism with long resonances in 1 Cor. 8:1: 'Knowledge puffs up, but love builds up.' This association, if not equation, of love and upbuilding is clearly crucial, but equally crucial is the concomitant downplaying of knowledge. Yet the same verb is used rather differently in 1 Cor. 8:10 where Paul warns that if those who are confident in their faith participate in temple meals, this may οἰκοδομέω—here generally translated 'encourage'—the weak to eat food dedicated to idols. The final use of the verb occurs in Paul's well-known summary at the end of that chapter: 'Everything is lawful, but not everything is upbuilding.' What 1 Cor. 8:10 reminds us is that even οἰκοδομέω is not always 'upbuilding', in the sense of 'edifying'; it is not good to be reinforced in an inappropriate practice.

This double edge becomes sharper in 1 Corinthians 14 where Paul is steering a typically subtle course in dealing with a potential crisis in the Corinthian community. The issue is the role of speaking in tongues. Paul has no problem with tongues in themselves, but the key verse on this topic contains two instances of the verb οἰκοδομέω: 'Those who speak in a tongue build up themselves, but those who prophesy build up the church' (1 Cor. 14:4). It is clear that there are here two kinds of upbuilding—upbuilding oneself and upbuilding the community— and also clear that in this context Paul prefers the second. It is a moot point how negatively Paul regards the upbuilding of the self and one still debated among Pauline scholars. Is it something to be deprecated as an expression of egotism, or is it a legitimate, even essential exercise, which should nevertheless be subordinated to the needs of the group? However we answer that, the issue is that 'upbuilding' is once again rendered ambivalent.

This is made clear in a reference in Galatians, where Paul uses the verb in the context of his argument against those in the Church who are seeking to reintroduce some form of obedience to law: 'If I build up again what I had torn down, then I demonstrate that I am a transgressor' (Gal. 2:18). Here upbuilding is definitely negative: it can be misdirected. 2 Corinthians then goes on to tie the idea of upbuilding explicitly to apostolic authority, when Paul writes that his authority is given for 'building up', not 'tearing down' (καθειρεσις). He picks up this contrast with a different nuance in ch. 13 of the same letter when he warns the Corinthians that he is writing severely to them so that when he comes he may not have to be severe in person in the use of his authority, 'given to build up, not tear down'. The implication is, however, that he certainly could use it in this fashion. Yet, in 1 Thess. 5:11, Paul uses the verb entirely positively as part of his culminating charge to the community: 'Therefore encourage one another and build each other up, as indeed you are doing'.

So, for Paul, upbuilding is, in Kierkegaardian terms, a 'work of love' when carried out in a community. As such, it is something that an apostle's authority is directed towards and is the duty of each member of a Christian community. However, the relationship between individual upbuilding and the communal experience is shadowed by ambiguity, and 'upbuilding' in itself can be misdirected. Building oneself up at the expense of, or in isolation from, the community is to be frowned upon. How then does this accord with Kierkegaard's use of the term?

Upbuilding in Kierkegaard's Understanding

As I indicated earlier, in the *Eighteen Upbuilding Discourses* themselves there is no developed discussion of the term 'upbuilding' and, indeed, there are surprisingly few references to the term. For that we have to turn elsewhere in the authorship, with an awareness of all the caveats as to the differences in genre, date and ascribed authorship of the texts we might compare.

It turns out that the most extended explanation of what upbuilding means is to be found in *Works of Love*, the second series. Kierkegaard begins by expounding Paul's phrase from 1 Cor. 8:1: 'love builds up'. The argument of this deliberation is that the phrase is definitional; it is love that builds up, and building up is what love does. All language about things spiritual is metaphorical, and biblical language is no exception. The metaphor of 'building up' is one such key metaphor.

Kierkegaard then goes on to explore the common usage of the word *opbyggelig* in Danish, laying stress on the element 'op' as of special significance. This is interesting, because the Greek root of the word does not contain the same directional element: here Kierkegaard is making theological points from the etymology of the Danish. His point is that *at opbyggelige* entails building from the ground up. Foundations are essential.

In equating love with upbuilding, Kierkegaard's point is both restrictive and expansive. The word upbuilding can only be used of situations where love is present, but, since love can be present anywhere and everywhere, any action or event can be upbuilding. 'A discourse about what can be upbuilding would therefore be the most interminable discourse of all discourses, inasmuch as everything can be that', he warns (WOL, 215).

The Pauline roots of this discussion are clear, and indeed the whole of *Works of Love* is a running commentary on 1 Corinthians 13, seeking to show how Paul in this chapter is specifying more precisely how love acts in order to be upbuilding. Given that focus, Paul appears by name less than might be expected. Kierkegaard does not cite him explicitly and indeed seems, probably justifiably, to assume that his readers do not need to be told that particular concepts and turns of phrase are Pauline. When he does attribute them, he often simply refers to 'Holy Scripture' rather than Paul as the source. He does mention the potential paradox that Paul seems to commend himself, but this, Kierkegaard explains, is done in love and therefore is upbuilding (cp. 2 Cor. 12:9).

This hints at the most obvious difference between Paul and Kierkegaard in this regard. Paul's concern is with the community, and indeed his letter is addressed to a group, not an individual. Kierkegaard explicitly addresses one single reader. Indeed, one might ask if the single reader, alone at home, could not run the risk of being regarded as upbuilding herself at the expense of community in Paul's terms. Is reading an upbuilding discourse in such a way more like seeking the private edification of speaking in tongues rather than aspiring to the kind of public engagement that prophecy entails?

The equation of upbuilding with love, however, cannot be made glibly and indeed does not really help us with the question of definition. If everything can be upbuilding, then what content does the term have? The key question then becomes to track down what makes the potentially upbuilding 'everything' actually upbuilding in a particular case.

Kierkegaard's answer appears both in a journal entry of 1847 and in *Christian Discourses*. In his journal, Kierkegaard equates the upbuilding with the *terrifying* [*forfærdende*]: '—*first of all* one must scrupulously try to find the *terrifying* and then scrupulously once again—then one finds the *upbuilding*. Alas, as a rule we try scrupulously in neither the first instance nor the second' (WOL, 413).[7]

Kierkegaard expands on this point in *Christian Discourses*, using his habitual medical analogy to explain at more length the place of terror in upbuilding. Upbuilding is not for the healthy, but the sick. For those who (mistakenly) think they are healthy, then, it is as terrifying as falling into the hands of a doctor who summarily treats them as sick (see CD, 96). No protests of health will avail.

In the course of this discussion, Kierkegaard explicitly offers the key to the puzzle of detecting the upbuilding: 'The terrifying is to the upbuilding what the divining rod is to the spring [*Thi det Forfærdende er i Forhold til det Opbyggelige som Ønskeqvisten i Forhold til Kildespringet*]' is the memorable phrase with which he sums this up. He could hardly be clearer. If we wish to find the upbuilding in upbuilding discourses, then they are upbuilding insofar as they are terrifying.

This may not be the first adjective we might apply to the *Eighteen Upbuilding Discourses* and the point could legitimately be made that this is a later formulation at a point when Kierkegaard's thought may have developed along these lines. Yet the terrifying is explicitly discussed in the discourse on 'Preserving One's Soul in Patience' and again the discourse 'Against Cowardliness'. In both cases, the point is made that the terrifying in itself may simply prompt the reader to flight or to denial, neither of which allow for upbuilding. The crucial element is that the reader should be aware of the danger and then stand one's ground.

To reapply Kierkegaard's medical metaphor, the diagnosis of a fatal disease may lead the patient either to denial or to refuse a cure, but that step is still essential if a cure is to be effected. Indeed, in curing addiction, accepting the terrifying realization that one is potentially fatally ill is in itself the first step to recovery. The point is the terror; one can know intellectually that one's conduct is destructive, but the turning point comes when this thought becomes terrifying. The terrifying *is* the upbuilding, Kierkegaard would answer, but only to those who are truly terrified.

This sterner note is detectable in Paul, as we have seen. Throughout 2 Corinthians, Paul interweaves his suffering, his apparent weakness and ineffectiveness in person with the distress, or indeed fear, that his letters instill, and that he at once disclaims and reinforces, all in the name of upbuilding. The following crucial quotation is effectively the culmination of the letter, as it immediately precedes his final greetings: 'This is why I write these things when I am absent, that when I come I may not have to be harsh in my use of authority—the authority that the Lord gave me for building you up, not for tearing you down' (2 Cor. 13:10).

Written at a distance, the letter serves to terrify, so that upbuilding may occur when Paul meets them face-to-face. This severity puts Kierkegaard's insistence on building from the foundations upwards in another light. In order to do this, it may first be necessary to raze a defective building to the ground; as Paul again warned, building on what is intrinsically flawed is worse than useless. Yet Kierkegaard seems to be going beyond Paul in making this the 'divining rod' or defining feature of the upbuilding, especially given the rather consolatory tone of many of the discourses.

In his defence, an immediate onslaught may not be the most productive way to terrify the reader and in any case the writer without authority cannot wave the stick of that authority at the reader in the way that the apostle can. Any connoisseur of horror literature will know that it is far more effective to begin with the familiar and the cosy and then subtly to suggest that there is something nasty in the woodshed. There is an art of seduction at work here, not entirely dissimilar from the proceedings of the Seducer in *Either/Or*. Read with an eye to the terrifying, the *Upbuilding Discourses* are a good deal less innocuous than they seem.

'The Thorn in the Flesh'

A full examination of the theme of the terrifying and its relationship to Pauline categories throughout the discourses is beyond the scope of the time allotted, so I want now to turn to one particular discourse to see what light it can shed on this. The discourse, 'The Thorn in the Flesh,' is one of the *Four Upbuilding Discourses* of 1844. Lev Shestov in his *Kierkegaard and the Existential Philosophy* calls it 'one of his most remarkable discourses, remarkable for its profundity and for its stunning power of expression.'[8] Kierkegaard begins by a reflection on the way that a biblical phrase can pass into common parlance, and thereby seemingly lose its significance. The corollary of this, though, is that the full terror of its significance can be reawakened unexpectedly, shattering the comfort of the one who attends to it. This intriguingly echoes Gershom Scholem's point in a letter on which Derrida has commented, where he warns that reviving Hebrew as the everyday language of Israel risks a volcanic explosion as the apocalyptic potential of the language is smuggled into the most mundane transactions.

One such devalued phrase is the 'thorn in the flesh', Kierkegaard argues, which in common parlance may denote a minor if persistent irritant, but which for Paul describes an 'angel' or messenger of Satan, sent to him just at the point when he has received unspeakable revelations and has been transported to the third heaven. Just as he gains the highest prize possible for a human being, he is called back to earth and afflicted. What marks Paul out as an apostle, Kierkegaard claims, is that he is able to welcome this visitation of the angel of Satan as an act of benevolence by God.

Once we have got back to Paul as the source of the phrase, Kierkegaard reminds us that we need to read the text. Here Kierkegaard satirizes the way in which scholarly and other readers have misunderstood this verse, a tendency exacerbated by the permission everyone seems to assume they have to solve what is presented as a riddle.[9] One thing we must not do, he warns, is presume to use this verse as comfort for our petty sufferings, or to imagine that sufferings are not to be welcomed. We are not to measure our own suffering, but just remember that even— or especially—the greatest warriors of faith can be laid low. The whole point is—to terrify us.

What is terrifying in the contemplation of Paul's account of the thorn in the flesh is that it is not just a matter of ordinary suffering; name your suffering, Paul had to undergo it more than anyone, states Kierkegaard, but he did not label any of these mundane sufferings, severe as they were, as his 'thorn in the flesh.' This particular suffering was intimately related to the blessing he received in being taken up in heaven.

We might explain the point here as follows. At the moment of entering this indescribable state, inescapably, the possibility of being deprived of that bliss is posited. Only the person privileged with this glimpse can truly conceive the pain of then being shut out of heaven. We might try to imagine it, but can no more imagine the pain it would mean than we can truly imagine heaven. But just that unimaginable pain fell to Paul; the assault by Satan's angel occurs in order to deny him the bliss of the 'third heaven' and recall him to earth. This is a suffering even worse than death, Kierkegaard insists, because it involves the loss of the eternal, not just the temporal, and it casts the shadow of a possibility of change in God. What a truly terrifying prospect.

Yet it is a mistake to think that this is something unique to the apostle, Kierkegaard goes on to say. There would be no point in writing about it if it were not a possibility for all Christians—both the bliss and the suffering. To be spared the suffering is not a blessing, as it would also entail being denied the bliss.[10]

What, then, is the role of Paul in all this? He is both the greatest and the least—unfit to be an apostle because of his past, but in some ways all the fitter to be an apostle because of his humility and humiliation.[11] This also helps us understand, within the *Discourses*, what constitutes the apostolic authority that the author of the *Discourses* disclaims for himself. That apostolicity is manifest in the ability to discover the work of Providence within suffering, and suffering of the highest metaphysical order.

That, too, is the function of Paul in the other two discourses in which he appears. In 'Strengthening in the Inner Being', Paul's apostolicity is shown in the fact that, in his correspondence with the Ephesians, what concerns him over his imprisonment and sufferings in Rome is that they will dismay the Ephesians and cause them to lose heart. Indeed, Kierkegaard suggests that he may have suspected that he had become a cause of offence to them. In response, he urges them to understand that his sufferings are *their* glory, something that Kierkegaard describes as a miracle. It would be admirable enough for him to see his sufferings as his own glory, but he goes a startling step further.

Similarly, in 'The Expectancy of Eternal Salvation', Paul's ability to turn suffering to blessing shows his apostolic gift. Kierkegaard quotes Paul's words, 'Our hardship, which is brief and light, procures for us an eternal weight of glory beyond all measure' and conjectures that the reader who knew nothing of Paul would suppose that he had led a relatively quiet life, not without suffering, perhaps, but never put to the extreme test. The reality, Kierkegaard stresses, was quite the opposite and sober reflection would conclude, 'A life like that is certainly an everlasting affliction and not to be endured—an everlasting affliction' (EUD, 262). Yet again, Paul triumphs over this. Experience, Kierkegaard marvels, 'is scarcely capable of lifting the apostolic sufferings to place them on the scale, but Paul understands that heaven's salvation has an eternal overweight' (EUD, 263).

Paul as apostle is terrifying, because he sets a standard of suffering that makes the suffering of his readers, and Kierkegaard's readers, pale in comparison, yet by the same token he is upbuilding, because he shows that such suffering can be turned to blessing if it is regarded as blessing. What is striking, however, is that it is Paul who is the example, not Christ. There is no mention of Christ's sufferings, of the persecution, mistreatment and crucifixion, and no summons to imitate Christ in these discourses.

Kierkegaard versus Paul

I hope, then, that we have seen Paul's significance for the concept of upbuilding and for the strategy of the *Upbuilding Discourses*. In the final paragraphs of this essay, however, I want to say something about Paul as a problem for Kierkegaard, and thus for the *Upbuilding Discourses* as texts, a problem that hinges on the vexed question of authority which Kierkegaard makes such a feature of in the preface. There is, as I suggested earlier, matter enough here for subsequent research, so all I can do here is raise issues that may be pursued in further work.

Compare these two journal entries. In the first, Kierkegaard reacts to the doubts that historical criticism was casting on the authenticity of certain traditionally Pauline letters:

> Suppose that doubt hit upon and come up with a kind of probability that Paul's letters were not by Paul and that Paul never lived at all—what then? Well, scholarly orthodoxy might give up hope. The believer might simply turn to God in prayer, saying: How can all this hang together? I cannot cope with all this scholarship, but I stick to Paul's teaching and you, my God, will not allow me to live in error, whatever the critics prove about Paul's existence. I take what I read here in Paul and this I refer to you, O God and then you will keep me from being led into error through my reading. (JP, 214)

Contrast this unquestioning reliance on Paul's authority, albeit that the authority is in the end God's, with this particularly unwieldy sentence—the syntax may itself be a significant symptom of the conflict here—from a late journal entry:

> And so it is my observation (which is so extremely necessary, particularly in Protestantism, because all Christendom's knavish tricks are connected with a continued effort, under the name of progress, of getting rid of the master and taking one's stand with the disciple, and then taking advantage of that fact that the apostle, who personally did not compromise, gave in a little and while perfecting Christianity, threw Christianity away completely [!], turning it upside down, getting it to be the opposite of what it is in the Christian proclamation)—my observation that the apostle's proclamation in the quoted examples [on marriage and the drinking of wine] does not have the passion of the unconditioned, as the master's did. (JP, 3213)

The accusation that Paul 'threw Christianity away completely' is, to say the least, surprising, especially when Kierkegaard prefaces this passage with the disclaimer, 'No one, unless he deliberately wants to, can misunderstand me, as if I did not show the apostle the honour due him.'

Elsewhere, Kierkegaard castigates Luther for making Paul a corrective to Christ and failing to see that Paul represents a reduction rather than an advance in Christian teaching. Kierkegaard, and here his thought owes much to his pietistic heritage, sees Paul as representing an accommodation with human sinfulness in the face of the absolute ethical demands of the gospel, replacing the idea of Christ as the prototype, the one to be imitated, with Christ the redeemer, who exonerates us from the effort of imitation.

Yet, as we have seen, in the *Upbuilding Discourses* Kierkegaard does precisely the same. It is Paul's sufferings and Paul's fortitude that are held up to us. Quite deliberately, Kierkegaard in these discourses refrains from any discussion of Jesus' sufferings, precisely because the reader cannot aspire to the kind of identification with Christ that is possible with Paul. Paul remains within the bounds of the possible, humanly speaking, whereas Christ brings the absolute paradox to the fore.

And yet Paul has apostolic authority. Who, then, is Kierkegaard to presume to criticize him and on what grounds? Kierkegaard's writings on this topic show not only in content but also in their convoluted style that he is aware of and made uncomfortable by the possible implications of this line of argument. His disclaimers of any apostolic authority of his own are so often repeated that the claim begins to register. Someone who constantly protests, 'But, hey, I'm really just an ordinary guy like the rest of you,' invites the response, 'Whoever thought you weren't?' At the same time, as is clear from the first entry above, he is the one who opposes external tests for revelation or apostolicity. If we were so foolish as to acclaim Kierkegaard as an apostle, how could he disprove it? By the argument of the first quotation cited above, if the sincere believer decides that a piece of writing is apostolic, even flying in the face of historical research, providence will preserve him from error. In a journal entry, Kierkegaard comes close to acknowledging the ambiguity of his position: 'I am able to provide a point from which the qualifications of an apostle may in some measure be scrutinized. But what disarray if I myself were to cause the confusion' (JP, 6532).

Kierkegaard could, if he chose, this entry implies, confuse the whole category of the apostolic, but restrains himself. For Kierkegaard, Paul's tolerance of human weakness and embrace of those who have not fully committed themselves to the suffering of Christianity weakens the community as the Church runs the risk of simply becoming another herd because its members are not yet able to build the bonds of love. What builds up the community may fatally compromise the individual.

For Paul, Kierkegaard here may be underestimating the role of grace and the importance of the Church as a community that builds its members up into the body of Christ, rather than expecting each of them to be an imitator of Christ. A preoccupation with one's own upbuilding may damage the community and ultimately be detrimental to one's own growth as a Christian disciple. Paul, Kierkegaard's paradigm of upbuilding, also unsettles his account of what the upbuilding may be.

Another way of putting this may be as simple as the fact that Paul writes out of the paradoxical conviction that, unworthy as he manifestly is, he is an apostle of Jesus, called while a sinner and indeed an active enemy of the Church to serve as one of the elect of God. Paul never asks or discusses whether he is a Christian; for him to live is Christ. Kierkegaard, even in his latest attacks on the Church, writes as one who lays no claim to being a Christian but who is obsessed with knowing what a Christian might be. He has a different consciousness of his own unworthiness to lay claim to that term, whereas Paul, to his own astonishment, is unable to deny that Christ is the basis of his identity. What builds one up, may knock another down; not all upbuilding is edifying.

As a final word, it is always a sobering thought to consider what Kierkegaard would have made of you, my reader, and, even more, me as author, spending our time and mental energy in poring over the minutiae of the antecedents, structure, genesis, coherence and influence of his *Upbuilding Discourses*. In the parable which prefaces Part One of *Upbuilding Discourses in Various Spirits*, he writes of a woman who devoted all her skill to embroidering an altarcloth. He imagines her distress if the details of her needlework became the focus of attention, distracting the worshippers from their devotions (UD, 5–6). The only excuse we can offer to him, I suspect, is such reading becomes in itself an occasion for upbuilding: not the upbuilding of scholarly reputations and of personal intellectual and spiritual prejudices, but of mutual upbuilding in engagement with the deep question that Kierkegaard is pointing us to.

One mark of such upbuilding, we have learned, will be the terrifying. What is it that would terrify us the most, individually and collectively, as his readers? What would really frighten us? Is it worth taking some time, individually and collectively, to ponder that question? Might that be the point at which, individually and collectively, we have most to gain? It may not be the usual thing to wish one's reader, although such things are the price of engaging with Kierkegaard, but my concluding hope for us both is that, in our reading of his works, we have a terrible time.

Notes

1. On this, see particularly George Pattison, *Kierkegaard's Upbuilding Discourses: Philosophy, Literature and Theology* (London: Routledge, 2002).

2. Lori Unger Brandt, 'Paul as Herald of Grace and Paradigm of Christian Living', *KR:SRR* 2, pp. 189–205.

3. Andrew J. Burgess, 'The Apostle Paul in the Strategic Humor of Kierkegaard's 1843–4 Upbuilding Discourses', *Proceedings of the Kierkegaard Round Table Session in WCP and the One-day Kierkegaard Conference in Seoul, Korea* (Seoul: Korea Kierkegaard Academy: Institute of Philosophy, Seoul National University, 2008), pp. 88–98.

4. The work in question is *Tresindstyve opbyggelige Taler over Johannes eller retter Jesu Christi Aabenbaring*, Thomas Balle's Danish translation, dating from 1765, of Johann Albrecht Bengel's *Sechzig erbauliche Reden über die Offenbarung Johannis oder vielmehr Jesu Christi* (Stuttgart: Johann Christoph Erhardt, 1747). A copy of the German original was in Kierkegaard's library.

5. See George Pattison 'The Art of Upbuilding', in Robert L. Perkins (ed.), *International Kierkegaard Commentary. V. Eighteen Upbuilding Discourses* (Macon: Mercer University Press, 2003), pp. 77–89 (85, 78).

6. In the Gospels it is used exclusively in its literal sense, for instance in the parable of the man who built houses on sand and rock. It is only in Acts and Paul's letters, and once in 1 Peter, that it is used metaphorically. In Acts it appears in this way twice. The first time is in a summary verse in ch. 9 (9:31) to report that the Church throughout Judaea, Galilee and Samaria was being 'built up', living in peace and increasing in numbers. The second time is in a speech given by Paul (and that is noteworthy) to the elders of Ephesus when he tells them that the message of God's grace is able to 'build them up' (20:32). This reinforces the association between Paul and this term. It is in Paul's letters, particularly in 1 Corinthians, that the word takes on metaphorical significance.

7. It is notable that the Hongs' translation of this entry in the notes to WOL uses 'terrifying' for *forfærdende*, whereas JP uses 'dismaying', very possibly echoing the use of the latter word in Lowrie's translation of *Christian Discourses*, 102. The context seems to justify the strongest possible translation, however, and the Hongs' second thoughts are carried through to their own translation of *Christian Discourses*.

8. Lev Shestov, *Kierkegaard and the Existential Philosophy* (trans. Elinor Hewitt; Athens: Ohio University Press, 1969), p. 45.

9. As an example, and perhaps also influential on Kierkegaard, Carl Emil Scharling, the New Testament professor with whom Kierkegaard studied this text at university, writes as follows in his crib book for his students entitled *Epistolam Pauli ad Corinthios Posteriorem annotationibus in usum Juvenum theologiae studiosorum* (Copenhagen: C.A. Reitzel, 1840): 'De natura et ratione illius σκόλοπος interpretes diversissimas proposuerunt conjecturas: Nonnulli de adversariis vel de adversario certo quodam—alii de morbo quodam vel infirmitate corporis—alii de libidinibus sensualitatis vel de gravibus et continuis animi tentationibus etc cogitarunt. At nullum certum exstat criterium, unde accuratior cognition hujus rei peti possit' (102) [As to

the nature and reason for this σκόλοπος, interpreters have proposed diverse conjectures: some think of enemies or one particular enemy—others of some sickness or bodily weakness—others of sensual desires or grave and continual temptations of the soul. But there is no certain criterion by which a more accurate understanding of this matter could be found (my translation)].

10. Kierkegaard's own hypothesis as to what constituted the thorn in the flesh is that Paul is scarred by the memory of having kicked against the pricks, of his persecution of Christians: a 'recollection that festers in the flesh like a thorn' (EUD, 340). Even when Paul preaches Christ crucified, that recalls to him the shouts of the Jews for Christ to be crucified. And where was Paul at the crucifixion? That we do not know, but the implication Kierkegaard leaves hanging is that he would have been one of those shouting in the crowd. What we do know is that Paul was present when Stephen was stoned, so that every time he called people to the Way it reminded him of the people of the Way whom he had had killed.

All this the apostle is able to regard as a benefit from God, however. He is recalled to his past, but the unimaginable thing is that God can forget the past. Paul's strength is that he regards Satan's angel as God's emissary—and Kierkegaard permits himself a humorous empathy with the discomfiture of the devil in this situation. Nevertheless, the past can recur as the future. In time, there is no security. We cannot run past time. Enigmatically, Kierkegaard then speaks to the one who knows that the discourse is about, who knows fulfillment—except for the one word lacking. As this is an upbuilding discourse, is that word Christ? The one who does not know is then reminded that the problem is impatience, which makes magnifies the smallest gap and delay in to an abyss which allows the terrifying recrudescence of the past with all the borrowed strength of the future.

11. It is also intriguing that here we have a response of Paul to something that is inexpressible and somehow related to the problem of tongues in the Corinthian Church. Just as the one who speaks in tongues does not edify the congregation, so the man who speaks of the unspeakable glories of heaven cannot build up his companions. What he can best do is awaken them to their own incapacity to conceive the heavens and the infinite distance that separates them from heaven. The inexpressible, the upbuilding and the terrifying go together here.

FORGIVING THE UNFORGIVABLE: KIERKEGAARD, DERRIDA AND THE SCANDAL OF FORGIVENESS

Two months to the day before Kierkegaard's death on 11 November, 1855, a terrifying article of his on 'Divine Justice' appeared in *The Moment* no. 8. In it, Kierkegaard addresses the problem of the apparent triumph of tyranny, injustice and evil in the world. How is this to be reconciled with the justice of God? Kierkegaard's argument is that divine justice appears precisely in allowing great sinners to go unpunished within time, so that their crimes can fully mature:

> Yes, tremble that there are crimes that need all of time in order to come into existence, that occasionally, perhaps out of consideration for the rest of us, cannot be punished in this life. Tremble, but do not accuse God's justice; no, tremble at the thought of this (how frightful it sounds when said this way!) dreadful advantage of only being punished in eternity... But the criminal whose distinction was that he cannot be punished in this world consequently cannot be saved; by not being punished within time, he cannot be saved for eternity. (*MLW* 306)

This echo of a theology to be found in the psalms[1] is highly disturbing for our modern sensibilities, conscious as we are of the hideous record of genocide and crimes against humanity of the twentieth century. It combines two possibilities of outrage. The first is the notion that God consciously permits these criminals to commit monstrous crimes against innocent victims. Despite Kierkegaard's assurances, this seems like gross injustice. The second, perhaps contradictory, one is that this formulation seems to leave no space for forgiveness either by God or the victims.

In both respects this passage points to the problematic concept of the unforgivable. Can the perpetrators of crimes on this scale be forgiven for them? If not, does the existence of unforgivable acts mean there is a limit to God's forgiveness and, if so, what are the consequences for his love? More problematic still, this may lead to the further question: Is it forgivable that God has permitted these acts? In this essay, I want to examine the place of the category of the unforgivable in Kierkegaard's work and how his insights relate to current debates on the issue.

One author who has written influentially on the question of the unforgivable in relation to the Holocaust and other crimes against humanity is Vladimir Jankélévitch.[2] For Jankélévitch, as for many other writers,[3] the word 'unforgivable' is entirely appropriate for these crimes because of their scale and the fact that those most directly affected are by their death in no position to offer forgiveness. Forgiveness, he argues, cannot be granted unless asked for; forgiveness is not 'for swine'; it depends on the residual humanity and some identification with the victim by the guilty party. With reference to the *Shoah*, Jankélévitch argues further that no finite penalty can meet such a crime and, following Hannah Arendt,[4] asserts that human beings cannot forgive what they cannot punish. For this reason, too, these crimes are unforgivable. Indeed, Jankélévitch insists that it is a duty *not* to forgive in the name of the dead. To do so may lead to the unforgivable crime and its victims being forgotten.

Jankélévitch's work finds a respectful but critical response in Jacques Derrida's essay 'Le Siècle et le Pardon.'[5] Derrida both acknowledges and directly counters Jankélévitch's position. Such crimes are indeed unforgivable, but this does not rule out forgiveness. On the contrary, Derrida holds to the paradoxical assertion that 'forgiveness forgives only the unforgivable.'[6] To forgive what is forgivable, after all, is tautologous. The very act of deciding that a given situation is forgivable is tantamount to forgiving it. It is only when faced with the unforgivable that the work of forgiveness becomes appropriate or required. Indeed, it is the existence of the unforgivable which is the condition for forgiveness: 'One neither can nor should forgive, there is no forgiveness, if there is any such thing, except where there is the unforgivable.'[7]

Derrida takes impossibility as the condition of pure forgiveness: 'Pure, unconditional forgiveness, in order to have its proper meaning, should have no "meaning", no finality, no intelligibility, even. It is a folly of the impossible [*une folie de l'impossible*]. It would be necessary to follow without weakening the consequence of this paradox or aporia.'[8] Or, as he puts it earlier in the same essay, 'Forgiveness ought to proclaim itself as the impossible itself.'[9] But the impossibility of forgiveness, humanly speaking, does not mean that it never happens. On the contrary, 'it is perhaps the only thing that happens, which surprises, like a revolution, the ordinary course of history, politics and law.'[10] Forgiveness is the exceptional interruption.

This paradoxical formulation, that forgiveness can only forgive the unforgivable, has a Kierkegaardian ring to it and the argument in this essay will be that Derrida's account has striking similarities to elements of Kierkegaard's understanding of the matter, even though the quotation above might suggest that Kierkegaard has more affinities with Jankélévitch.

It is at the point of the possible impossibility that Derrida's account coincides with a fundamental category in Kierkegaard's thought. 'What is decisive,' according to Anti-Climacus in *The Sickness unto Death*, 'is that with God everything is possible' (SUD, 38), echoing the words of Jesus in Mt. 19:26.[11] If there is one phrase that is pivotal to Kierkegaard, it is this statement, that 'with God everything is possible'—not merely that possible things are possible. This is the essence of the scandal, which is the characteristic of the incarnation, the impossible meeting point of the absolutely other categories of God and humanity, the scandal which provokes a response either of offence or faith. Only by encountering the impossible is the true scope of divine possibility opened up.[12]

Kierkegaard's account is rooted in his profound engagement with Christian theology, as is to be expected. For his part, Derrida also is highly conscious of the fundamental importance of the biblical tradition to any contemporary discussion of forgiveness and indeed discusses the problems of importing this 'Abrahamic' category into international politics in relation to non-Christian cultures. This makes it all the more interesting that he takes such a high view of forgiveness.

Derrida characterizes the Christian tradition as one that has at its heart a tension between conditional and unconditional forgiveness. Forgiveness is sometimes presented as a free and unconditional act, offered to guilty and innocent alike, which takes no account of repentance. At other times, repentance is presented as the necessary condition for forgiveness. Derrida does not try to reconcile these positions. Instead, he insists that the importance of the tradition lies in the fact that it holds these two together as 'irreconcilable and indissociable' strands.[13] Both the irreconcilability and the indissociability have to be taken on board.

Forgiveness in the Gospels

These assertions about the paradoxicality of the Christian tradition can certainly be verified from the New Testament. On the one hand, we find a demand for unconditional forgiveness of one's enemies: 'Love your enemies, do good to those who hate you. Bless those who curse you, pray for those who abuse you' (Lk. 6:27). No repentance is here implied. On the other hand, we find passages which require repentance as the condition for forgiveness. Take for instance, Lk. 17:3: 'Take heed to yourselves: if your brother sins, rebuke him, and if he repents, forgive him, and if he sins against you seven times in the day, and turns to you seven times, and says "I repent," you must forgive him.' Here the forgiveness, although freely offered, is clearly conditional on repentance.

Furthermore, Mt. 6:1-15 makes it absolutely clear that one's own forgiveness is conditional not just on repentance, but on one's willingness to forgive others: 'For if you forgive men their trespasses, your heavenly Father also will forgive you; but if you do not forgive men their trespasses, neither will your Father forgive your trespasses.' Luke 6:37 puts the point even more succinctly: 'Forgive and you will be forgiven.' Here there is a reciprocity in forgiveness, not just a conditionality, which seems to sit uneasily with the proclamation of free forgiveness.

These paradoxes of forgiveness in the New Testament go further than Derrida takes us. It is in the New Testament, after all, where the disturbing concept of the unforgivable sin is first found. For all its talk of sin, punishment and the withholding of divine forgiveness, the Old Testament knows no category of sin that is in principle unforgivable. Jesus sets out the parameters of the unforgivable sin in Mt. 12:31-32 (see also Mk 3:29; Lk. 12:10): 'Therefore I tell you, every sin and blasphemy will be forgiven men, but the blasphemy against the Spirit will not be forgiven. And whoever says a word against the Son of man will be forgiven; but whoever speaks against the Holy Spirit will not be forgiven, either in this age or in the age to come.'

The exact nature of the sin against the Holy Spirit has been anxiously debated by those who fear they may have unwittingly fallen into it, as if by avoiding that one sin, they assure themselves of divine forgiveness. In *Sickness unto Death*, Anti-Climacus defines it in terms of the willful opposition to the truth of Christianity and the person of the God–man. In this, he seems to contradict the biblical teaching, which is clear that the sin which is unforgivable is speaking against the Holy Spirit. Matthew and Luke explicitly state that 'whoever says a word against the Son of Man will be forgiven.' This conflation is typical of Kierkegaard's tendency to elevate Christ at the expense, so to speak, of the spirit. The unforgivable sin thus becomes related to the denial of the truth of Christianity. This runs the risk of being interpreted as a matter of doctrinal assent, and is perhaps a distraction from a more fruitful definition to be found elsewhere in his work.

Kierkegaard recounts an anecdote about a person who had become convinced that he had sinned against the Holy Spirit and that for him there was no mercy. Kierkegaard suggests, 'Perhaps the sin against the Holy Spirit was rather the pride with which he would not forgive himself. There is also a severity in condemning oneself and not wanting to hear about grace which is nothing but sin' (JP, 4029). The unforgivable sin, then, is not to forgive oneself, or not to acknowledge that one is forgiven: the two come to the same thing in Kierkegaard's eyes. In *Sickness unto Death* there is an entire section entitled, 'The Sin of Despairing of the Forgiveness of Sins (Offense)' [Part Two B.B] (SD, 113–24). In the final paragraph of the section, we find the matter expressed as follows: '…despair of the forgiveness of sins is offense. And offense is the intensification of sin' (SD, 124). In the conclusion of the book which immediately follows, Anti-Climacus characterizes the sin against the Holy Spirit as 'the positive form of being offended' (SD, 125).

The offence of forgiveness is brought to a head when the same Jesus who warns of the unforgivable sin speaks the following words from the cross, as Luke records them: 'Father, forgive them: they know not what they do' (Lk. 23:34). On the understanding of forgiveness put forward by Jankélévitch, for instance, this speech contains not one, but several absurdities. Jesus, who speaks the words, does not directly mention himself or his situation, nor is the speech addressed to the ones who need forgiveness, those who are crucifying him. Instead he evokes the Father to forgive on his behalf. To put this another way, what Jesus does *not* say is 'I forgive you.' In fact, he never once speaks these words in the Gospels. 'Your sins are forgiven' is what he customarily says. Forgiveness here is referred to God as the third party. The New Testament's model is consistently contrary to the common view that forgiveness has to be a transaction between one who asks forgiveness and the offended party. What sense does it make to invite another to forgive?

Furthermore, the speech itself indicates that those crucifying him would not understand or see its application because 'they know not what they do.' This forgiveness is in no sense a response to repentance. Not only are the crucifiers unrepentant, they are not even aware what it is they have to repent for. Nor do they cease doing what they are doing. As we have seen, Jankélévitch takes it as read that those who do not seek forgiveness cannot be forgiven, and the Gospels themselves speak of the need for repentance.

Kierkegaard and Forgiveness

It is on these paradoxes that Kierkegaard's account of forgiveness stakes its validity. The sin which defines sin is to lack faith in divine possibility, but as Anti-Climacus is so careful to explain, possibility without necessity is no possibility at all. The notion of the unforgivable sin, which would seem to justify despair of forgiveness, marks the necessity which faith must acknowledge while still maintaining that 'with God all things are possible.' The denial of possibility is the unforgivable. All sin is sin against the Holy Spirit, because all sin is a failure, in one way or another, to live in the light of the incomprehensible fact that 'with God all things are possible.'

Meditating on Paul's hymn to love in 1 Corinthians 13, Paul Ricoeur reflects that 'If love excuses everything, then that everything includes the unforgivable.'[14] The paradox is that it is the Holy Spirit which is the bearer of possibility. This includes the impossible possibility that the unforgivable sin against the Holy Spirit can be and is forgiven. But if this is true, who can forgive except God? Derrida himself raises, but then explicitly leaves open, the question of whether pardoning a person, as opposed to an act, needs what he calls 'some absolute witness, God, for example, that God who required that one forgives the other in order to deserve to be forgiven in one's turn.'[15]

We may turn here to the account of forgiveness implied by the rubric that dominates the end of *Works of Love*, what Kierkegaard calls the 'divine like for like'. This is not a discussion of the *lex talionis*, equal retribution, but of a 'vertical' conception of 'like for like' deriving from Christ's words to the centurion from Capernaum: 'Be it done to you as you have believed' (Mt. 8:13). Christianity is a God-relationship and relations to others are relations in, through and under God. Indeed, Kierkegaard goes so far as to say,

> God is actually himself this pure like for like, the pure rendition of how you yourself are. If there is anger in you, then God is anger in you; if there is leniency and mercifulness in you, then God is merciful in you... God's relation to a human being is at every moment to infinitize what that human being is at every moment. (WL, 384)

But if every human being is a sinner, this locks us into an inescapable reciprocity of being visited with our sins. Yet, what is impossible for humanity is possible for God who can act as 'absolute witness' in Derrida's phrase.

For the unrepentant sinner, forgiveness is subjectively not seen as possible, because there is no awareness of sin. Either the sinner considers her conduct irreproachable, or else the sinner takes the view that the sin is forgivable, and therefore, feels no need to be forgiven. Indeed, if forgiveness is withheld in these conditions, the sinner is the one who will feel aggrieved. It is only once that one is convinced of one's sin that forgiveness arises as a need, and then it seems to be an impossibility. The mediation between divine love and the sense of forgiveness is the category of the unforgivable. On this view, it is the fact that the sin against the Holy Spirit is unforgivable that makes Jesus' words of forgiveness during the crucifixion possible. Far from being a contradiction, the two are paradoxically bound together. Only because there is unforgivable sin is forgiveness meaningful, as only a God who does not forgive can forgive. Only in being forgiven can we discover our need to be forgiven. Only when we become convinced of our unforgivableness can we understand why we need to be forgiven.

Forgiving and Forgetting

But what of the consequences of this forgiveness? How does Kierkegaard deal with the charge raised by Jankélévitch and others that forgiveness leads to the unacceptable possibility of forgetting the crime and its victims? Kierkegaard's most nuanced reading of the relationship between forgiveness and forgetting comes in the section towards the end of *Works of Love* on 'Love Hides a Multitude of Sins'. Forgiveness is not the same as ignorance, which is blind to sin. Rather, 'forgiveness removes what cannot be denied to be sin' (WL, 294). Forgiveness here is like faith, in that it concerns the unseen in the seen. However, it is the opposite motion from faith. Faith holds to the unseen in the seen. The faithful and unfaithful may experience the same event, but the faithful testify to the presence and activity of the unseen, of the eternal, in the momentary event. By a reverse analogy, forgiveness does not cease to see the sinful act, but believes that forgiveness takes sin away:

> The one who loves sees the sin he forgives, but he believes that forgiveness takes it away. This cannot be seen, whereas the sin can indeed be seen; on the other hand, if the sin did not exist to be seen, it could not be forgiven either... Blessed is the believer, he believes what he cannot see; blessed is the one who loves, he believes away that which he indeed can see! (WL, 295)

Far from the evil being negated, it never ceases to be the object of attention. The one who forgives does not blind himself to sin but in fact sees more than the unforgiving: he sees not just the sin but the sin *and* the forgiveness it entails.

Does this then give us as human beings the license to act as if sin had never occurred? Kierkegaard's answer is a clear 'No.' From the human standpoint, as opposed to the divine, Kierkegaard is clear that forgetting is itself sin. In *The Gospel of Sufferings* II [But How Can the Burden Be Light If the Suffering Is Heavy?] (UD, 230–47) Kierkegaard makes it absolutely clear that forgiveness does *not* involve forgetting that sin has occurred. In this discourse, Kierkegaard explicitly condemns the desire for all to be forgiven and forgotten as the characteristic of the 'light-minded' person. However, it is no solution to go to the other extreme as does the 'heavy-minded' person who cannot let go of his sin and so cannot believe.

For the believer, Kierkegaard explains, everything is *not* forgotten, but it *is* forgotten in forgiveness. In a typically paradoxical sentence, Kierkegaard writes, 'Every time you recollect the forgiveness, it [sin] is forgotten; but when you forget the forgiveness, it is not forgotten, and then the forgiveness is wasted' (UD, 247). The believer must not, indeed cannot, forget he is forgiven, because it is out of forgiveness that his new life springs. 'A man rests in the forgiveness of sins when the thought of God does not remind him of the sin but that it is forgiven, when the past is not a memory of how much he trespassed but of how much he has been forgiven' (JP, 1209).

Does that mean that crimes like the Holocaust can be forgotten? On the contrary, they have to be remembered all the more as a point where the divine 'nevertheless' impinges on human history. Does it mean that reparations to those who suffered in the Holocaust and punishment of those who perpetrated it can be set aside? By no means: these are matters of love to our neighbours. What it does mean is that we cannot seek to seal the Holocaust off as a unique and inhuman invasion into history. On the contrary, it is a uniquely potent manifestation of the most universal aspect of the human condition: the sin against the Holy Ghost which is the human life closed to God's gift of possibility.

Kierkegaard would be misrepresented if he were put forward as an advocate of the idea that forgiveness obliterates the past and undoes evil. Indeed, his position may give evil a stronger metaphysical basis than do, for instance, Hegel or Schelling, who follow Augustine's notion of evil as privative and therefore ultimately unreal in the face of the good. Though it is difficult to be specific here on Kierkegaard's view on the metaphysics of evil, there is evidence, at least in Vigilius Haufniensis's *The Concept of Anxiety*, of a rather different attitude which resonates with his different understanding of forgiveness:

> If (*sit venia verbo* [pardon the expression]) freedom remains in the good, then it knows nothing at all of evil. In this sense one may say about God (if anyone misunderstands this, it is not my fault) that he knows nothing of evil. By this I by no means say that evil is merely the negative, *das Aufzuhebende* [that which is to be annulled]; on the contrary, that God knows nothing of evil, that he neither can nor will know of it, is the absolute punishment of evil. In this sense the preposition *apo* [away from] is used in the New Testament to signify removal from God, or if I dare put it this way, God's ignoring of evil. If one conceives of God finitely, it is indeed convenient for evil if God ignores it, but because God is the infinite, his ignoring is the living annihilation, for evil cannot dispense with God, even merely in order to be evil (CA, 112).

Kierkegaard explains that when God forgives, sin, in a startling phrase, is 'hidden behind God's back.' It does not cease to have existed, but it ceases to be regarded. In this special sense, God 'forgets' sin, and here forgetting has the same structure as hope, but in reverse. Whereas hope gives being to what does not (yet) exist, forgetting removes being from what nevertheless exists. What is forgotten is not the same as that which never existed, or indeed as that which has ceased to exist. It is that which is disregarded in love.

It is precisely because evil partakes in some sense of existence that God can subject it to 'living annihilation', rather than its simply vanishing when ignored. The 'forgotten' evil is not rendered non-existent by God's forgetting. Far then from being the champion of forgiveness as a forgetting of evil actions which renders them unreal, Kierkegaard's account depends on a stronger sense of evil's reality than the Augustinian tradition seems to countenance. It depends on the necessity of the remembrance of past evil, precisely in so far as it has become the occasion for divine forgiveness.

One corollary of this is that forgiveness for Kierkegaard does not mean that the ill consequences of one's sin will be eradicated, but they will cease to be seen as punishment. They will become suffering that can be borne with Christian fortitude as they are not inflicted by God on one estranged from God, but they can be offered to God who will bear them with and for us as he would any other suffering (see here JP, 1222).

This provides a way to understand the rather grim quotation with which we began. The fate of the one who persists in sin is precisely—to be ignored. Just as God 'makes nothing' of evil by putting it behind his back, so he 'makes nothing' of the human being who chooses to make nothing of God. In the article in *The Moment* 8 entitled 'Tremble— Because in One Sense It Is So Infinitely Easy to Fool God', Kierkegaard puts it this way: 'For an omnipotent being it must, if one may speak this way, be an immense effort to be obliged to look after a nothing, to be aware of a nothing, to be concerned about a nothing. And then this nothing wants to fool him—O man, shudder, it is done so infinitely easily' (MLW, 307).

But God's greatest punishment for us is to ignore us—just as he makes nothing of evil. A journal entry reiterates this point:

> It is much easier to fool God than my neighbour. Why? Because my neighbour is insignificant enough to keep a sharp eye on me. But, but, but that God is easiest to fool means: God punishes—how genuinely majestic—by ignoring… And therefore—what dreadful punishment!— worldly life goes on splendidly for us and humankind makes great strides in physical discoveries etc.—but God ignores us. (JP, 2563)

The human being is only sustained in existence by God's loving forbearance which restrains his omnipotence. The human being who in the end sins by refusing to believe in the forgiveness of sins is not simply 'made nothing of', he *is* nothing. As such, there can be no salvation for him, for how can 'nothing' be saved? Paradoxically, as ever, in Kierkegaard's understanding it is only by realizing our dependence on God that we can receive the gift of being an individual in the face of God.

Though Kierkegaard does not make this explicit, there is a divine like for like implied in the fate of those who are not punished in time. The transition out of time for all human beings is death—for those who refuse God, physical death is inevitable. For the Christian, *The Sickness unto Death* argues, physical death itself is not a punishment, but a task we can take up with and in Christ. Far more to be feared is the 'sickness unto death', the despair that cannot die. Those, however, who have lived a life where they live by the terror of inflicting physical pain and death on others, gain the like for like. They have lived by the credo that death is the worst that can happen and have used that threat mercilessly against their fellow citizens. In death, they meet that punishment and become the victims themselves of death as terror. Having ignored God, they are ignored by God.

The Scandal of Forgiveness

This offers no easy answer to the problem of sin, of human suffering and divine responsibility. By all human standards, scandal is the proper reaction to Jesus' claim to forgive sin, as Anti-Climacus points out in *The Sickness unto Death*:

> The Jews had a perfect right to be offended by Christ because he claimed to forgive sins. It takes a singularly high degree of spiritlessness (that is, as ordinarily found in Christendom), if one is not a believer (and if one is a believer, one does believe that Christ was God), not to be offended at someone's claim to forgive sins. And in the next place, it takes an equally singular spiritlessness not to be offended at the very idea that sin can be forgiven. For the human understanding, this is most impossible—but I do not therefore laud as genius the inability to believe it, for it *shall* be believed. (SUD, 116)

Jankélévitch is a modern witness to this justifiable sense of scandal. Kierkegaard's contribution, as so often, and here I think his thought is profoundly in accord with the New Testament, is to heighten the scandal by insisting that the unforgivable *is forgiven*. Paradoxical as it seems, at one level this is simply a restatement of the banal scandal that evil occurs—and yet the world continues with all the implications for God's love, power and justice that have been mentioned before. Kierkegaard's answer demands a further question, one that was raised at the beginning of this essay, and it is this: Can we forgive God for forgiving the unforgivable?

A remark of Derrida's bears repeating in this context. Asked, 'Can one forgive God?', his reply was illuminating. Insofar as human beings constantly seem to *judge* God, he said, it makes sense to ask the question of forgiving God.[16] Believers, according to Derrida, are those who have decided *a priori* to forgive God. The life of faith, then, is lived in the constant temptation *not* to forgive God.

Confronting the Holocaust, and other such crimes, we may see a God who is impotent or careless of human life, or both. It is a moot point whether it is easier to forgive God his apparent cruelty or his apparent weakness. In *The Sickness unto Death*, however, Anti-Climacus delves deeper to explain the problem at the heart of the need to forgive God. What God must be forgiven is the infliction of human misery as the inescapable consequence of the possibility of offence inseparable from his love:

> What a rare act of love, what unfathomable grief of love, that even God
> cannot remove the possibility that this act of love reverses itself for
> a person and becomes the most extreme misery—something that in
> another sense God does not want to do, cannot want to do...therefore
> he can—it is possible—he can by his love make a person as miserable
> as one otherwise never could be. What an unfathomable conflict in
> love! Yet in love he does not have the heart to desist from completing
> this act of love—alas, even though it makes a person more miserable
> than he otherwise would ever have been! (SUD, 126)

Here it is God who is faced with an impossibility. By loving the human
being, by offering the possibility of the forgiveness of sin, God also
introduces the possibility of offence, and thus of despair. To paraphrase
both Derrida and Kierkegaard, to continue to believe in a God of love
and justice after the experiences of the twentieth century is evidence
either of spiritlessness or of a *folie de l'impossible*. The culture of despair
is an understandable reaction to these horrors whether it expresses
itself as a facile and unseeing optimism, a defiant cynicism, a desperate
displacement in consumerism, or a spiritless apathy. Not to believe,
however, gives victory to the despair which is not only the reaction to
evil but its cause in the first place. In a moving reflection on Primo Levi's
writings out of the experience of concentration camps, Ettore Rocca
sees the murder in the camps as the outcome of the modern culture
of despair: 'The sickness unto death in its final stage is sickness unto
extermination; the culture of despair in its fulfillment is the culture of
the concentration camps.'[17]

If Kierkegaard is to be believed, this outcome is ultimately a
consequence of God's love. That in turn means that what God has to
be forgiven is his love, which is offered to all. It leads to his acceptance
of those we cannot accept, his forgiveness of those we cannot forgive,
and most pertinently, his forgiveness of us. The subjective motion
of accepting the forgiveness of sins is to forgive God his temerity, his
weakness, and his harshness, for loving us. This is the other side of the
divine like for like.

The Power to Forgive

Here, humanly, we encounter the impossible possibility. But here, too,
may be the answer to the question that Derrida poses himself at the end
of his essay on forgiveness.

> What I dream of, what I try to think of as the 'purity' of a forgiveness worthy the name, would be forgiveness without power: *unconditional but without sovereignty.* The most difficult task, at the same time necessary and apparently impossible, would then be to dissociate unconditionality from sovereignty. Will that be done some day? Don't hold your breath, as the saying goes. But since the hypothesis of this unpresentable task is announced, even as a dream for thought, this folly is perhaps not so foolish...[18]

The word from the cross is the word of forgiveness from the point of utter powerlessness. All sovereignty has been renounced. In addressing his prayer to the Father—'Father, forgive them...'—Jesus does not even claim the power to forgive. Nor is any condition made for their forgiveness. Kierkegaard makes this connection between impotence, forgiveness and the crucifixion explicit in a journal entry: 'That supreme power is impotence is seen in the impotence of Christ, the only one who never got justice for even his death became a benefaction, even to his murderers' (JP, 4154).

This is the point, too, of the well known passage in the journal where Kierkegaard explains that human freedom is only possible because of God's omnipotence (JP, 1251). Only omnipotence has the power to restrain itself enough to leave space for freedom, or to use the terms of the present discussion, only omnipotence is sovereign enough to be able to renounce its sovereignty. In any situation where human sovereignty is involved, be it of the king or the state, the potential abusiveness of a claim to pardon also is present.[19]

In the *Christian Discourse* entitled, 'The Joy of It: That the Weaker You Become, the Stronger God Becomes in You', Kierkegaard explores the mystery of omnipotence which can require love from a human being. God creates human beings from nothing, which is wonder enough, but then says to them: 'become something even in relation to me.'

In human relations it is the power of the mighty that requires something from you, his love that gives in. But this is not so in your relationship with God. There is no earthly power for whom you are nothing, therefore it is his power that requires. But for God you are nothing, and therefore it is his love, just as it made you to be something, that requires something of you. It is said that God's omnipotence crushes a human being. But this is not so; no human being is so much that God needs omnipotence to crush him, because for omnipotence he is nothing (CD, 128).

God's power is not to be understood by extrapolation from human power. Human power has to take the existing human being as a given and therefore has to exercise itself if it wishes to influence or subdue him. God is not powerful; he is omnipotent. This is a difference of kind and not degree. In relationship to a human being, God does not require to exercise power because, in the face of omnipotence, a human being is nothing. It is only God's love that imparts to the human being the existence that enables a relationship to God. Because of this, it can look as if God is weak and that it is the human being who has the power if the human being chooses to keep the strength imparted to him by God to himself. But 'the one who is strong without God is weak' (CD, 130) and any human declaration of independence is merely defiance.

Yet, as we have seen, for Kierkegaard, 'what is decisive is that with God everything is possible.' It becomes decisive precisely at the point where humanly speaking there is no possibility. In his discourse on 'The Joy of It: That Hardship Does Not Take Away But Procures Hope,' Kierkegaard reminds us that though the impossibility of the forgiveness of sins provokes either scandal or a spiritless acceptance in this age, the third and proper response to it is wonder:

> The highest is proclaimed, the most marvelous, but no one wonders. It is proclaimed that there is forgiveness of sins, but no one says, 'It is impossible.' Scarcely anyone turns away offended and says, 'It is impossible'; even less does anyone say it in wonder and as the one who says it who would like it to be true but does not dare to believe it, the one who still does not want to let go of it but unhappily loves this pronouncement that he does not dare to believe even less is it said by one who just believes it, one whose repentance is mitigated into a quiet sorrow that in turn is transfigured into a blessed joy, the one who therefore, expressing his unspeakable gratitude to God, refreshes his soul by repeating, 'It is impossible!' Oh, blessed refreshment, that the one who was brought close to despair because it was it was impossible now believes it, blessedly believes it, but in his soul's wonder continues to say, 'It is impossible!' (CD, 107)

Not to believe gives victory to the despair which is not only the reaction to but the cause of the evil in the first place. The Holocaust shows what despair can do. Forgiveness as God's possibility becomes decisive just where there is no human possibility of forgiveness—in the face of the unforgivable.

Notes

1. In Psalm 73, the psalmist confesses that he has almost lost faith because the wicked seem to prosper mightily at the expense of the righteous. However, in

the temple he receives a vision of the ultimate downfall of the wicked despite present appearances and his confidence in divine justice is restored. A similar protest and reassurance is to be found in Psalm 94, which goes on to rejoice in the blessedness of being punished while in the meantime the Lord digs a pit for the prosperous wicked. The wicked themselves think to deceive God as they say to themselves in midst of their crimes, 'The Lord does not see, the God of Jacob does not perceive' (Ps. 94:7). This finds an echo in the fact that Kierkegaard follows the article on 'Divine Justice' in *The Moment* no. 8 with one entitled 'Tremble—Because in One Sense It Is So Infinitely Easy to Fool God!'

2. Jankélévitch's main works on the subject, the two essays 'Dans l'honneur et la dignité' (1948) and 'Pardonner?' (1971), are collected in his *L'Imprescriptible* (Paris: Éditions du Seuil, 1986).

3. See here, for instance, many of the contributors to the Symposium edited by Harry James Cargas and Bonny V. Fetterman, which forms the second part of Simon Wiesenthal, *The Sunflower: On the Possibilities and Limits of Forgiveness* (New York: Schocken Books, rev. and expanded edn, 1998). This powerful text raises many of the questions this essay addresses in a particularly pointed and poignant way.

4. Hannah Arendt, *The Human Condition* (Chicago: University of Chicago Press, 1958).

5. 'Le Siècle et le Pardon: Entretien avec Michel Wievorka' first appeared in *Monde de débats* 9, December 1999, and is reprinted in Jacques Derrida, *Foi et Savoir* suivi de *Le Siècle et le Pardon (Entretien avec Michel Wievorka)* (Paris: Editions du Seuil, 2000), pp. 101–133. The essay is an outcome of three years' consideration of forgiveness in Derrida's seminar. Translations in the text of the present essay are my own.

6. Derrida, *Le Siècle et le Pardon*, p. 108.

7. Derrida, *Le Siècle et le Pardon*, p. 108

8. Derrida, *Le Siècle et le Pardon*, pp. 119–20

9. Derrida, *Le Siècle et le Pardon*, p. 109.

10. Derrida, *Le Siècle et le Pardon*, p. 109.

11. See also Mk 10:27; 14:36; Lk. 1:37.

12. For a compelling and too little known reading of Kierkegaardian category of offence, especially in relation to the Gospels, see David McCracken, *The Scandal of the Gospels: Jesus, Story and Offense* (New York: Oxford University Press, 1994), especially ch. 4, 'Offense or Faith: The Kierkegaardian Choice,' pp. 41–68.

13. Derrida, *Le Siècle et le Pardon*, p. 119.

14. Paul Ricoeur, *La mémoire, l'histoire, l'oubli* (Paris: Éditions du Seuil, 2000), p. 605. Ricoeur here relies on the standard French translation of Paul's phrase *panta stegei* in 1 Cor. 13:5 as 'elle [la charité] excuse tout'. Most English translations take the verb *stegein* to mean 'endure' or 'bear with'. The epilogue to this book (pp. 591–656) is entitled 'Le pardon difficile' and engages extensively with both Jankélévitch and Derrida. Ricoeur agrees explicitly with Derrida that forgiveness is wedded to the unforgivable, but regards it, as his title indicates, as difficult rather than impossible. He takes the line that forgiveness is an irreducible, and therefore inexplicable, given, like love.

Kierkegaard is given practically the last word in the book, but interestingly, in a passing reference to the lilies and the birds and their lesson to man of his own magnificence. Kierkegaard's own discussions of forgiveness are not dealt with.

15. Derrida, *Le Siècle et le Pardon*, p. 113.
16. This was a response to a question from the audience after Derrida's lecture on 'Forgiveness', delivered on 14 October, 1999, at 'Questioning God', the second conference on Religion and Postmodernism held at Villanova University, Philadelphia PA, USA.
17. Ettore Rocca, 'La Memoria, il Silenzio e lo Straniero: Søren Kierkegaard, Primo Levi e i Campi di Sterminio,' *Quaderni di Studi Kierkegaardiani* 1 (2000), pp. 115–25 (125).
18. Derrida, *Le Siècle et le Pardon*, p. 133.
19. In a journal entry Kierkegaard writes that forgiveness is the prerogative only of the divine and that the sinner is justified in saying to human forgiveness,

> No, thank you, may I rather ask to be punished and suffer my punishment and be spared your miserable, wretched forgiveness, which, even if I were properly saved and become somewhat meritorious, would probably turn up again and in the form of envy the forgiveness would be charged to my account. (JP, 1224)

Human forgiveness, in this passage, does not cease to see the sin and refuses to *forget* it.

Bibliography

Allchin, A. M. *N.F.S. Grundtvig: An Introduction to his Life and Work*. London: Darton, Longman and Todd, 1997.

Anselm. 'Why God Became a Man.' In *Anselm of Canterbury*, III. Ed. and trans. J. Hopkins and H. Richardson; Toronto: Edwin Mellen Press, 1976.

Arendt, Hannah. *The Human Condition*. Chicago: University of Chicago Press, 1958.

Aristotle. *De Interpretatione*. In *The Works of Aristotle*, I. Ed. W.D. Ross; Oxford: Clarendon Press, 1926.

Auden, W.H. *Collected Poems*. Ed. Edward Mendelson; London: Faber & Faber, 1994.

Augustine. *City of God*. Trans. H. Bettenson; Harmondsworth: Penguin, 1972.

Bataille, Georges. *Eroticism*. Trans. M. Dalwood; London: Marion Boyars, 1987.

Bauman, Zygmunt. *Mortality, Immortality and Other Life Strategies*. Cambridge: Polity Press, 1992.

Beal, Timothy K. 'Intertextuality'. In *Handbook of Postmodern Biblical Interpretation*. Ed. A.K.M. Adam; St Louis: Chalice Press, 2000.

Bengel, Johann Albrecht. *Tresindstyve obyggelige Taler over Johannes eller retter Jesu Christi Aabenbaring*. Copenhagen: 1765. [Trans. Thomas Balle of *Sechzig erbauliche Reden über die Offenbarung Johannis oder vielmehr Jesu Christi*. Stuttgart: Johann Christoph Erhardt, 1747.]

Bolt, P.G. 'What Were the Sadducees Reading? An Enquiry into the Literary Background of Mark 12:18-23.' *Tyndale Bulletin* 45 (1994), pp. 369–94.

Borges, Jorge Luis. *Selected Non-fictions*. Ed. Eliot Weinberger; trans. Esther Allen, Suzanne Jill Levine and Eliot Weinberger; Viking: New York, 1999.

Brandt, Lori Unger. 'Paul as Herald of Grace and Paradigm of Christian Living.' *KR:SRR* 2, pp. 189–205.

Brooks, Peter. *Reading for the Plot: Design and Intention in Narrative*. Cambridge, MA: Harvard University Press, 1992.

Browning, R. *The Poems: Volume 2*. Ed. J. Pettigrew; supplemented and completed by T. J. Collins; Harmondsworth: Penguin Books, 1981.

Burgess, Andrew J. 'A Word-Experiment on the Category of the Comic.' In *International Kierkegaard Commentary: The Corsair Affair*. Ed. Robert L. Perkins; Macon, GA: Mercer University Press, 1990, pp. 85–122.

— 'The Apostle Paul in the Strategic Humor of Kierkegaard's 1843–4 Upbuilding Discourses.' In *Proceedings of the Kierkegaard Round Table Session in WCP and the One-day Kierkegaard Conference in Seoul, Korea* (Seoul: Korea Kierkegaard Academy: Institute of Philosophy, Seoul National University, 2008), pp. 88–98.

Calvino, Italo. *Invisible Cities*. Trans. W. Weaver; London: Pan Books, 1979.

Carroll, Lewis. *Alice's Adventures in Wonderland* and *Through the Looking Glass*. Harmondsworth: Puffin, 1962.

Cassirer, Heinz W. *God's New Covenant*. Grand Rapids: Eerdmans, 1989.

Clark, K., and M. Holquist. *Mikhail Bakhtin*. Cambridge: Belknap/Harvard, 1984.

Cousland, J.R.C. 'Tobit: A Comedy in Error?' *Catholic Biblical Quarterly* 65 (2001), pp. 535–53.

Dahmer, L. *A Father's Story: One Man's Anguish at Confronting the Evil in his Son*. London: Little, Brown & Co, 1994.

Derrida, Jacques. *Foi et Savoir* suivi de *Le Siècle et le Pardon (Entretien avec Michel Wievorka)*. Paris: Editions du Seuil, 2000.

— *Aporias*. Trans. T.Dutoit; Stanford: Stanford University Press, 1993.

— *Dissemination*. Trans. Barbara Johnson; London: The Athlone Press, 1981.

Dickinson, Emily. *Selected Letters*. Ed. T.H. Johnson; Cambridge, MA: Belknap Press, 1990.

Drew, Philip. *The Poetry of Browning: A Critical Introduction*. London, Methuen and Co, 1970.

Freud, Sigmund. *Jokes and Their Relation to the Unconscious*. Pelican Freud Library, VI; Trans. James Strachey; Harmondsworth: Penguin, 1976.

Fuller, John. *W.H. Auden: A Commentary*. London: Faber & Faber, 1998.

Gamble, Harry Y. 'The New Testament Canon: Recent Research and the Status Quaestionis'. In *The Canon Debate*. Ed. L.M. McDonald and J.A. Sanders. Peabody, MA: Hendrickson Publishers, 2002.

Genette, Gérard. *Seuils*. Paris: Éditions du Seuil, 1987.

Görres, Ida Friederike. *Broken Lights: Diaries and Letters 1951–59*. Trans. B. Waldstein-Wartenberg; Westminster, MA: Newman Press, 1964.

Greene, Graham. *Collected Stories*. London: The Bodley Head and William Heinemann, 1972.

Hall, Amy Laura. *Kierkegaard and the Treachery of Love*. Cambridge: Cambridge University Press, 2002.

Hegel, G.W. *Lectures on the Philosophy of Religion*. Ed. and trans. P.C. Hodgson; 3 vols.; Berkeley, CA: University of California Press, 1985.

— *The Phenomenology of Spirit*. Trans. A.V. Miller; Oxford: Clarendon Press, 1977.

Hiemstra, Anne. 'Browning: History, Myth and Higher Criticism'. Unpublished PhD thesis; New York: Columbia University, 1996.

Jankélévitch, Vladimir. *L'Imprescriptible*. Paris: Éditions du Seuil, 1986.

Kierkegaard, Søren. *Purity of Heart Is to Will One Thing: Spiritual Preparation for Confession*. Trans. with an introductory essay by Douglas V. Steere; New York: Harper and Row, 1948.

— *The Concept of Dread*. Trans. W. Lowrie; Oxford: Oxford University Press, 1944.

— *Concluding Unscientific Postscript*. Trans. David F. Swenson and Walter Lowrie; Princeton: Princeton University Press, 1941.

Kirmmse, Bruce H. *Encounters with Kierkegaard: A Life as Seen by His Contemporaries*. Princeton: Princeton University Press, 1996.

— *Kierkegaard in Golden Age Denmark*. Bloomington: Indiana University Press, 1990.

LaCocque, André and Paul Ricoeur. *Thinking Biblically: Exegetical and Hermeneutical Studies*. Trans. David Pellauer; Chicago: University of Chicago Press, 1998.

Lichtenberg, Georg Christoph. *Aphorismen, Schriften, Briefe*. Munich: Carl Hauser, 1974.

Lippitt, John. *Humour and Irony in Kierkegaard's Thought*. Basingstoke: MacMillan, 2000.

Lowrie, Walter. *A Short Life of Kierkegaard*. Princeton: Princeton University Press, 1942.

Luther, Martin. *Luther's Works*. XXXV. *Word and Sacrament I*. Ed. T. Bachmann; Philadelphia: Muhlenberg Press, 1960.

— 'Preface to the Book of Tobit [1534]'. In *Luther's Works*. XXXV. *Words and Sacraments I*. Ed. and trans. E. Theodore Bachmann; Philadelphia: Muhlenberg Press, 1960, pp. 345–47.

— 'Preface to the Epistles of St James and St Jude'. In *Luther's Works*. XXXV. *Word and Sacrament I*. Ed. and trans. E. Theodore Bachmann; Philadelphia: Muhlenberg Press, 1960, pp. 361–62.

Luther, Martin. *Dr Martin Luthers Werke Kritische Gesamtausgabe: Tischreden 1–6*. Weimar: Hermann Böhlhaus Nachfolger, 1912.

Marino, Gordon D. *Kierkegaard in the Present Age*. Milwaukee: Marquette University Press, 2001.

Martin, Ralph P. *James*. Word Biblical Commentary, 48; Waco: Word Books, 1968.

Mayor, J.B. *The Epistle of St. James: The Greek Text with Introduction, Notes and Comment*. Grand Rapids: Zondervan, 1951 (1897).

McCracken, David. 'Narration and Comedy in the Book of Tobit'. *Journal of Biblical Literature* 114 (1995), pp. 401–18.

— *The Scandal of the Gospels: Jesus, Story and Offense*. Oxford: Oxford University Press, 1994.

Menn, E.M. *Judah and Tamar (Genesis 38) in Ancient Jewish Exegesis*. Leiden: Brill, 1997.

Metzger, Bruce. *The Canon of the New Testament: Its Origin, Development and Significance*. Oxford: Clarendon Press, 1987.

Munro, Neil [Hugh Foulis]. *Para Handy and Other Tales*. Edinburgh: William Blackwood and Sons, 1948.

Nancy, Jean-Luc. *The Inoperative Community*. Ed. P. Connor; Minneapolis: Minnesota University Press, 1991.

Nickelsburg, George W.E. 'Tobit, Genesis and the *Odyssey*: A Complex Web of Intertextuality'. In *Mimesis and Intertextuality in Antiquity and Christianity*. Ed. D.R. MacDonald; Harrisburg, PA: Trinity Press International, 2001.

Noble, P.R. *The Canonical Approach: A Critical Reconstruction of the Hermeneutics of Brevard S. Childs*. Leiden: E.J.Brill, 1995.

Norris, Christopher. *Derrida*. London: Fontana, 1987.

Oden, Thomas C. *The Humor of Kierkegaard: An Anthology*. Princeton: Princeton University Press, 2004.

Pattison, George. *Kierkegaard's Upbuilding Discourses: Philosophy, Literature and Theology*. London: Routledge, 2002.

Pattison, George. 'The Art of Upbuilding'. In *International Kierkegaard Commentary*. V. *Eighteen Upbuilding Discourses*. Ed. Robert L. Perkins; Macon: Mercer University Press, 2003, pp. 77–90.

Pelikan, Jaroslav. *Fools for Christ: Essays on the True, the Good and the Beautiful*. Eugene: Wipf and Stock, 1955.

Pessoa, Fernando. *The Book of Disquiet*. London: Serpents Tail, 1994.

Pevear, Richard. 'Introduction'. In *The Brothers Karamazov*. London: Vintage, 1990, pp. xi–xviii.

Polk, Timothy H. *The Biblical Kierkegaard: Reading by the Rule of Faith*. Macon, GA: Mercer University Press, 1997.

Pons, Jolita. *Stealing a Gift: Kierkegaard's Pseudonyms and the Bible*. New York: Fordham University Press, 2004.

Poole, Roger. *Kierkegaard: The Indirect Communication*. Charlottesville: University Press of Virginia, 1993.

Pyper, Hugh S. 'The Stage and Stages in a Christian Authorship'. In *International Kierkegaard Commentary*. XVII. *Christian Discourses* and *The Crisis and a Crisis in the Life of an Actress*. Ed. R.L. Perkins; Macon, GA: Mercer University Press, 2004.

Raymond, William. *The Infinite Moment and Other Essays on Robert Browning*. Toronto: University of Toronto Press, 2nd edn, 1965.

Ricoeur, Paul. *La mémoire, l'histoire, l'oubli*. Paris: Éditions du Seuil, 2000.

Rocca, Ettore. 'La Memoria, il Silenzio e lo Straniero: Søren Kierkegaard, Primo Levi e i Campi di Sterminio'. *Quaderni di Studi Kierkegaardiani* 1 (2000), pp. 115–25.

Rogerson, John. *Myth in Old Testament Interpretation*. BZAW, 134. Berlin: De Gruyter, 1974.

Rosas, L. Joseph, III. *Scripture in the Thought of Søren Kierkegaard*. Nashville: Broadman and Holman, 1994.

Scharling, Carl Emil. *Epistolam Pauli ad Corinthios Posteriorem annotationibus in usum Juvenum theologiae studiosorum*. Copenhagen: C.A. Reitzel, 1840.

Schleiermacher, F.E.D. *The Christian Faith*. Trans. H.R. Mackintosh and J.S. Stewart; Edinburgh: T&T Clark, 1976.

Sharrock, Roger. 'Browning and History'. In *Writers and Their Backgrounds: Robert Browning*. Ed. Isobel Armstrong; London: G. Bell and Sons, 1974.

Shaw, W. David. *The Lucid Veil: Poetic Truth in the Victorian Age*. London: The Athlone Press, 1987.

Shestov, Lev. *Kierkegaard and the Existential Philosophy*. Trans. Elinor Hewitt; Athens: Ohio University Press, 1969.

Sophocles. *Antigone*. In *The Three Theban Plays*. Trans. R. Fagles; Harmondsworth: Penguin, 1984.

Spark, Muriel. 'What Images Return'. In *Scotland: An Anthology*. Ed. Douglas Dunn; London: Fontana, 1992, pp. 117–20.

Steiner, George. *After Babel: Aspects of Language and Translation*. Oxford: Oxford University Press, 3rd edn, 1998.

Steiner, George. *Antigones*. Oxford: Oxford University Press, 1984.

Taylor, Mark C. *Kierkegaard's Pseudonymous Authorship: A Study of Time and the Self*. Princeton: Princeton University Press, 1975.

Weber, Samuel. *The Legend of Freud*. Minneapolis: University of Minnesota Press, 1982.

Weisberg, D. 'The Widow of Our Discontent: Levirate Marriage in Israel and the Bible'. *JSOT* 28 (2004), pp. 403–29.

Wiesenthal, Simon. *The Sunflower: On the Possibilities and Limits of Forgiveness*. New York: Schocken Books, rev. and expanded edn, 1998.

Williams, Rowan. 'God and Risk (2)'. In *The Divine Risk*. Ed. Richard Holloway; London: Darton, Longman and Todd, 1990.

Woolford, John. 'Sources and Resources in Browning's Early Reading'. In *Writers and Their Backgrounds: Robert Browning*. Ed. Isobel Armstrong; London: G. Bell and Sons, 1974.

Zimmermann, Frank. *The Book of Tobit*. New York: Harper and Brothers, 1958.

Index of Biblical References

Genesis
1:28   118
2–3   82
4:17   70
6:1–4   118
19   71
22   47
38   121

Deuteronomy
25:5–10   121–2
28:52–55   68

Judges   48

Ruth
4:6   122

2 Samuel
12   32

2 Kings
5   124
6   69

2 Chronicles
36:10   26

Psalms
73   158
94   158

Ezekiel
33:30–33   30–32

Habakkuk
3:17–19   7

Zechariah   26

Malachi   26

Judith   28

Mark
3:29   148

Matthew
6:1–15   148
8:13   150
12:31–32   148

Luke
6:27   148
6:37   148
12:10   148
17:3   148
23:34   149

John
5:2–18   5
21:15   77

Acts
9:31   143
20:32   143

Romans
5:12–14   95
6:1–11   54
6:3–5   77
7:9–11   54

I Corinthians   37
8:1   134
8:10   133

13   135, 150
14   133
15:22   95

2 Corinthians   134, 136
12:9   134
13   134, 137

Ephesians
2:5   77, 139

Galatians
2:19–20   54

1 Thessalonians   ·
5:11   134

James   82,
            95–96
1:13–15   84, 88
1:17   12
1:17–24   88
1:22–25   35
1:23–24   92
3:6   87

Tobit
1:6   117
5:14   117

Sirach   28
25:22   118

Book of Mormon
Moroni
10:3–5   21

3 Nephi   29

Index of Authors

Adam, A.K.M. 30
Adler, A.P. 36
Allchin, A.M. 28
Anselm of Canterbury 54
Arendt, H. 146
Aristotle 65–6
Auden, W.H. 3–6, 9
Augustine of Hippo 71, 79, 82, 152

Bachmann, H. 119
Badiou, A. 131
Bakhtin M. 30
Balle, T. 143
Bataille, G. 75
Bauer, G.L. 95
Baumann, Z. 70, 79
Beal, T. 23
Beauchamp, P. 89
Bengel, J.A. 143
Birkedal, V. 95
Bloom, H. 69
Bolt, P. 127
Borges, J.L. 46
Brandt, L.U. 130, 143
Brooks, P. 106
Browning, R. 45–6
Burgess, A. 99, 109, 111, 114, 130, 132, 143

Cargas, H.C. 159
Cassirer, H.W. 80
Calvin, J. 28
Calvino, I. 72, 79
Carroll, L. 104, 114
Clark, K. 30
Clausen, N.H. 18–20, 95, 119, 127
Cousland, J.R.C. 117–8, 123, 125, 127

Dahmer, L. 68, 79
Dahmer, J. 68
Derrida, J. 45, 70, 79, 103, 114, 137, 145–60
Dostoevsky, F. 1–2
Drew, P. 51
Dickinson, E. 73, 79, 80
Eichhorn, J. 95

Fetterman, B.V. 159
Freud, S. 104–12, 114

Gabler, J. 95
Gamble, H. 29
Genette, G. 100–2, 114
Görres, I. 48
Greene, G. 115–6, 127
Grundtvig, N.F.S. 18–20

Hall, A.L. 47
Hegel, G.F. 54–57, 70, 76, 79, 152
Heidegger, M. 70
Hiemstra, A. 51
Holquist, M. 30
Hong, E.H. 143, 159
Hong, H.G. 143, 159

Jankélévitch, V. 146, 151, 155, 158
Joyce, J. 2

Kafka, F. 46
Kingsland, W.G. 46
Kirkconnell , W.G. 28
Kirmmse, B. 29, 95
Kristeva, J. 30

Lacan, J. 45

Lessing, G.E. 51
Levi, P. 156
Lichtenberg, J.G. 39
LaCocque, A. 97
Lippitt, J.L. 129
Lowrie, W. 81, 93, 128
Lund, P.W. 83
Luther, M. 15, 17,18, 22, 35, 37, 85, 116,
   119, 127, 141

McCracken, D. 115, 117–9, 123, 125,
   127, 159
MacDonald, D.R. 128
Mandela, N. 11
Marino, G. 48
Martin, R.P. 96
Mayor, J.B. 96
Menn, E.M. 128
Metzger, B. 16
Munro, N. (Hugh Foulis) 41–2
Mynster, J.P.

Nancy, J.-L. 79–80
Nickelsburg, G.W.E. 128
Nietzsche, F. 3
Noble, P. 15
Norris, C. 104, 114

Oecolampadius 28

Pattison, G. 131, 143
Pelikan, J. 20
Perkins, R.L. 31
Pessoa, F. 73, 79
Plato 36
Polk, T. 47, 95
Poole, R. 95

Proust, M. 2

Ricoeur P. 88, 96, 150, 159
Rocca, E. 156, 160
Rogerson, J. 95

Scharling, C. E. 143
Schelling, F.W.J. 152
Schleiermacher, F.E.D. 19–20, 29
Scholem, G. 137
Scott, W. 100
Shakespeare, W. 36, 125
Shestov, L. 137, 143
Smith, E. 30
Smith, J. 30
Snow, L. 30
Sophocles 69, 79
Spark, M. 6
Steiner, G. 68, 71, 79, 91, 98,
Strong, P. 11

Taylor, M.C. 91, 98
Troels-Lund, T.F. 12–13

Virgil 2

Weber, S. 105–6, 114

Weil, S. 3
Weisberg, D. 122, 129
Wiesenthal, S. 159
Williams, R. 49
Woodhouse, B. 133

Zimmerman, F. 121–2, 128
Žižek, S. 131